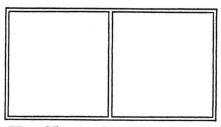

He Slew the Dreamer

He Slew the Dreamer

MY SEARCH, WITH JAMES EARL RAY,
FOR THE TRUTH ABOUT THE MURDER OF
MARTIN LUTHER KING

William Bradford Huie

DELACORTE PRESS • NEW YORK

And they said one to another, Behold, this dreamer cometh. Come now therefore, and let us slay him . . . and we shall see what will become of his dreams.

GENESIS 37 : 19–20

(In Memphis, Tennessee, the motel room outside which Dr. King was slain has been converted into a shrine which is now a tourist attraction. On a wall at the spot where Dr. King fell is inscribed this quotation from Genesis. My title, *He Slew the Dreamer,* is derived from it. WBH)

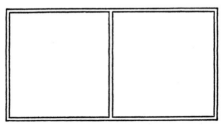

He Slew the Dreamer

One

When a forty-year-old habitual criminal named James Earl Ray was arrested in London on June 8, 1968, and charged with the murder of Dr. Martin Luther King, Jr., I decided to try to persuade him to sell me information. That he would ever give or sell information to any agent of the law seemed unlikely; that he would ever give information at any trial seemed even less likely. And no suspect or defendant in the United States can be compelled to give information. So what Ray knew could be learned and used only if someone like me could deal with him.

Through his attorney, Arthur J. Hanes, of Birmingham, Alabama, I sent this letter to Ray:

Dear Mr. Ray:
I'm interested in dealing with you. I'm told that you read, so perhaps you have read some of my books or magazine stories. My latest books, *Three Lives for Mississippi* and *The Klansman,* are about murder planned and done by groups of men to try to prevent racial change. Both these books are being filmed. I want to find the truth about how the murder of Dr. King was planned and done. I want to publish this truth, then film it.

1

Do you want to help me? Obviously you were involved in Dr. King's murder. You bought a rifle in Birmingham; you were in Memphis with this rifle and left it at the murder scene; you fled the scene in a white Mustang which you had also bought in Birmingham, then you abandoned the Mustang in Atlanta and fled to Canada and England. Evidence of these actions and movements is convincing. There are also indications that you may have had accomplices.

To the charge of murder I assume you will plead not guilty, so I'm not suggesting that you sell me a legal confession of murder. I am suggesting that you assist me in recreating your experience during the period between your escape and your arrest. You escaped from the Missouri State Penitentiary on April 23, 1967. Dr. King was murdered in Memphis on April 4, 1968. You were arrested in London on June 8, 1968. I am suggesting that for a price you tell me where you were each day between April 23, 1967, and June 8, 1968. I'll want to know what you were doing, what name you were using, whom you talked with, and how and from whom you got money.

If you sell me such information, will you further jeopardize yourself? I don't know. That's for you to decide. I know that a large number of Americans are disturbed by "the assassinations." Meaning the murders of the two Kennedys and of Dr. King. These Americans yearn to know the whole truth about why and how these murders were done, and what these murders tell us about our society. To any man who helps explain the murder of Dr. King, even if he is the murderer, these Americans will feel some measure of gratitude.

So I think you might help yourself by helping me. There is an old saying: To understand is to forgive. It isn't entirely true, but it is partially true. You might help yourself by helping me to help others understand you.

If you want to deal with me, I will have a contract drawn for us to sign, and I will pay you a substantial sum. You can use the money to pay your lawyers or in any way you choose. Through your lawyers we can begin communicating in writing. I can send in questions; you can send out answers. After you have been returned to Memphis, I will go to the judge to whom your case is assigned and show him the contract existing between us. You can ask the judge to allow you to talk with me. The judge's decision, at first, may be against you, but at some point, perhaps after your

trial has begun, I believe he will allow you to talk with me. Until
then we can do our best by writing to one another, and by communicating orally through your attorneys.

Sincerely,

WILLIAM BRADFORD HUIE

When Ray replied that he wanted to deal with me, contracts were
signed, and I made an initial payment of $10,000. I paid this
money to James Earl Ray, who had personally signed the contract,
and Ray assigned the $10,000 to Arthur J. Hanes. For me this was
a calculated risk: I didn't know what I might get for the money.
Ray had served a total of 13 years in four different prisons, so he
would have an "old con's" reluctance to identify accomplices. He
had practiced deception all his life, so even about himself how
much truth would he tell me? I could accept as truth only what I
could verify; and verication is often difficult and sometimes impossible. Nevertheless, I had decided to pay my money and make the
effort.

His first statement to me was that he didn't kill Dr. King. He
said that, as instructed, he bought the rifle in Birmingham, carried
it to Memphis, and took a room at the rooming house at 3:15 P.M.
on April 4. He said he didn't know anybody was to be killed, didn't
know that Dr. King was in Memphis. He said that, when he heard
the shot at 6:01 P.M., he was sitting in the Mustang on Main
Street. The "other man" came running down the stairs, dropped
the rifle on the sidewalk, jumped into the back seat of the Mustang,
covered up with a sheet, and he (Ray) drove away. About eight
blocks from the rooming house, he said, the "other man" told him
to stop, then jumped out of the car, after which he (Ray) drove on
toward Atlanta.

I regarded this account as neither true nor false, only as a beginning between a criminal accustomed to lying and a reporter seeking the truth. I thought that the truth could come only after weeks,
perhaps months, of my working with Ray, pulling and hauling,
checking, challenging, correcting, until two plus two finally equaled
four.

When Ray was returned to Memphis on July 19, 1968, he was
lodged in the Shelby County Jail under conditions which made reflection and writing difficult. Four ordinary cells had been con-

verted into one cell. All windows had been covered with sheet steel, necessitating air conditioning and continuous lighting. Television cameras watched Ray continuously. To sleep he had to wear a mask. Guards were always in the cell with him, often playing gin rummy. But, despite these conditions, Ray began writing. He was given a table, and I sent him a dictionary, tablets, pens, road maps of the entire United States, Canada and Mexico, and blank diaries for 1967 and 1968. I asked him to make at least one entry on every page of the diaries from April 23, 1967, to June 8, 1968. On the maps I asked him to trace all his travels.

The case was assigned to Judge W. Preston Battle, and on Wednesday, August 14, 1968, I called on Judge Battle in his office in the Shelby County Courthouse. I explained my contracts with Ray and told the judge what I wanted to do. He said he would not allow Ray to talk with me prior to his trial. Pointedly, however, the judge issued no order to interfere with my communicating in writing with Ray. He allowed Ray and me to communicate in writing which was never read by any agent of the law other than Ray's attorney.

As Ray began writing, I began trying to understand him, to see him in my mind as a person, to imagine how he felt and thought. And whenever I begin trying to understand a man, I always start with his birth date. When was he born in relation to the Depression? Or to the wars? I was born in 1910, so I was out of college in 1931, a $20-a-week reporter writing about hungry people who were trying to survive and be somebody. I have always been aware that the year as well as the condition of my birth affected how I thought and felt and acted. In 1953 I wrote a book about Eddie Slovik, the only American since the Civil War to be shot by the Army for cowardice (*The Execution of Private Slovik*). Eddie Slovik was born in 1920, and a prison supervisor helped me to understand Eddie, whom I never met, by telling me this:

> Here in the Michigan reformatory I was Eddie's supervisor for about three of his teen-age years. I never had a boy I liked more. He was good-hearted, a good worker, and with a little luck I figured he could make a pretty good citizen.
>
> Well, he fouled up in the Army and Eisenhower had him shot. I'm not going to make any excuses for Eddie. A man's only a man

and he stands up to life as best he can and takes what comes to him. Men in my business don't offer excuses for boys; we just try to help. But if you want to understand Eddie Slovik as he was, and not as he ought to have been, then you've got to understand the year and the condition of his birth.

Men in my business know that there are good years and bad years to be born in the United States. It's like those good years and bad years for wine in France. There are good years and bad years to be born in a city like Detroit. And, brother, let's face it: if your old man was a Polack punch press operator making automobile fenders, then 1920 was a bad year to be born.

If you were born in 1920 and your old man was a fender maker, then when you were ten and eleven and twelve your old man didn't make many fenders because Ford and General Motors and Chrysler weren't selling many. Your old man had plenty of time to lie at home drunk and beat up the kids and the old woman. Your mother couldn't get much scrubbing to do for other folks, so she had time to drink and fight while the kids foraged in the streets. The welfare paid your rent and gave you potatoes; and if you were twelve years old in that situation in 1932, then everybody you knew was hungry and fighting and stealing and drinking and in trouble. You were scared. And you came out of it—unless you were unusual—either weak and scared and feeling inferior, or else rebellious and resentful and full of hate, wanting to fight and maybe kill somebody.

Eddie Slovik, a petty thief at fifteen, came out of it weak and scared and feeling inferior.

James Earl Ray was born in Alton, Illinois, on March 10, 1928. That, too, was a bad year if your father was described as a laborer, a drifter, a ditchdigger, indifferent to his children, a frequenter of poolrooms, often unemployed and away from home. In 1929 the family moved across the Mississippi River to St. Louis; then, in 1932, it moved northward past Huckleberry Finn country to Ewing, Missouri: population 324. Ray's mother, Lucille Maher, was nineteen when he was born. During Depression years, she bore eight more children, in dirt-floor poverty, and broke down into alcoholism. In a neglected area of a Catholic cemetery at Godfrey, Illinois, I found her grave. "LUCILLE MARY RYAN. 1909–1961." The spelling on the gravestone is significant. It should be "LUCILLE

MAHER RAY." But the Rays either couldn't spell or else they had
so little feeling of identity that they couldn't care. When, in the
early 1940s, the family broke up and the children went to live in
orphanages or with relatives, they spelled their names in different
ways: Ray, Rayns, Raines, Ryan.

People who remember the mother say she had a hard life: she
had been raised a Catholic and she tried, but she was pregnant so
often; she sometimes had only potatoes to feed her children; her
husband didn't help her much; she couldn't keep her children
warm in winter, so she just went to pieces. Her second child, Mar-
jorie, caught fire from the kitchen stove and burned to death when
she was six.

A woman who taught in the Ewing school in the 1930s told me:
"The mother was desperately poor but she was proud. I remember
once when Jimmy broke his leg playing on the school grounds. His
mother came to me a few days later and asked if I would drive her
and Jimmy to Quincy [Illinois] to see the doctor. I can still see her
carrying Jimmy, who was almost as big as she was, down to the
car and putting him in the back seat so he could rest his cast on the
seat. We made the trip several times and one day she asked me if
I liked chicken. I said yes, and she said that she had some young
ones and that when they grew a little more she'd fix two for me. She
said it would help pay for the gasoline. About a month later she
came over with a box of fried chicken. I hated to take it, but of
course I had to."

School records are not kind to Jimmy. They say that he "violated all regulations," that he was "shiftless," that he was "seldom
if ever polite," that his appearance was "repulsive." He failed the
first grade and had to repeat it, possibly because he was absent 48
of the 190 school days. Thereafter he was absent about a third of
each school year. His IQ was average: a second-grade examination
showed it at 108. When he was in the sixth grade, he was branded
a thief for stealing the lunch money. But his sixth-grade teacher
says: "The boy had some pride. He told me he thought the other
children laughed at him because of his patched clothes."

In the eighth grade, when he was fifteen, Jimmy dropped out.
That was 1942–1943, the last year for the Rays in Ewing. The
family broke up. The mother and some of the children went to

Adams, Illinois, then to Quincy, where the three younger children became wards of the court and were placed in the Catholic Children's Home at Alton. Jimmy Ray went to live with his grandmother, Mary Katherine Maher. The two lived briefly on a farm in Missouri, then moved to Alton. The 1945 Alton city directory lists Mrs. Maher and James Ray as residing at 538 East Broadway.

At sixteen, in 1944, James Ray got a job at a tannery operated by the now defunct International Shoe Company at Hartford, Illinois, five miles southeast of Alton. He worked there for almost two years, and here is what is remembered about those years:

> He did not get into trouble. When he enlisted in the Army in 1946, about three weeks before he was eighteen, he had no police record. His younger brothers, John and Jerry, both had records before they were eighteen. But James Ray was clean until he went into the Army.
>
> Above everything else in the world James Ray valued a savings account. He was a teen-age miser. In a little less than two years at the tannery (he was laid off in December, 1945, when the company began closing down) he accumulated $1,100 in a savings bank. He didn't smoke, and with girls he was "backward and bashful and left them alone."
>
> He was valued by his employers. His grandmother, his great aunt, and his uncle described him as "a good boy, neat, responsible, dependable." His grandmother said: "His boss in the tannery was a man from Germany who taught Jimmy the trade of dyeing leather. Jimmy had the job of mixing dyes. He got promoted. And he squirreled away every dollar he possibly could. He meant to be somebody and have something."
>
> He was a "loner." He just "didn't strike up with anybody." The exception was his boss, an older man, the German who taught him the dyeing trade, a man named Henry who is still living. Henry was said to be a Nazi sympathizer, an admirer of Hitler. A restaurant operator recalls: "I remember young Ray and Henry. About twice a week they'd come in—this went on for a year or so. They'd sometimes stand and wait 15 minutes just to sit at the two stools at the end of the counter so they could talk without anybody hearing their conversation." Ray would buy his wartime ration of cigarettes each week for Henry, but not for any of his relatives.

Six weeks after he lost his job at the tannery, on February 19, 1946, Ray enlisted in the Army at a recruiting station in East St. Louis (Army serial number RA 16163129). He took basic training at Camp Crowder, Missouri, and further training at Fort Sheridan, Illinois, and Camp Lee, Virginia. On July 18, 1946, he left Camp Kilmer, New Jersey, for Bremerhaven, Germany. He was a private in the military police.

After several months in Germany, he began to drink and fight. He was transferred to the infantry, then got his first taste of prison, in an Army stockade: three months at hard labor for being drunk and resisting arrest. On December 23, 1948, he was discharged honorably for "ineptness and lack of adaptability to military service" (discharge number AR 615-369).

His first arrest as a civilian was in Alton on January 1, 1949, for a traffic violation. Then he drifted to Chicago and California, where he began his civilian prison career in the Los Angeles County Jail: eight months for burglary. He was arrested in Cedar Rapids, Iowa, for vagrancy on April 18, 1950, one of several arrests for vagrancy. He next landed in the Illinois State Prison at Pontiac for armed robbery of a taxi driver in Chicago. He served almost two years.

On September 30, 1954, he was arrested for burglary in Edwardsville, Illinois. He was released on bond posted by a professional bondsman. But this case never came to trial because, on March 23, 1955, Ray was arrested and charged with "forging the endorsement on a U. S. Post Office Money Order." For this offense Ray served in the federal prison at Leavenworth, Kansas, until April 1958.

Here is the official report on the post-office offense, taken from the Leavenworth Admission Summary:

> On March 7, 1955, the U. S. Post Office at Kellerville, Illinois, was burglarized and sixty-six blank U. S. Postal Money Orders and the office validating stamp were stolen. The following day at Alton, Illinois, an unsuccessful attempt was made to cash one of these stolen money orders. Successful attempts then followed at various places, including Hot Springs National Park, Arkansas, and Tallahassee, Florida, and it was finally learned that Ray and his co-defendant, Walter Terry Rife, were the persons who were

cashing these stolen and forged money orders. When Ray and Rife were apprehended, thirty-four of the stolen money orders were found hidden under the dash above the glove compartment in the automobile, all of which had been dated and stamped with the validating stamp and some of which had been made out ready for cashing.

Through admissions by Ray and Rife all of the sixty-six money orders were accounted for but two. Then Ray admitted cashing one at a luggage store in Kansas City, Kansas, and Rife admitted cashing one at Miami Beach, Florida. Thus the entire group of sixty-six money orders has been accounted for. Postal Inspectors found in the room occupied by Ray and Rife a quantity of merchandise they had acquired by passing the money orders, and this merchandise was returned to the persons from whom it was secured by fraud.

Other than to admit that he had gone on a nation-wide spree of cashing these money orders, Ray had no further information to give and no statement to make.

Ray is a 27-year-old white male, of medium physique, weighing 168 pounds and standing 71 inches tall. He has had good health in the past. He complains of chronic difficulty in breathing through his nose, frequent headaches, and thinks he may be allergic to the climate in this region. He denies history of narcotic addiction, venereal disease, major mental illness, tuberculosis or convulsive disorders. Blood pressure 118/74. Vision: 20/20. Audiogram within average limits. Urinalysis negative. Kohlmor non-reactive.

Ray's employment record shows that he had jobs in Chicago both before and after his term in the Los Angeles County Jail. From July to September 1949 he worked for Dryden Rubber Company, Chicago, as a laborer for $1.10 an hour. When he returned from Los Angeles to Chicago, he worked for Nee Products Company for 90 cents an hour from April to July 1950. He worked for the Arbey Corporation from July 1950 to June 1951; and the Borg-Erickson Company from August 1951 to May 1952. He had obtained a social security card.

The judge who sentenced Ray to Leavenworth in 1955 was Federal District Judge Charles Evans Whittaker, who later served as Associate Justice of the U. S. Supreme Court (from 1957 to 1962).

Here is an excerpt from Leavenworth's Annual Review of Ray's case, dated October 9, 1956:

> During the last year he has completed courses in Spanish, Composition, Typing, and Culinary Sanitation. He is presently enrolled in Applied English and Elementary Vocabulary.
>
> Ray is a Catholic by preference who does not attend services and does not desire religious instruction. He is indifferent toward his religious obligations.
>
> He apparently lacks foresight, or is afraid of the future, as he absolutely refuses to look forward. He claims that he can do his time better if he doesn't think. He further claims that he doesn't have any trouble at this time, has all the economic security that one needs, and apparently is enjoying his present situation.

On April 5, 1958, Ray was released from Leavenworth with this report:

> He is being given Conditional Release from this institution today. On his admission here in 1955 he was placed under medium custody and assigned to the Fire Department. He remained on this assignment until September 15, 1955, when he was re-assigned to the Paint Shop. On September 12, 1957, he was approved for our Honor Farm but was never actually transferred to the Farm due to the fact that he did not feel that he could live in an Honor Farm Dormitory because they are integrated. He was therefore never given Honor status. He was assigned to our bakery where he has remained until his Conditional Release.
>
> Release plans call for Ray to return to his place of conviction in Kansas City, Missouri, where he will reside alone. He has been referred to both federal and state employment assistance agencies. He is being released with a total of $99.33 in his personal account, of which $64.70 is being given to him in cash. The remaining $35.63 is being forwarded to the U. S. Post Office in Kansas City. Ray is also being given $1 in bus fare to Kansas City.

Apparently he went straight for about a year. He helped his uncle paint several houses, but quit and accused his uncle of cheating him. He began using a variety of aliases. He was suspected of the armed robbery of a food store in Alton, but he was next arrested for the armed robbery of a Kroger supermarket in St. Louis on October 10, 1959. The arrest came 20 minutes after the robbery, and police recovered the $120 he and an accomplice had taken. Under Missouri's habitual-criminal law, on October 26, 1959, Ray was sentenced to 20 years at the Missouri State Penitentiary at Jefferson City.

At the conclusion of his trial at the Municipal Courts Building in St. Louis, Ray jerked away from deputies and ran free for ten minutes until the deputies trapped him still inside the building. Most of his crimes had been characterized by ineptitude, often ludicrous ineptitude.

A Progress Report from the Missouri State Penitentiary in 1965 contains these assertions:

> Ray was received here March 17, 1960. He is assigned to the bakery where he has won good to excellent ratings on his work. There has been only one serious conduct violation. In 1961 he attempted to escape. His brother Jerry corresponds regularly and visits about once every eight months. He sometimes hears from his brother John. If he is paroled, he prefers to live with his brother Jerry in Wheeling, Illinois. He would accept almost any type of employment. He claims three years experience in bakeries.
>
> Institutionally this 37-year-old single white man has done well enough to merit consideration for parole. He denies use of narcotics and claims to be a light drinker. His record of arrests dates over a sixteen-year period. He seems to be pretty well established in this type of anti-social behavior. He will probably continue to make a fair institutional adjustment. Prognosis for making a successful adjustment in society is considered marginal at best.

In 1966, during his seventh year at the Missouri State Penitentiary, Ray, at his own request, was given a series of psychiatric examinations. From September 8 to October 21, 1966, he was confined during examination at the Missouri State Mental Hospital No. 1 at Fulton. Then, after his return to the penitentiary at Jefferson City, he was examined by Dr. Henry V. Guhleman, Jr. In a report to the Missouri Board of Probation and Parole Dr. Guhleman wrote:

> This 38-year-old white male was seen for psychiatric evaluation on December 13, 1966. He was admitted here in March, 1960, to serve a twenty-year sentence for armed robbery. He is presently charged with an escape attempt in March, 1966, and has recently

been returned after an evaluation at Fulton State Hospital. He has requested an independent psychiatric evaluation following their evaluation.

Ray is an interesting and rather complicated individual. He reports that within the last year he has had physical difficulties involving a number of somatic complaints such as pain in the "solar plexus, tachycardia and intracranial tension." When we commented that these were rather large words, he reported that he had been reading up in the prison's medical literature. He stated that he thought at times he had cancer or heart trouble but that he no longer feels this way. On certain days he has rather severe head pains, but this is only intermittent. He is now on librium and works intermittently on a construction job.

Ray has never been married, though he has lived for brief periods with women. This man's basic problem revolves around what appears to be an increasingly severe obsessive compulsive trend. He states that at the age of ten he awoke one night and thought he had lost his eye sight. He became quite fearful. These various fears confront him from time to time and in a typical obsessive compulsive way he feels he must do certain things in order to avoid what he feels is going to occur and might result in harm to him.

For instance, he describes a feeling of fear which can be alleviated if he takes his glass of water which he is drinking, sets it on the table, and moves it back and forth several times. He also describes at length some rather marked obsessive compulsive features but is reluctant to go into them in detail. Indeed he just started to discuss this with the people at Fulton prior to his being sent back here. He appears worried and his brow is creased. It is evident that this man does have an underlying obsessive compulsive personality. He is of the opinion that his recent escape attempt was the result of undue anxiety and tension with the need to actually do something. He is fearful that this might lead into more serious difficulties.

At the present time there is no evidence of delusions, hallucinations or paranoid ideas. There is only evidence of this rather deep underlying obsessive personality trend. This is not psychotic in nature but severely neurotic.

It is doubtful that he should be considered for parole. He is in need of psychiatric help. Certainly he is becoming increasingly concerned about himself.

The report of the Fulton State Hospital on the intensive examination of James Earl Ray is dated October 24, 1966. Of Ray's mental status the report says:

> He is oriented for time, place and person. His memory is unimpaired for both recent and remote events. He is coherent, alert, relevant, and there are no hallucinations or delusions. He appeared to be somewhat tense and anxious and at times showed some mild depression but not of psychotic proportions. He has a good verbal assessment of reality but in the past he has used poor judgment. He has an IQ of 105 which places him within the average range of intellectual functioning. Tests showed no evidence of a psychosis.
>
> This patient has been observed, studied and tested. No symptoms or signs indicating a mental disease or defect could be found. Although he showed signs of anxiety and depression, these could not be considered of psychotic proportions.
>
> DIAGNOSIS: Sociopathic Personality, Antisocial Type with anxiety and depressive features.

The superintendent of the Missouri State Hospital at Fulton is Dr. D. B. Peterson. I asked him if James Earl Ray is capable of planned killing for money.

"Certainly he is," replied the doctor. "Any man who commits armed robbery indicates that he may be willing to kill for gain if necessary. There is very little difference between armed robbery and planned killing for money."

Then I asked: "Is Ray capable of killing in the hope of winning some sort of distinction or approval for himself? Is he capable of killing in the hope of relieving his anxiety, enhancing his self-respect?"

The doctor answered: "Perhaps. He is so consumed with self-consideration that he is incapable of considering the rights of any other individual. Certainly he is incapable of being considerate of the welfare of society as a whole."

This, then, is what his record shows James Earl Ray to be: a man with a deprived childhood who developed into a habitual criminal who should never be paroled from prison, an antisocial man capable of murder and incapable of considering the rights of any other human being. Once I understood what Ray is, I was ready to confront the obvious questions.

Did Ray make the decision to kill Dr. King? If not, who did make the decision and then used Ray to do the killing?

Did Ku Klux Klansmen make the decision? Certainly some Klansmen are killers. I know them. I have dealt with them. I have paid them for information, as has the U. S. Department of Justice. They planned and committed the ritual castration of Edward Aaron. They planned and committed the murder of James Chaney, Andrew Goodman and Michael Schwerner. They murdered four children in a Birmingham church. They murdered Viola Liuzzo, Lemuel Penn and Vernon Dahmer. I confronted them in the Ruby McCollum case. No one knows better than I that some Klansmen are killers.

But Klansmen don't kill for pay. Nor do they pay killers. Klansmen kill from religious conviction. The average Klan killer attends church and has no previous criminal record. Klansmen hated Dr. King. But they didn't hate him so intensely in 1968 as they did in 1963 or 1964 or 1965, or even in 1955, when he first defeated them with the Montgomery bus boycott. Had the Klansmen who are killers wanted to kill Dr. King in 1968, they would have killed him themselves. They would not have used a criminal outsider like Ray.

Did Negro militants use Ray to kill Dr. King? By 1968 some Negro militants hated Dr. King. He conceded that they might kill him. A few Negro militants welcomed the racial violence which followed Dr. King's murder by a white man. They might have been capable of conspiring with a white criminal and paying him to fire the shot. But would Ray have sold himself to Negroes? A man who declined Honor status at Leavenworth because he chose not to sleep in an integrated Honor Farm Dormitory?

Did Memphis police or Memphis businessmen use Ray to kill Dr. King? Some of them hated Dr. King. But they would not have wanted him killed in Memphis. And a fugitive like Ray would not have risked meeting with them.

What about the Mafia? These are criminals who usually murder only their criminal competitors. They have been known to murder a noncriminal who refuses to pay them tribute, but the typical

Mafia murder victim is a criminal whose death is shrugged off by the police as good riddance. The Mafia would hesitate to murder any man whose death would set off an outcry which might threaten the Mafia. The Mafia were not in competition with Dr. King; and the Mafia had no reason to incite Negro-white conflict. Some Mafia members can be hired to arrange a murder. But if a member of the Mafia had been hired to arrange the murder of Dr. King, he, in turn, would have hired an experienced killer, not James Earl Ray.

What about lesser criminals—men who do not belong to the Mafia or to any other organized criminal group, but who can be hired to kill or to arrange a killing; men who for a few thousand dollars might find a fugitive like Ray and use him as a triggerman, a decoy, or some other sort of accomplice? If this was the answer, who supplied the few thousand dollars?

I know—and know of—wealthy or well-off men who are not criminals in any ordinary sense but who believe that the United States of America must be changed into some sort of police state. They believe that this nation's social and racial problems are so acute that order can be maintained only by massive force. These Americans, who consider themselves patriots, are willing to incite bloody black-white conflict so that it can be used as the excuse to employ this force. These citizens want black gunmen to ambush white police. They want black vandals to destroy property; and they want television to show the vandals in action. They contributed money to Malcolm X when he urged black Americans to murder and vandalize white Americans. They are contributing to Malcolm's successors, and they contributed to the Presidential campaign of George C. Wallace, who advocates order by force. Did men like these give money to some white criminal who then used Ray in the murder of Dr. King?

Did Fidel Castro or some other Communist arrange the murder of Dr. King to exacerbate the racial problem in the United States? If so, why would Ray have been used? And had Ray been used, wouldn't his escape to a Communist country have been arranged? Or his death? When Communists arrange a murder in an anti-Communist country, the murderer is usually a dependable Communist and a trained killer, and he is seldom found and brought to trial.

Or did Ray act entirely on his own? He knows how to support

himself with burglary, forgery, smuggling and armed robbery.
Could he, alone, have decided on the murder, planned it, financed
it by committing other crimes, then committed it, all in the expectation of winning status among criminals, self-approval, perhaps
public approval and reward?

Every agent of the law assigned to this case was asking these
questions of himself and others. But the agents couldn't ask Ray. I
could. So the task I had undertaken was to try to buy from Ray
expressions which might lead to the answers.

Two

James Earl Ray described for me his escape from prison on April 23, 1967. Using a ball-point pen and ruled, yellow, legal-size paper, he wrote:

> In April 1967 I had been in the Missouri State Prison at Jefferson City for seven years. During these years my brother Jerry visited me on the average of once every eight months. Once or twice my brother John came. They were my only visitors. I've never been close to marrying. No woman has ever thought much of me. I've never thought I was financially able to marry; and marrying would have interfered with my travels. I was thirty-nine, and I had spent about thirteen of my years in jail. But I wasn't a sadist or a masochist or a homosexual, and I had never taken dope.
>
> In prison I worked mostly in the kitchen. During yardtime I sometimes gambled. I read detective books and *True* and *Argosy* and books about how to change yourself and get along. But mostly I studied how to break out and how to get capital and I. D. [identifying cards and documents] after I broke out.
>
> On April 23 [1967] I was ready again to try to break out. I had nothing to lose since eighteen more years were hanging over me

and I had nobody on the outside and no "good behavior" on the inside working for me. I thought I "behaved" all right in prison. I did my work, was quiet and clean, and I didn't fight or disturb anybody. I didn't even snore or jerk or holler in my sleep. I don't smoke, so I sold my "commissary" to other prisoners and accumulated cash in my shoes. But I was always trying to break out, and that's called a crime in itself and they try you for it and add to your sentence. As long as you keep trying to break out you can never get out legally, no matter how short your original sentence was. I had already tried to break out three times and failed; I was awaiting trial for attempted escape; I had just got out of isolation for the last attempt; and the warden had sent me word what to expect if I was caught trying again. So this time I *had* to get out! Then I had to use self-discipline and not get caught after I got out. And just as soon as I could accumulate enough capital and I. D., I had to get out of the United States and into some country I couldn't be extradited from.

April 23rd was a Sunday. I was working the 11 A.M. to 7 P.M. shift in the bread slicing room, so I was allowed to eat in the kitchen. When I came for breakfast at 8 A.M. I brought with me in a sack 20 candy bars, a comb, a razor and blades, a piece of mirror, soap, and a transistor radio. The sack attracted no attention: kitchen personnel are allowed to shower and shave in a bathroom in the kitchen. I ate a good breakfast of about six eggs since I knew this might be my last meal for a while. Then I went to the bread room where I had hidden a white shirt and a pair of standard green prison pants that I had dyed black with stencil ink. [Remember that Ray had been trained to mix dyes in the tannery when he was seventeen.] I put the dyed pants on, then I put my green prison pants and green shirt on top of them. I transferred the items in the sack to my pockets, then stuffed the sack under my shirts. I went down the elevator to the ground floor and out onto the loading dock.

In the kitchen cooks use a 4-foot-long hook to pull pans around. I had one of these hooks in my hand. I stood there on the dock watching the guard on the tower. I had studied his actions. They all act different. Some of them doze, but they must call in every 15 minutes. So if you take any action you must do it right after you see them call in. I watched this guard call in, saw his head drop, then I ran the 75 feet to the wall.

The wall is 23 feet high, but there is a truck tunnel through it, and where the wall meets the tunnel there is a water pipe that runs up about 6 feet. I got on top of the elbow of this water pipe, and with that hook, using some cracks and crevices, I got to the top, then swung down and dropped.

This account of Ray's escape is true up to where he says he went over the wall. He didn't go over the wall. He went through the tunnel gate with the aid of accomplices who are still in the prison. He lied to me to protect these accomplices—something I knew he had to do under his prison code. So in *Look* magazine I published his account, along with his diagram showing how he went over the wall. I published this false diagram to show Ray that I was willing to help him protect his accomplices in lesser crimes if he would help me establish the truth about the murder. Here now is the truth about the escape:

The prison bakery bakes bread not only for the 1,500 men in the main prison but also for those who live on the prison's several nearby farms. This bread, in April 1967, was trucked to the farms in boxes about four feet long, three feet wide and three feet deep. On the morning of Ray's escape, after the boxes were filled, Ray got into one of them, crushing the soft, sliced, freshly baked bread, and the top was put on. Then, when the boxes were loaded into a truck, the heavy box with Ray in it was placed on top of the others. Without opening any of the boxes, guards passed the truck through the tunnel exit. The truck cleared the prison area, and when it stopped at a street intersection near the Missouri River bridge, Ray jumped out.

It was a well-planned escape. John Ray had visited James Ray in the prison on April 22. That James Ray could plan this escape, finance it and persuade other prisoners to help him at risk to themselves indicates that he had matured during his seven years at "Jeff City." He was no longer reckless and inept; he had become careful and crafty. (To prevent further such use of bread boxes, prison officials reduced the size of the boxes to where they are now too small for a man to hide in.)

Ray's written account of his escape after he jumped out of the truck is not challenged by prison authorities and seems to be true:

I had accumulated about $300 in prison which I had in my shoes, along with a social security number. [Not a card, only the number of a card issued to him as John L. Rayns in 1951. In 1944 a card was issued to him as James Earl Ray.] I ran to the railroad tracks and along the river until I was sure nobody could see me. Then I took off my prison clothes and hid the green pants but kept the green shirt so I could wear it at night when it was cold. I put the shirt and other articles in the sack. I went down the track to a railroad bridge under which I hid for the day, listening to the radio for the announcement of my escape. I didn't hear anything, and I found out later that the warden didn't report me missing because he thought I was hiding inside the prison.

I had traveled east from the prison, toward St. Louis, but I knew the police would think I would go there [he having been born near East St. Louis], so when it was dark I crossed the bridge and headed back the other way toward Kansas City. I walked all that night, except for short rests to eat candy bars. It was a little cold, but I wasn't complaining.

The 2nd day I hid and slept and listened to radio reports. Then I walked all night. I looked at the stars a lot. I hadn't seen them for quite a while. On the 3rd day I ran out of candy bars. I slept, and since the area is mostly bluffs, I could see a long way along the highway. Now and then I saw highway patrol cars, and I naturally figured they were after me. On the radio I heard the report that I had escaped.

While walking at night, when I approached a house along the railroad track that had strong lights that lighted the track, I had to detour, over rough ground and through creeks. This was causing my feet to swell, and I began having trouble getting my shoes on if I took them off. On the 3rd night I found a trailer sitting by the river. I broke in and took half a bottle of wine and some food. Also a blanket and some pants as it was cold. Then I found a place in the woods and got comfortable. I ate, and drank the wine, and covered up with the blanket, and when I woke up it was raining on me. The wine must have got me. I got up and walked the rest of the night.

The 4th day I slept and watched, but I couldn't risk taking my shoes off because I'd never get them back on. The 4th night I walked, but on those feet I couldn't walk far.

By daylight on the 5th day it was raining. I decided to build a fire. I had got some matches out of the trailer. I found a tunnel about 4 feet high under the railroad, and I got in there and built a fire. When the fire was going good, I heard a motor. Two railroad workers got off the motor car and came down to check on the smoke. I had stomped the fire out, but too late. I told them I had been hunting and got wet and started the fire to dry out. They said okay and left. They were the first humans I had spoken to since my escape. I stayed there the rest of the day, trying to help my feet, but I couldn't even rub them since I couldn't take my shoes off.

The 5th night I hobbled on. I had plenty of water to drink because there were many springs along the track, and I could hear them running. Just before daylight I saw the lights of a town big enough to risk going into. So I hid, and waited all the 6th day, and tried to clean up the best I could. I decided the heat must be off by now. So when night came I walked into the town, bought two cans of beer and some sandwiches, and went back to the railroad. Later that night I caught a train back to St. Louis. There I bought some over-sized shoes and a jacket. I took a cab to East St. Louis where I called a friend who drove me to Edwardsville, where I caught a bus for Chicago.

Note this further evidence that Ray is no longer inept but has become crafty. In six difficult days he takes only one risk: that of burglarizing the trailer. He avoids the highways, walks on the railroad. He moves only at night, hides during daylight. That the two railroad men failed to suspect him of being an escaped convict is typical of his criminal experience. Nobody thinks he "looks like a criminal." Everybody says he "looks just like everybody else." He can go unnoticed almost anywhere.

He had the additional advantage of not being regarded as an important fugitive. His escape made no headlines: it was merely announced, barely reported. The prison issued a routine Wanted poster, offering the minimum $50 reward. This poster carried an incorrect set of fingerprints, an error acknowledged and corrected in a second poster.

This poster error—the nationwide circulation of a wrong set of fingerprints—is being exploited by the assassination mythmakers. Many people, both in the United States and abroad, believe that Ray was "let out" of the prison on order of the Central Intelligence Agency and the Federal Bureau of Investigation so that these agencies could "use him as a decoy just as they used Oswald in the murder of John F. Kennedy." The "two sets of fingerprints" is said to be a CIA-FBI device to create "two Rays" who could later employ "two white Mustangs" and "two Canadian passports" so that "one Ray" could be chased and captured while the "other Ray" escaped to roam free until the CIA-FBI needs him for another assassination.

On August 21, 1968, 16 months after Ray's escape and three weeks after he began writing to me, I flew to Chicago to see if he was telling me the truth about the date of his arrival there after his escape. In a rented car, I drove down Diversey Parkway to North Sheffield Avenue, using a diagram Ray had drawn. I found the red-brick house he described: 2731 North Sheffield, a two-story-plus-basement rooming house. I told the managers, Mr. and Mrs. Donnelly, that I was looking for a man who disappeared after being in the Army, a man named John Rayns, who might have stayed in their house late in April or early in May 1967. Mr. Donnelly produced his book, and there it was, in Ray's handwriting: "John Larry Rayns 4-30-67."

"I remember him," Mrs. Donnelly said. "He had foot trouble when he came here. He could hardly walk for several days. He stayed in the back basement room. A nice, quiet fellow, neat and clean. He paid $14 a week for his room, and he always paid promptly. He was tidy and careful about his garbage. He stayed here six or eight weeks, got mail several times; and when he left he said he had to go to Canada on business. I sure hope nothing has happened to him."

I didnt tell the Donnellys what had happened to the nice, quiet fellow named John Rayns. During five months of publicity they had never suspected that John Rayns was Eric S. Galt and James Earl Ray.

On May 3, 1967, John Larry Rayns, on his fourth day after arriving in Chicago and his tenth day after escaping from prison, read this advertisement in the Male Help Wanted section of *The Chicago Tribune:*

> Kitchen man and dishwasher. 6-day wk. $94.
> For north suburban restaurant. Call Indian
> Trail at HI 6-1703.

Ray got this job, and thereby caused me to meet and astonish three fine, friendly people. It happened this way:

Winnetka, Illinois, on Lake Michigan, 18 miles north of the Chicago Loop, is an incorporated village of 13,500 affluent white people. It's a fashionable suburb just north of Evanston and Northwestern University. One of Winnetka's soundest institutions is the Indian Trail Restaurant, in a white, single-story brick building across from the post office. The restaurant is the creation of two sisters, Clara and Elly Struve, together with Clara's husband, Harvey Klingeman, who is Pennsylvania Dutch and a Rotarian. For 34 years the Indian Trail has been a favored place for suburban families to lunch and dine in one of its three art-filled rooms. Some of the 78 employees have worked there since 1934, when the Klingemans and Elly Struve rescued the restaurant from its third Depression failure.

The Klingeman family is the American success story. Industry, efficiency, responsibility, devotion, thrift, accumulation, humanitarianism. Hardworking parents whose four sons and one daughter all have attended college and lead comfortable, rewarding lives. The oldest son, a Ph.D., teaches at Oregon State at Corvallis, Oregon. The middle son is a reserve Marine and is a senior at Michigan State University. Clara Struve Klingeman was born in Haifa, where her father was the U. S. consul. The family belonged to a Quaker-like sect, the Temple Society; and Mrs. Klingeman today is a Congregationalist, a serene, white-haired, kind-eyed woman who radiates belief in the essential goodness of every human being.

About 9:30 A.M., August 21, 1968, I walked into the Indian Trail. The door was open, but there were no customers since there is no service until lunchtime. I went into the busy kitchen and found Mrs. Klingeman giving instructions. She took me for a salesman and invited me to join her for coffee and Danish pastry. I told her I was a writer from Alabama, and I wondered if she remembered an employee named John Rayns.

"Of course, I remember John," she said smiling. "Such a nice man. He was here for two or three months and we so regretted to see him go. He came here as a dishwasher. But during his first week we saw that he could be more than a dishwasher. So we promoted him to the steam table and raised his wages. He was quiet, neat, efficient, and so dependable. He was never late a minute, though he had to ride the buses for perhaps 15 miles each way. I felt sorry for him when he arrived here. He had been on a hunting trip, and his feet were sore. My sister got one of those long bandages from the hospital and showed him how to bind his feet, and he seemed so appreciative. I hope he is well. We wrote him after he left and told him how much we valued him and how we'd always have a job waiting for him. Do you know where he is now?"

I hesitated, temporarily overwhelmed by the ironies. "Yes," I said, "I know where he is. But first tell me: Hasn't anyone been here recently asking you about John Rayns?"

"No," she said, her curiosity rising. "You are the only person who has asked me about him since he left."

"That surprises me almost as much as I am going to surprise you," I said. "You see, John Rayns is really James Earl Ray, and he's in jail in Memphis, accused of the murder of Dr. Martin Luther King."

I'll never forget the astonishment, followed quickly by anguish, in Mrs. Klingeman's eyes. For a long interval she didn't speak. Then she asked: "Are you sure? It seems impossible. You mean he is the man we have read so much about? So cruel? So senseless? So shameful?"

I nodded, and she went on: "I don't know what to say. Dr. King spoke in Winnetka several years ago, and we went to hear him. He was such a good man. And I would have trusted John Rayns in my home to baby-sit with my grandchildren. It's frightening to learn that one can be so mistaken about people."

"Well," I said, "maybe you weren't so mistaken about the man you knew. Maybe he *was* reliable while he worked for you. He's prouder of his experience here than he is of anything else in his life. He urged me to 'learn about' him by talking first with you. You are the only employer who ever valued him and paid him $117 a week."

The earning record of John L. Rayns, furnished me by Mrs. Klingeman, shows that he received eight weekly checks, from May 7 to June 25, 1967. The social security number is 318-24-7098. The W-2 form shows that his taxable earnings were $813.66, with

$112.60 withheld for federal income tax, and $36.72 withheld for social security.

I lunched at the Indian Trail as the guest of Mr. and Mrs. Klingeman. The sister who gave Ray the bandage was not Miss Elly Struve, one of the three owners of the restaurant, who is now in poor health, but Mrs. Gertrude Struve Paulus, who prepares salads in the kitchen. She worked near Ray and often talked with him.

"He would never initiate a conversation," Mrs. Paulus told me. "He seemed lonely and shy. But once I had asked him something, like how he felt, he would talk. We talked about Bremerhaven [Germany]: he had been there in the Army, and I knew it years ago. And once or twice I kidded him about the girls. But he didn't like it. He was not a man who liked the girls."

"No, he didn't," I said. "That's one of the published errors about him, about how he is always consorting with prostitutes. When he has sought the company of women, it has been only in the hope of getting their help in establishing identity. When he came here, he had been in prison for seven years. Yet, in two months in Chicago, there is no evidence that he was once even close to a woman. Apparently, he has no sexual interest in women. He gets angry whenever I mention women to him."

"Yes," said Mrs. Paulus, "I recognized that in him. He is not a man for the girls. During his last week he said that he hated to leave here, but he had to go back to the boats in order to keep his seaman's license. That's the way he put it: He 'had to go back to the boats.' "

(That Ray doesn't "like girls" was one of my early misconceptions of him. Prison records make clear that he is not a homosexual, but his first attorney, Arthur Hanes, concluded that he is a "limp wrist." When I found that Ray, after escaping from prison, went three months without having a woman, I concluded that he was some sort of neuter. Later, however, in Canada and Mexico, he consorted with women in something like a normal male manner. Here is how he explained his conduct in Chicago: "There's nothing strange about me not looking for a woman in Chicago. I had waited seven years so I could wait a few weeks longer. A woman is a risk for a fugitive. She might report you to the police. And a woman costs money, and I was trying to accumulate capital as fast as I could without risking a holdup." So Ray's avoiding women in Chicago was only further evidence that he had become a disciplined criminal, determined not to be caught again.)

Of the 78 employees of the Indian Trail Restaurant, about 22, normally, are Negroes. Several Negroes worked close to Ray and with him, but no one remembers any indication that he disliked them.

One recollection seems important. For seven weeks at the restaurant John Rayns received not a single telephone call. But during the week he left, he received "three or four pressing calls" that seemed to excite him.

After a new employee has worked at the Indian Trail for six weeks, Mrs. Klingeman and her chief assistants prepare a "Six-Week Report" on his "Work Habits." Here is their report on John L. Rayns:

> Reports promptly for work.
> No odor of drinking—no salary advances.
> Took direction, retained instructions.
> Quiet, never raised voice, no foul talk or stories.
>
> Stood up against: Hot kitchen, steam table, and oven heat. Not bothered by working in limited space. When working fast, no conflicts with kitchen employees or busy, excited waitresses. No complaints against food, pay, hours, co-workers or management.
>
> No references to past work experiences—no expressions of any strong feelings or attitudes.
>
> *Impression:* A reliable man of excellent potential for food service industry.

Ray quit his job with this hand-printed letter, dated June 27, 1967, and mailed from Quincy, Illinois:

> Dear Mrs. Klingeman:
> I have been offered a job on a ship so will take it. I guess George [another employee] will be back this week so everything will be allright. If I have any pay coming just send it to the address below and they can send it wherever I am.
>
> Thanks,
[Signed] JOHN

John L. Rayns,
PO Box 293,
Winnetka, Illinois

(So Ray had rented a box in the post office directly across the street from the restaurant.)

Along with Ray's last check, mailed to the post-office box in Winnetka, Mr. Klingeman sent this letter:

Dear John:

It is with very much regret, with us, that you have left the Indian Trail.

Mrs. Klingeman spoke to me again and again of the quality (and her personal interest) in your good work here. She had also built hope that you would stay and learn all she knows. She was also most willing to go along (if given the opportunity) to do all possible to make you feel more and more happy working here.

She and I both wish you well. Please know you are always welcome.

HARVEY A. KLINGEMAN

On the day I was there, the Indian Trail served lunch to about 550 people, mostly women, some of whom had to wait in line. Mrs. Klingeman was busy, so I didn't leave until after the last customer had left. Then Mrs. Klingeman said to me: "I have been wondering why I remember John Rayns so clearly. I have just gone through our records where I saw the names of a dozen men who worked for us for short periods a year or so ago, and I have no recollection of any of them. Yet when you mentioned John, I remembered him instantly. So there was something unique about him, and it must have been something good. His story saddens me terribly—such a waste of life! But you can say for me that whatever he is and whatever he has done, while he was here, we saw a little spark of dignity in John Rayns."

The weeks following my visit were difficult for Mr. and Mrs. Klingeman. They began to fear that some people would blame them for employing a fugitive who became an accused assassin. They feared that a few people might even suspect that they had "known something." They informed the FBI of what I had revealed to them, and FBI agents invaded the restaurant and seized its files. The agents brought photographs of men, and they wanted to know if anybody had ever seen one of them with Ray. The agents also had recordings of voices, and they wanted to know if any of these voices could be recognized as having telephoned for Ray.

On October 29, 1968, I published in *Look* some of the story of Ray and the Klingemans, and this brought an army of reporters and photographers to the Indian Trail. In a telephone conversation Mrs. Klingeman told me: "You just can't imagine how your visit changed our lives. It has been an overwhelming experience which I wish we could have avoided. In one way we have been fortunate. Nobody seems to blame us. We haven't been denounced or threatened. Everybody seems to understand that we did no more than hire a man. We didn't know what he had done or might do. I suppose that from now on we must clear every prospective employee with the police. But somehow I hate to admit that we must do that here in the United States."

Back in Memphis, I told Ray about my visit to the Indian Trail and asked him why he quit his good job there. He replied:

> Yes, I had a good job there, and I hated to quit. I was earning far more money than I had ever earned in my life. But you know why I had to quit. I had been there two months, and since I had used that name and social security number before, I thought the FBI would be on me if I risked another month there. I see now that I over-estimated them. After they run out of informers they lose their imagination.
>
> I accumulated a little capital there. I bought a 1960 Chrysler for $100. I saw it advertised in the *Tribune,* and I bought it from an individual, so I didn't need to show I. D. to get it, only money. With the car I got a car title and a temporary driver's license to use for I. D. This left me with $450. But I still had to have a name and some I. D. for that new name. I couldn't use Rayns much longer and I could never use Ray again.
>
> So what I needed was to get to Canada. While I was staying at the Donnellys in Chicago I wrote to the Canadian embassy for information on immigration. The reply was one of the letters the Donnellys say I got. In prison I studied about how a broker named Burell or Birrell got a Canadian passport and escaped to South America.

(Lowell McAfee Birrell was indicted by federal and New York County juries in several multimillion-dollar stock swindles. *The New York Times* and other newspapers carried a story on September 4, 1959, explaining how Birrell, through a friend, obtained a Canadian passport, with which he escaped to Brazil, which then had no extradition treaty with the United States. In its issue of February 27, 1962, *Look* published a story showing Birrell and two other "million-dollar fugitives" living luxuriously in Rio de Janeiro. An overline said: "Scot-free within Brazil's borders, the three are safe from extradition." The *Look* story explained again how Birrell had entered Brazil on a "false Canadian passport made out in the name of Lowell McAfee." Ray memorized Birrell's escape story.)

While he was working at the Indian Trail Restaurant, was Ray planning to murder Dr. King ten months later?

A man who claims to have been a fellow prisoner of Ray's at both Leavenworth and Jefferson City has declared that, after the murder of President Kennedy, a prisoner at Jefferson City speculated that "somebody has made a million dollars"; that a second prisoner then speculated that "the man who murders King will make another million"; and that, on hearing this speculation, James Earl Ray said: "That's the million I'm gonna collect." So just as some Americans believe that the CIA-FBI, prior to April 23, 1967, decided to kill Dr. King and then arranged Ray's escape in order to use him, others believe, with more reason, that Ray decided on the murder three years before he managed to escape.

I studied Ray's way of life in Chicago to see if his behavior evidenced any such intent to murder Dr. King. When he wasn't at work, or traveling to or from work, he spent most of his time in his room. He told me:

> Usually I drank two cans of beer every night in my room. I read *The Chicago Tribune*, listened to the transistor radio, and sometimes read murder mysteries or books about Canada and Latin America. Naturally, most of my thinking was about how to live outside the U. S. About two nights a week I sat for a while in a bar on Diversey, drinking vodka and orange juice, since I don't like the taste of whiskey. This bar was the same place I bought my groceries: it was a bar-delicatessen.

Because Ray read *The Chicago Tribune,* I examined each edition of this newspaper published during May and June 1967. I looked for a report that Dr. King had visited Chicago during this period: I thought Ray might have seen him. But no such visit was reported. I then looked for stories on Dr. King which might have caused Ray to decide to murder him, or which might have reminded Ray of a previous decision to murder him. On May 1, 1967, there was this story:

WESTMORELAND TRIP HIT IN KING SERMON

Dr. Martin Luther King today accused President Johnson of bringing Gen. William Westmoreland home to silence dissent against the Vietnam war and encourage support for escalation of the conflict.

"I don't know about you," said Dr. King, "but I ain't gonna study war no more."

The congregation, which included Stokeley Carmichael, a Black Power advocate, interrupted Dr. King twice with applause during his sermon and gave him a standing ovation when he was finished.

Dr. King said: "Every young man in this country who believes this war is abominable and unjust should file as a conscientious objector."

Dr. King's position on Vietnam would not have caused Ray to decide to murder him. Because Ray hates the Army. He hates General Eisenhower. I was told that, in 1952, Ray was a supporter of the late Senator Joe McCarthy. He liked to watch the senator on television. Not, however, because of McCarthy's anti-Communism, but because Ray thought McCarthy was anti-Army.

Here is a story, in *The Tribune* of June 18, 1967, which might have irritated Ray if he read it:

RIGHTS BATTLE ENTERS COSTLY PHASE: DR. KING

Dr. Martin Luther King Jr. said today the movement for Negro equality has entered a new and more difficult phase because it will "cost the nation something."

"It didn't cost the nation anything to guarantee the right to vote, or to guarantee access to public accommodations, but we are dealing with issues now that will cost the nation something," the civil rights leader said on the ABC program *Issues and Answers*.

Dr. King added: "Many of the allies who were with us during the first phase of the movement will not be with us now because it does mean dispersing the ghetto, it does mean living next door to them, and it does mean the government pouring billions of dollars into programs to get rid of slums and poverty and deprivation, and I think this is why the civil rights movement has to restructure itself, in a sense to gear itself for an altogether new phase of struggle."

While Ray was in Chicago, apparently the only person he talked with who knew his real identity was his brother Jerry. Apparently he lived alone and frugally, trying to accumulate enough capital to reach Canada. Therefore the questions are: Was he going to Canada only to try to escape those 18 remaining years at Jefferson City? Or was the proposed trip also part of his plan to kill Dr. King? Was he seeking a Canadian passport to use after he had returned to the United States and murdered Dr. King?

After quitting his job at the Indian Trail Restaurant, and before leaving for Canada, Ray spent two weeks in the area where he was born. He wrote to me:

Except for the $450 and the old Chrysler I didn't have many possessions when I left Chicago. Just a few clothes, a sports jacket, and pants. On my way to East St. Louis the old Chrysler gave me trouble, but I got there. I sold that car for $50, and bought a '62 red Plymouth for $200. You can find where I bought it: from a dealer on Main Street coming out of East St. Louis toward Belleville. The car lot is between the 1500 and 2000 block on the left hand side of Main Street as you travel east. I used the Rayns name on the car title. I spent a night with the friend who took me to Edwardsville when I escaped. Then I went to Quincy and stayed six or seven days, and here are the names of two men there you can see, but don't write about them or they will be arrested for harboring me. I just want to show you that I've got friends who have known me all my life. And they think well of me.

From Quincy I went back to Chicago to pick up my last check

from the Indian Trail. The check was mailed to a box I had in the post office in Winnetka. Then I went back to East St. Louis and told my friends I was leaving the country and to tell my family. I didn't tell anybody which country I was going to. The last thing I did was get a new .38 pistol from a friend. But I didn't pay him for it then. I was just too short of capital.

I left East St. Louis on July 15th and spent the first night in a motel in Indianapolis. The next day I crossed from Detroit into Windsor [Canada], but since a lot of traffic was moving to Expo there was no trouble at the border, and I headed for Montreal.

Ray's being in the area of East St. Louis, Alton, and Quincy from July 1 to 15, 1967, leads to another question. On Thursday, July 13, 1967, in Alton, where Ray was born and where he had committed other robberies, a bank was robbed of $22,000 by two armed men in stocking-cap masks. If one of these bandits was James Earl Ray, the mystery of where he got the money to travel and live on before the murder of Dr. King would be solved. So there are people who believe that Ray was one of these bandits and that he got at least an even split of $11,000.

He insisted to me that he was not one of these bandits. And there are indications that he was not. He had never before robbed a bank. He had never had $2,000 at once. His behavior before and after this robbery doesn't seem to indicate that he expected to get, or that he got, $11,000 with a gun. Had he been planning to risk such a robbery in the United States after his escape, why would he have worked eight weeks in the kitchen of the Indian Trail? By working in that restaurant, he acquired no useful identification cards or records. He netted only about $200 in new capital. And had he acquired $11,000 on July 13, would he have been traveling toward Montreal on July 15 in a $200 red Plymouth?

What causes me to doubt that Ray robbed this bank is that in all of his writings to me he insists that his first objective after escaping from Jefferson City was a Canadian passport. Therefore I doubt that he would have risked committing a major crime in the United States before he went to Canada and sought the passport. But since he was in the area and has no alibi, he may have robbed the bank in Alton. He may have left most of the $11,000 in the

United States with someone he trusted while he drove to Canada in a ramshackle car.

Who would suspect the driver of a $200 Plymouth of being a successful bank robber?

Three

Behind the wheel of his beat-up red Plymouth, driving from Detroit to Montreal in July 1967, James Earl Ray apparently attracted no attention from his fellow Expo-bound tourists. He was bareheaded, with his thick black hair cut a bit longer than a crew cut. He wore no glasses. He was thirty-nine, but could be taken for thirty-five. He was five feet eleven inches and weighed only 165, so except for a paunch which he has a habit of rubbing, he looked thin. His nose looked sharp; his face, thin. He wore a light-blue sport shirt and dark pants, and in his pockets were about $280 and the pistol. As he drove along the MacDonald-Cartier Freeway (401), he was trying to choose a new name. He explains:

> I've used many different names, but picking a new one is never easy. I can't afford to pick something easy like Smith or Brown or Jones, because I might forget who I was if somebody suddenly asks me. My name has to be unusual so it'll stick in my memory and I'll always know who I am.

He chose "Eric S. Galt," and the fact that there is a real Eric S. Galt in Toronto has led to the speculation that this name was suggested to Ray and that this is more evidence that he was assisted in his escape, his travels, and in his murder of Dr. King. A more likely explanation is this: Between Detroit and Toronto he passed near the city of Galt; he saw "Galt" on exit markers and chose it as a surname. When he stopped for the night of July 16 at a Toronto motel, he looked through the Galts in the telephone directories; and in his process of seeking something different from the more common first names, he chose "Eric S." He was still John L. Rayns on the night of July 17, when he registered at the Bourgard Motel in Dorion, a few miles west of Montreal. His first use of "Eric S. Galt" was on July 18 in Montreal, when he signed a six-month lease on a room at the Har-K Apartments, 2589 East Notre Dame. The rent was $75 a month, and since Montreal was crowded with Expo visitors, he had to pay the first and last months' rent, a total of $150. He writes:

> One thing was certain: I never in my life intended to return to the United States. What hope was there for me back there? I intended to get a Canadian passport, then go by plane or ship to some country in Africa or South America from which I could never be extradited. The first thing I did in Montreal, even before I rented a room, was call a travel agency and ask what I.D. I needed to get a passport. I told them, of course, that I was a Canadian citizen. They said I didn't need any I.D., but I had to have another Canadian citizen who would swear that he had known me for two years. Later [in April, 1968, after the murder of Dr. King] I found out this wasn't true: you can get a Canadian passport simply by swearing you are a Canadian citizen, and you don't need anybody else to swear with you. But right then I thought I needed somebody else, so I began looking for him; and, in case I couldn't find him, I began trying to find a way to get on a ship without a passport. And, of course, I had to get some more capital, as I had only about $70 left after I paid for the room. But I can swear this: I was never going to cross that border back into the United States.

Is it true that Ray never intended to return to the United States? Had he been successful in obtaining a Canadian passport, would he have gone to some Latin American or African country and never attempted to kill Dr. King? Or was his being in Canada in July and August 1967 only a rehearsal for his later trip, only part of his preparation for the murder?

I think it may be true that he never intended to return to the United States. Had he been successful then, as he later was, in obtaining the Canadian passport, he might have gone to Africa or Latin America and never returned. But he didn't get the passport; he didn't apply for one. And he did return. He was in Canada from July 16 to August 21, 1967. He reached Birmingham, Alabama, on August 25, 1967. So on September 14, 1968, carrying with me Ray's diagrams and explanations, I flew to Montreal to try to confirm his story of what caused him to risk a return and what caused him to travel directly from Montreal to Birmingham, a city which Ray had never visited before but which was often visited by Dr. King.

I found where he had lived, and I Xeroxed the lease he signed. He hadn't remembered the house's number or name, but his diagram was accurate. Notre Dame is the east-west boulevard that for many blocks runs along the north bank of the St. Lawrence River. By the time you reach its 2500 block east, it has run down to cheap lodgings, warehouses and industries. The Har-K is a three-story hive of 57 rooms. Its sign says: "Welcome American and Canadian Artists." Across from it is a textile mill—Tex-made Cotton Yarns and Fabrics—which hums day and night. What may have attracted Ray, with his ambitions for Latin American travel, was a now shuttered nightclub, the Acapulco, on the ground-floor corner of the Har-K. Its extravagant yellow and red neon sign, now dark, promised "Acapulco Spectacles" in now dingy sombreros and serapes.

But Ray only slept at the Har-K. He lodged his hopes—and spent his days and evenings—with "the boats," about 30 blocks to the west. Each year Montreal is visited by 6,000 ships, which pour hundreds of seamen each day onto its docks and into its waterfront taverns and its club for merchant seamen, Mariners House, at 165 Place D'Youville. And since Montreal is the easiest big city in the world to bring contraband into and get contraband out of, it is an international crime center. Much of the contraband moving from Europe into the United States goes through Montreal. This includes most of the millions of dollars' worth of heroin which moves each year from the Middle East to Marseille to Montreal to New York.

Ray hung around the seamen's hiring hall and was told, "No

jobs." He hung around Mariners House, trying to educate himself. He wrote to me in detail about how he learned that this Mariners House had been built following the union of two formerly separate seamen's clubs, one Catholic and the other Protestant. From what I could learn, except during his Army service, Ray has never been aboard a ship. Yet ships must have been one of the fantasies which sustained him through thousands of lonely prison nights. He must have imagined himself sailing into and out of exotic harbors, watching the harbor lights, in many faraway places. He told other people, in addition to those at the Indian Trail Restaurant, that he was a seaman, temporarily home from the sea, to which he must soon return. He told me how, in Montreal, he shadowed seamen from tavern to tavern, hoping to steal "papers" from one who drank too much.

Ray frequented Neptune Tavern, 121 West Commissioners Street. I visited it. The ceiling lights are suspended from pilot wheels. There is a pilot wheel over the bottles back of the bar. The furniture is massive oak, in its natural color, and signs welcome all seamen, promise highest prices for English money, and inform you that "Nous Servons les Repas" (We Serve Meals). The menu is chalked on a blackboard furnished by Milson's Biere.

On his third and fourth evenings in the Neptune, Ray says he "sort of let the word get around" that he had had a little trouble down in the States, that he was looking for I.D. and capital, and just might be available for activities that didn't involve too much risk. This resulted in a "contact." A man whom Ray calls "Raoul" and describes to me as being a reddish-haired French Canadian about thirty-five, and whom Ray took to be a seaman, showed interest in him. They began cautious verbal exploration, with Raoul's hinting that, if Ray was willing to assist certain projects, Raoul might be able to provide Ray with I.D. and capital. Ray says this exploration continued during "at least eight meetings" over a period of three weeks.

(In the eight months he spent in the Shelby County Jail, Memphis, Ray wrote to me at great length about Raoul. In addition, he spent hours describing his activities with Raoul to his attorneys, Mr. Hanes and Percy Foreman. All three of us concluded that "Raoul," which is a common name in French Canada, is the name

Ray uses for any and all of his contacts and accomplices in crime between July 1967 and April 1968.)

Meanwhile, in Montreal, Ray had an immediate need for capital, and he told me he satisfied it in this way:

> On St. Catherine East, out past the 1400 block, there are a lot of nightclubs. Prostitutes hang out in these places, and in 1967, with the Expo crowds, they were doing big business. The procedure is that the girl leaves the club with you, and the two of you take a cab to an apartment run by whoever she is working for. I picked up one of these girls. I picked up the best-looking one I could find, as I figured she'd take me to the most prosperous place. We went to the apartment where I gave her $25 which she took to the office. When I left I wrote down the address. The next night I took my car and parked it close to that address. Then I went back to the club and picked up the same girl. We took a cab to the same house. I gave her another $25, but when she started to the office I put the gun on her and went with her. When she got the manager by knocking, I put the gun on him. We went into his room, and I made her take her stockings off and tie his hands and feet while he lay on the bed. He tried to hold out on me, but he must have figured I was down to about my last $5 and just might put a bullet in him. He pointed to a cabinet where I found about $800. Then I made the girl get under the bed and left. I hated to take a risk like that, but I figured if I held up a whorehouse they probably wouldn't report it, and I guess they didn't.

After I published this account of the whorehouse robbery, in *Look* in November 1968, Ray complained that I had made him look bad by quoting him as saying that he had got only $800. "I got more than that," he said. "I feel sure I told you that I got $1,700, which is what I did get." Then he made a further revelation. He said that he had told me "a little lie"—that he had once held up a whorehouse in this manner, but that it was not in Montreal in 1967, but in Chicago in 1959. "In Montreal in 1967," he explained, "I actually held up a food store and got $1,700. But I didn't want you to publish this, as I don't want the Canadians to put a 'hold' on me and try to take me back to Canada after I get out of prison in Tennessee. So I told you a true story but told you the wrong time I did it."

I then explained to Ray that I had sensed that his story of holding up the whorehouse was a lie; that I had assumed that he had actually held up a food store or a loan company or a branch bank in Montreal; that I had published his account of the whorehouse holdup to demonstrate again to him my willingness to protect him and his accomplices in lesser crimes in return for his signed agreement to tell me the complete truth about the murder of Dr. King. I also reassured him that, prior to his trial for the murder of Dr. King, I would not publish anything about his role in that murder which would further jeopardize him.

"Only after your trial," I wrote to him, "do I expect to publish the complete truth about the murder of Dr. King. This you and I have understood from the beginning. Prior to your trial I will publish only a partial account of your movements and activities down to March 22, 1968, which was two weeks before the murder. And prior to your trial I will publish only your statement that you were *involved* in the murder, and I won't reveal the extent of your involvement."

Ray then told me that we again understood one another. He further told me that a holdup in Canada in 1967 was less risky for him than a holdup in the United States. This, he said, was because, if he pulled a holdup in Canada and was caught in Canada, he would only be returned to the Missouri State Penitentiary, where a "hold" for Canada would be lodged against him. But if he pulled a holdup in any state of the United States other than Missouri and was then caught in the United States, he would first have to serve a prison sentence in the state where he pulled the holdup and then be returned to Missouri. This is why, he said, after his escape, he had waited until he reached Canada to pull a holdup.

Ray help up the food store in Montreal on either July 17 or 18, just before or just after he paid the $150 rent at the Har-K and before he began talking with Raoul at Neptune Tavern. (Ray says the holdup was on July 18, just *after* he paid the rent.) Because, with the $1,700 he got in the holdup, he began at once to make unusual expenditures.

On July 19, 1967, the day after he rented the room at Har-K, he spent about $300 for new clothes at Tip Top Tailors, 488 St. Catherine West. Tip Top is comparable to the Bond stores in the United States: you can buy a suit from $65 to $110, a sweater for

$20, and sport shirts for $10. Ray bought a new brown Botany suit, a pair of gray slacks, a red T-shirt, a yellow T-shirt, yellow swimming trunks, red pajamas, socks, underwear, neckties—the kind of clothes he had never owned before. He got a haircut and had his nails manicured at the Queen Elizabeth Hotel.

On July 21, 1967, he ordered a $150 tailor-made suit and was fitted for it at the English and Scotch Woolen Company, Montreal. He later notified this company to mail this suit to him at 2608 Highland Avenue, Birmingham, Alabama. It was so mailed and received.

Why was Ray dressing himself in such fashion? Because he planned to seek and find a woman, a "respectable Canadian woman," whom he would cultivate to the point where she would swear a lie for him, swear that she had known him for two years and that he was a Canadian citizen, and thereby help him get a Canadian passport. As a hunting ground for such a woman, Ray asked a travel agency to suggest a resort.

The agency suggested one of the most beautiful places on earth: the "Dean of the Laurentian Mountain Resorts," "incomparable, world-famous" Gray Rocks Inn, on Lake Ouimet, near St. Jovite and Mt. Tremblant, a place known to thousands of Canadian and American vacationers for golf, swimming, boating and riding in summer and for skiing in winter. Ray paid the agency $153 for minimum room and board for a single man for a week. On Monday, July 31, he put his new clothes in the decrepit old red Plymouth and drove 80 miles up the Laurentian Auto-route for the biggest week of the season, the week that would end on Sunday, August 6, with the running of the 200-mile road race at Mt. Tremblant.

A year and seven weeks later, I followed Ray's route to Gray Rocks. It was a perfect, brisk, sunny fall afternoon. The car was driven by a French-speaking private detective, and with us was Jim Hansen, a *Look* photographer who appreciates mountains and color. The trees in the Laurentians were turning—reds, browns, yellows—and we agreed that the red was the richest we had even seen.

Jim Hansen said: "I bet old Ray, down there in that cell in Memphis, wishes to hell he was back up here."

"Yeah," I said, "I guess he does. And I wish to hell that some of the other rascals I've trailed had led me to places like this."

Ray had found a woman. He had told me about her. He wanted me to find her and get her to tell me about him. So I was looking for her. She lives in Ottawa and works for the Canadian government.

When I reached Ottawa, I telephoned her. I assumed I'd frighten her. She'd resist a strange man insisting that she meet him and talk in confidence about an individual she met about a year before. I guessed that she had read the Galt-Ray stories, had been appalled and was trying to keep secret that she once knew the accused murderer of Dr. King. Her voice quavered on the telephone. She said: "You must have the wrong party. I have no idea what you are talking about. So why should we meet?"

"You needn't be afraid," I said. "I won't harm you. It's important that you tell me what you know about a man who has received a great deal of publicity."

"You mean," she said, "a man . . . a man . . . a man I met last summer at Gray Rocks?"

"Yes," I said, "and don't be afraid. No one in the United States knows your name except him and me and his lawyers. I'll keep it that way." If she refused to see me, she had to fear that I might go to the Canadian police. So she had no choice.

Still hesitant, she said she would meet me for lunch. I told her how to recognize me: a harmless-looking man of fifty-seven, no hair, a blue suit, in a rented gray Ford. She said she would be on a street corner at noon: a brunette in an orange dress, "less than forty, but not much less."

I had an hour to kill before I met her, so I walked on Parliament Hill. It's another majestic place, with vistas that rival Washington's. The Canadian Parliament was in session. Prime Minister Pierre Trudeau had delivered his message from the throne. With other sightseers, I watched the maple-leaf flags flying from spires atop tall towers. I looked at monuments to the uncommon valor of old wars. Then I got in the gray Ford and went to find the brunette in the orange dress.

I wondered how she would look. Since Ray had been widely described as a creep who quivered when a woman dance instructor touched him, I guessed that she had to be a shapeless frump. So when I spotted her on the corner and she got in the car, I was flabbergasted. Of the thousands of women who work for the Canadian government, she must be one of the most attractive. Not in the manner of a brainless sexpot, but in the manner of a cultivated, sensitive, efficient, tastefully dressed and coiffured mature woman. At almost any resort she could have her pick of the unattached men.

"I guess you know how frightened I am," she said. "And how frightened I was last April to learn what had happened to Eric Galt. I'm getting a divorce, but I have wonderful children to protect."

"I understand," I said. "All I want is for you to tell me about him. I've never met him. You have. He wants you to tell me. I need clues to his personality, to why he was involved in the murder of Dr. King."

"I'll tell you all I know," she said. "I don't feel ashamed. Only afraid, for my children, and for my position, which is a responsible one."

At a restaurant, we ordered lunch, and I said: "I suppose you have noticed how surprised I am at your looks and personality. I had expected a much less attractive woman. As a novelist, I have written many boy-meets-girl situations. But I can't imagine how you and James Earl Ray ever met and became friends. Tell me how it happened."

"Well, first," she said, "remember that I think of him as Eric. And I never knew him as a criminal or as an ex-convict or as a would-be murderer. I only knew him as a lonely man who seemed to be trying to have fun on vacation. Last year, after years of trouble with an aggressive man, I had taken steps to get my divorce. A woman friend and I drove to Gray Rocks for a long weekend and to see the auto race at Mt. Tremblant. We didn't stay at Gray Rocks Inn, but at a cheaper place in St. Jovite. On Sunday we saw the race. It lasted for hours, with men trying to kill themselves, all tremendously exciting. The evening was for celebration, fiesta, so, of course, we expected to drink and dance and mingle with many people, perhaps kiss, and even make love if we found attractive partners. It was that sort of an occasion.

"We began the evening," she continued, "in the lounge of the Gray Rocks Inn. We found it crowded, and people were drinking and dancing, and there was this lone man sitting at a table. He was neat and well-dressed and shy. I guess it was his shyness which attracted us. My friend said, 'Let's sit with this man,' and we introduced ourselves and sat down and ordered drinks and began trying to talk."

"So he didn't pick you up? You picked him up?"

"Yes, you might say that. But it wasn't a pickup, only a friendly meeting, like everybody does on such an occasion. We didn't expect it to last all evening. But Eric was a nice man. He was not a take-charge guy. He listened and didn't talk much. He was so unaggressive. All around us were aggressive men, trying to paw you and take you to their cars or rooms. Eric wasn't that way. He wasn't loud or boastful. He spent his money generously, but not wastefully, and he made nothing of it."

"Did he dance?"

She laughed. "I managed to get him on the floor. I love to dance. He was so clumsy, and he has no ear for music, but I tried to teach him, and he was good-natured about it."

"Where did he say he was from?"

"From Chicago. He said he worked with his brother in some sort of business. In fact, he was meeting his brother in Montreal next day. Later that evening, when we left Gray Rocks Inn and went to other crowded, celebrating places, we rode in his old car, and he apologized for it. He said it was his brother's wife's car, a second car used to haul groceries and things."

"As the evening wore on, did you ever think of ditching him for another man?"

She reflected. "No, I didn't," she said. "Naturally, after all that I read about him later, about him being boorish and brutal and loathsome, I've tried to analyze my feelings. I have asked myself how I could ever have been attracted to him. I guess I felt comfortable with Eric. He had such a lost-and-lonely manner. You didn't feel sorry for him, but you sort of wanted to help him have fun and not feel so lonely. As the evening wore on, he seemed to become more confident. And more protective toward me. When other men would make plays for me, Eric quietly warned them off.

I guess a woman likes that, especially one who feels she has been discarded."

"Did he get drunk? Did you?"

"No, neither of us got drunk. We drank a lot. But we both knew exactly what we were doing."

That evening she and I dined together and talked for hours. She told me about herself. She struck me as being honest, decent and generous, and I began to worry about hurting her. I'd never reveal her name, but how could I tell her story without someone finding her out? I kept coming back to Ray. "Tell me about sex," I said. "Did you go to Ray's room at Gray Rocks?"

"I did," she answered. "And I stayed till morning."

"Well, what about him? I had concluded that he is some sort of neuter. His prison record indicates he isn't homosexual. Yet when he got out on April 23, 1967, and reached Chicago, he avoided women. So what about him?"

"Nothing unusual," she said. "My experience has been limited. But with me, I thought he acted perfectly normal."

"That seems unbelievable," I said. "Except for perhaps a whore in Montreal, you must have been the first woman he had been in bed with in nearly eight years. He knows nothing about women. He has spent 13 years in jail! He's a loner. A fugitive. A criminal. He doesn't belong. You must have seemed overwhelming to him. Yet you say he is perfectly normal."

"He was," she insisted. "I saw him again in Montreal, then again when he came to see me in Ottawa. He is perfectly normal. As for how he found me, well, he was complimentary."

I smiled. "Did you see the film *Never on Sunday?* Where the overwhelming but generous woman puts the nervous young sailor at ease so that he can gather confidence and perform like a man and then imagine he has conquered the world? With you and Ray, it must have been something like that."

She smiled. "I saw *Never on Sunday,*" she said. "Maybe it was like that. Except I wasn't selling to Eric. I was giving."

I returned to the subject of money. "I'm surprised at your statement that Ray spent freely," I said. "In prison he was known as a hard man with a dollar. Whenever another prisoner owed him money for cigarettes, Ray kept after him until he got it. And after

Ray got his first job when he was seventeen, he saved a thousand dollars. He was a miser."

"Well," she said, "I didn't say he spent lavishly. He only spent adequately and didn't seem to begrudge it. When I cautioned him once about spending too much, he sort of smiled and said, 'There's more where that came from.' "

I laughed. "I guess that explains it," I said. "The money he spent while he was with you he had got at gun point in Montreal. I guess the easier money is come by, the easier it is to spend. What about Negroes? Did he ever indicate to you that he hated them?"

"Once," she said. "It was while we were having dinner in Montreal. I can't remember how the subject came up. But he said something like 'You got to live near niggers to know 'em.' He meant that he had no patience with the racial views of people like me who don't 'know niggers' and that all people who 'know niggers' hate them."

From Gray Rocks, the two women planned to visit Expo in Montreal on their way back to Ottawa. When Ray left Gray Rocks on Monday morning, August 7, he told them he had no address in Montreal, he was rushing back to meet his brother, but he would get an apartment and telephone them so they could stay with him that night. During the afternoon, he telephoned, gave them the Notre Dame address, and they drove there.

"I was only briefly alone with Eric that night," she said. "The three of us spent the evening in that Acapulco Club, in the apartment house, and I tried to teach Eric the Latin dances. He seemed much more serious, perhaps worried. He told me he wanted to come to Ottawa and talk to me about a serious matter. As for sleeping, it was ridiculous. He had tried to get another room and couldn't. So the three of us slept across his bed in his one little room. The place was not Gray Rocks: it was seedy and run-down, and Eric was embarrassed about it. When I left him next day, he said he would telephone, and he told me again that he was coming to Ottawa to talk about the serious matter. He was very serious."

"Then he came to Ottawa on August 19th?"

"Yes. He arrived here during the afternoon. He had kept in touch by telephone. He stayed in a motel on Montreal Road. But he was without a car here in Ottawa. We used my car, and I rode him around and showed him the sights."

"He still had the old car," I said. "He told me that he hid it from you, and told you he was without a car, trying to play on your sympathy."

"That sounds strange," she said. "But he was ashamed of that car. And here he seemed downright worried. For long periods as we rode around, or while we were together at the motel, he said nothing. He just looked at me, like he was trying to get up the nerve to say something. I showed him where I work, and all the government buildings and the headquarters of the Royal Canadian Mounted Police."

"That's what worried him," I said. "You see, he came here to decide whether to risk telling you some of the truth and asking you to help him get a passport by swearing that you had known him for two years. He told me that he had about decided to risk you, but when you showed him where you worked, and all the government buildings, and the Mountie headquarters—well, he said he just had to conclude that, if he told you the truth, you'd just naturally have to turn him down and probably deliver him to the Mounties."

She shook her head. "That's sad," she said. "I never suspected that. And maybe the saddest part is that, if he had told me, I guess I would have turned him down. I don't think I would have delivered him to the Mounties, but I couldn't have sworn a lie and helped him get the passport. When he left me, he said he had to meet a man in Windsor. But he insisted he would see me again. He wrote to me from the States. His last letter came in March of this year [three weeks before the murder]. He wanted to know when I was taking my vacation so that he could meet me. I kept his letters. But then, of course, when the stories came out, I tore them up, hoping no one would ever find out I had known him."

Just as I caused trouble for Mr. and Mrs. Klingeman at the Indian Trail Restaurant by revealing to them, to the FBI and to the public that they had once employed Ray, I caused even more trouble for this woman in Canada. When, in *Look*, in November 1968, I published a portion of my conversation with her, I tried to protect her. I omitted her name and disguised her in several ways. But I had not foreseen the extent of the excitement the story would cause in Canada.

The day *Look* went on sale I received excited calls from Canadian publishers, some of whom I have written for in the past. They insisted that I provide them the woman's name and address. They said: "This is now a Parliamentary matter for us. A Member of Parliament has called for an investigation and said that this woman must be found and questioned."

"I'll never tell you who she is," I said, "and I plead with you not to try to find her. I have published all she knows. Exposing her would be cruel and unnecessary. She is an honest, decent woman, guilty of no offense, unless sexual adventuring among consenting adults on holiday in the Laurentians has become a crime in Canada. Please leave her alone."

That didn't stop them. I had revealed that she was a government worker living in Ottawa, and that, with another woman, she had registered at a motel in or near St. Jovite on the weekend of August 6, 1967. That was enough to send reporters digging into every record in that area. Near midnight one night my telephone rang in Alabama, and I was given an ultimatum: "We've found her! We know who she is. But she won't speak to us. If you'll call her and persuade her to talk with us, we'll protect her like you did. But if you won't call her and she won't talk, then we're going to publish her name. So you've got to call her."

"You can go to hell," I said. "I'm sorry I inhabit the same planet with people like you."

These reporters then resorted to the dirtiest of all the old tricks. A voice called her and identified himself as Arthur J. Hanes, of Birmingham, Alabama, counsel for James Earl Ray. The voice said that he believed it would be best for her to talk with the Canadian reporters and trust them not to reveal her name.

She then telephoned me. "I can't understand," she said, "why Mr. Hanes would call me and advise me to talk to reporters."

"Oh, God!" I said, "the bastards have tricked you. Mr. Hanes hasn't called you. They had someone call you and pretend to be Mr. Hanes." To "Mr. Hanes" she had not agreed to talk to reporters, but, frightened and taken by surprise at night, she had revealed enough to "Mr. Hanes" to indicate that she was the person the reporters were seeking.

I couldn't sleep the rest of that night. I told my wife: "I should never have written a line about that woman. And I'm sorry I ever began work on this story. A man like Ray can't meet anybody without hurting him. And I can't dig up Ray's story without hurting all the people he has met."

Assured by their unfair telephone call in the middle of the night, several Canadian newspapers published her name. Then the Canadian Broadcasting Corporation showed her picture on television. She surprised them by fighting back. With her friends and employers standing with her, she engaged a lawyer and sued the newspapers and the CBC.

A month later two men came to my home in Alabama. They were officials of the Canadian government and the CBC. (CBC, like the BBC in Britain, is a government corporation.) They told me about the suit pending against them, and they wanted me to be a witness in any trial.

"You can count on my being there," I assured them. "But I will be a witness for her, not for you. You hurt her ruthlessly and needlessly. So she has a valid claim against you."

After he returned from Gray Rocks to Montreal, and before he went to Ottawa to see the woman—between August 8 and 18— Ray says he talked at least five more times with Raoul in the Neptune Tavern. And Ray says Raoul made him this proposition:

1. That Ray would meet Raoul in the railroad station at Windsor at 3 P.M. on Monday, August 21, 1967.

2. That Ray would make two trips across the border from Windsor to Detroit for Raoul, using first the tunnel and then the bridge crossing, carrying packages of contraband concealed in the old red Plymouth.

3. That Ray would then sell the Plymouth and go by train or bus to Birmingham, Alabama. There Ray would "accumulate I.D." and wait for instructions by general-delivery mail.

4. That Raoul would pay "living expenses" and come to Birmingham and buy Ray a "suitable car."

5. That after a few weeks or months, after a little joint activity, Raoul would pay Ray $12,000 and give him a passport and "other I.D." and help him go "anywhere in the world."

6. That Ray would ask no questions. (Ray told me: "Every time I tried to ask Raoul a question, he told me straight to remember that he wasn't paying me to ask questions.") Raoul did, however, tell Ray that he (Raoul) spent some of his time in New Orleans, and he gave Ray a New Orleans telephone number.

Ray wrote to me:

> Well, I didn't know what to do about Raoul's proposition. If I took this proposition, I had to go back to the States and risk the Missouri Pen again. I didn't want to do that. I had sworn I'd never go back. But I was running out of capital again, and I didn't want to risk another holdup in Canada. I couldn't get on a ship. I couldn't get I.D. I had come to Canada to get a passport, and I hadn't yet got it. So I told Raoul okay I'd meet him in Windsor. But I didn't know then whether I'd meet him or not. The woman in Ottawa seemed to like me. She was my last chance. I hadn't had time to talk to her in Montreal about the passport. So now I was going to Ottawa and tell her something about myself, and if she'd help me get the passport, I wasn't going to meet Raoul. With a passport, I'd pull another holdup and get some capital and go on to Africa or South America just like I had planned to do.
>
> When I got to Ottawa things just didn't seem to go right. The woman still seemed to like me; she went out of her way for me; but she was just too close to the government. I decided I just couldn't afford to risk telling her anything. There was too much danger that she might turn me in. So I had to give up on her, and leave her, and head for Windsor to meet Raoul.

What truth is there in this? Did Ray actually find a criminal accomplice in a Montreal waterfront tavern who persuaded him to go to Birmingham? If so, was that accomplice already involved in a plot to murder Dr. King? And was Ray, knowingly or unknowingly, then and there drawn into this plot? Or did Ray and this accomplice merely agree to cooperate in crimes other than murder? Ray wrote:

On my way to Birmingham, Raoul wanted me to make two trips across the border at Windsor-Detroit. I guess he figured I wouldn't attract much attention in my old red Plymouth for which I had paid $200. I arrived at the Windsor railroad station a few minutes before 3 P.M. and waited about 30 minutes. Raoul came in with an attache case and said let's go. On the way to the tunnel we stopped and he took three packages out and put them behind the back part of the seat where you rest your back. We rode a little further toward the tunnel, and I let him out after he told me where to meet him on the other side. He said he'd cross in a cab. I went through the customs all right, and when he met me in Detroit he directed me to a side street where he removed the packages. We then drove to the Detroit bus station where he went in after telling me to go back to the Windsor railroad station and wait for him. I had waited about 10 minutes at the railroad station when he arrived in a cab. Then it was the same procedure, he told me to go over the bridge to Detroit, not through the tunnel.

Waiting in line at the bridge, I noticed that the customs officers were shaking down about every other car. So I remembered the TV set in the trunk that I had bought in Montreal. Hoping to keep them from shaking down my car, I declared this TV set. I had to pull out of traffic, into a special lane, and the officers not only looked at the TV set but really shook down the car. I thought they were going to find the packages, but they didn't go quite that far. This procedure took about 30 minutes, and cost me $4.50 duty on the TV set.

Raoul was nervous when I met him. He asked me what had taken me so long, and I showed him the receipt for the import tax. We parked on a side street where he got his three packages and gave me $750. He told me to sell the old car and go to Birmingham where he'd write me a general delivery letter telling me where and when to meet him. He again repeated the telephone number where I could contact him in New Orleans in an emergency. He said he'd bring me the money for a new car. I asked him again what I was expected to do, and he said for me not to worry, it would be relatively safe. I then drove him again to the Detroit bus station and left for Chicago. I spent that night in a motel about five miles east of Gary, Indiana. Next day I went into Chicago and gave the red Plymouth to my brother Jerry who had lent me $100 before I went to Canada. Then I caught a train for Birmingham.

Ray's first attorney, Arthur Hanes, once worked as an FBI agent on the Mexican border. Ray's second attorney, Percy Foreman, has defended men said to be members of the Mafia, some of whom direct the running of heroin across the Canadian border. Mr. Hanes spent about a hundred hours in conversation with Ray in the Memphis jail. Mr. Foreman spent about 40 hours. Both these well-informed lawyers believe that Ray made some sort of criminal contact in Montreal and that he crossed the border at Windsor-Detroit in the manner he describes.

"The way he tells it is standard operating procedure for bringing heroin in from Canada," Mr. Foreman said. "Men like Raoul in Montreal are always looking for Americans like Ray; and the Raouls always cross the border in planes, taxicabs or buses, while the Rays cross in their cars. Since Ray looked like an upright citizen to Mrs. Klingeman and to the woman in Canada, a Raoul would have picked him in a minute as a good bet to get across the border without the heroin being found in his car."

If it's true that Ray got $750 from a Raoul, then there is no mystery about how he financed himself, his travels and his appetites between April 23, 1967, when he escaped from prison, and August 25, 1967, when he arrived in Birmingham. He had $300 when he broke out; he earned about $670 net at the Indian Trail; he got $1,700 in the holdup in Montreal; and the $750 at the border. Total: $3,420.

Four

Ray's traveling directly from Montreal to Birmingham, Alabama, in late August 1967; his buying an expensive (for him) car in Birmingham; his staying in Alabama for six weeks and obtaining a driver's license there so that he could give 2608 Highland Avenue, Birmingham, as his "permanent address" for the next seven months: these actions tempt one to believe that the decision to kill Dr. King already had been made, either by Ray or by someone else, and that Ray was standing by to implement it. Else why, of all the states in the union, would Ray have gone to Alabama? He had never been in Alabama, except to drive across a portion of it in 1954 when he was forging postal money orders. So the temptation is to believe that Ray must have gone to Alabama because (1) Alabama was the scene of Dr. King's victories; (2) Dr. King often could be found in Alabama; and (3) Alabama was the home of some of Dr. King's more virulent enemies. It is indeed difficult not to concede that Ray's spending six weeks in Alabama was somehow connected with the subsequent murder.

In Alabama, as in every other place in this story, the only clues to the truth are (1) the ascertainable facts, (2) what Ray says, (3)

statements of persons who say they met Ray and (4) what Ray's
known behavior seems to indicate.

It is a fact that Ray traveled from Chicago to Birmingham on
the Illinois Central Railroad and arrived in Birmingham at Ter-
minal Station. Within four blocks of that station, he spent the night
of August 25, 1967, at the Granada Hotel, 2230 Fourth Avenue
North. There, because he had I.D. for it, including a social security
card, he used his old alias, John L. Rayns. Next day, as Eric S.
Galt, he took room and board at a house managed by Peter Nicho-
las Cherpes at 2608 Highland Avenue. On the registration card
Ray identified Eric S. Galt as a shipbuilder recently employed at a
shipyard in Pascagoula, Mississippi.

Ray said:

> Raoul had said in Montreal and in Detroit that he would find
> a meeting place in Birmingham and mail me the address and time.
> I then had very little I.D. for the Galt name, but when I asked
> for Eric Galt's mail at the general delivery window I was lucky:
> the postal clerk found a letter and, hiding the address from me,
> asked me for my middle initial. I said *S*, and it was addressed to
> Eric S. Galt, so he gave it to me. That's all that clerk asked for.
> If, like some clerks, he had asked me for a social security card, or
> a driver's license, or anything with Galt on it, I'd have been up
> the creek. But I got my letter, about my second or third day in
> Birmingham [Monday, August 28, 1967].
>
> In the letter Raoul told me to meet him that night in the Starlite
> Cafe, on Fifth Avenue North, right across the street from the
> U. S. post office. I met him and he told me to get a good car,
> around $2,000. Next day I found such a car and described it to
> him that night at the Starlite. He said it sounded okay, and next
> morning on the street he gave me $2,000 in 100 and 50 and 20-
> dollar bills. The car was a white 1966 Mustang, with red interior
> and about 18,000 miles on it. The only thing I didn't like about
> it was the color. Raoul didn't like that either, but he said go ahead
> and get it. At his request I gave Raoul a set of keys to the car,
> and he took my home address and telephone number and said
> he'd either write or call me in maybe six weeks. He also gave me
> $500 for living expenses and another $500 to buy some camera
> equipment he described to me. He said for me just to lie low,
> get some I.D. with the car, and stay out of trouble.

In trying to check what Ray says, I discovered these additional facts in Birmingham:

During the morning of Monday, August 28, 1967, Ray, as Eric S. Galt, rented safety deposit box 5517 at the Birmingham Trust National Bank in downtown Birmingham. He gave as a reference a fictitious Karl Galt, 2515 Lafayette Street, St. Louis, Missouri. The bank's log on this box, the record showing each time it was unlocked, is significant. It shows that the box was not unlocked when Ray rented it, but that he returned that afternoon, at 2:32 P.M. and had access to the box for five minutes. This means that on August 28 he put things *into* the box; he couldn't have taken anything out, as this was his first access. The log shows further that the box was unlocked, and Ray had access to it, on September 5 from 1:52 to 1:58 P.M., on September 21 from 11:04 to 11:08 A.M., and on September 28 from 10:16 to 10:19 A.M.

Therefore, Ray had access to this box only four times: on August 28, when he put something in; on September 5 and 21, when he could have either put in or taken out; and on September 28, when, preparing to leave Birmingham, he emptied the box. Bank officials closed the record on the box on December 13, 1967, after receiving the "customer's key" through the mail from Baton Rouge, Louisiana.

After Ray was identified as the suspected murderer of Dr. King, *The Birmingham News* reported that Ray used money from this bank box to buy the car. But the seller of the car, William D. Paisley, Jr., and his father, William D. Paisley, both of 701 South 48th Street, Birmingham, tell this story:

The white Mustang was advertised for sale for $1,995 in *The Birmingham News* of Sunday, August 27, 1967. On the afternoon of Tuesday, August 29, Ray telephoned the Paisley home. Mrs. Paisley advised him to call back around 6 P.M., when her husband would be there. Ray called soon after 6, wanted to see the car and was advised how to reach the Paisley home. He arrived in a cab a little after 7. Mr. Paisley offered to let him test-drive the car, but Ray declined, saying he had no Alabama driver's license. Mr. Paisley then drove Ray around the block in the car, and Ray said: "I'll take it off your hands." Ray then explained that he "did business" at the Birmingham Trust National Bank, where he offered to meet Mr. Paisley next morning at 10 A.M. and pay him in cash. Mr. Paisley said that he would want to deposit the money in the First National Bank, across the street from Birmingham Trust, and the two agreed to meet next morning in front of the First National Bank, from where they would cross the street to Birmingham Trust to get the cash. Mr. Paisley and his son then drove Ray back to downtown Birmingham, where Ray got out about five blocks from the Starlite Cafe.

Next morning Mr. Paisley met Ray in front of the First National Bank, expecting to go with Ray across the street to Birmingham Trust. But Ray surprised Mr. Paisley by saying that he already had the money, and he caused Mr. Paisley some apprehension by promptly counting out an even $2,000. "Man, let's be careful with this kind of money," Mr. Paisley cautioned, "right here on 20th Street in broad daylight." Mr. Paisley walked directly into the First National Bank, deposited $1,995, and brought $5 in change to Ray. Then he took Ray to a parking lot and gave him two sets of keys and the car.

Until he bought this Mustang, the most expensive car Ray had ever owned had cost him $350. And there is no evidence that Ray, ever before in his life, had had $2,000 in hand at one time. (Ray gave me a detailed accounting of his cash on hand, his receipts and his expenditures from the day of his escape from prison to the day of his capture in London. According to this report, Ray had the least money, only $90, on July 18, 1967, after he paid the $150 rent to the Har-K Apartments in Montreal. Then he got $1,700 in Canadian currency in the food-store holdup. He spent $1,000 in Canadian currency while he was in Canada; then Raoul gave him $750 in both Canadian and U. S. currencies in Detroit. Ray reports that his ticket from Chicago to Birmingham cost $40, and that he arrived in Birmingham with $1,500, about half in U. S. currency and half in Canadian currency. While he was in Birmingham, then while he was in Mexico and California, Ray continued to carry some Canadian currency. A week before he murdered Dr. King, Ray went to a bank in Atlanta, Georgia, and converted $300 of Canadian currency into U. S. currency. And when Ray reached Canada, after the murder, he had with him Canadian currency, which he had obtained in the holdup in Montreal or from Raoul.)

Mr. Paisley's deposit slip shows that Ray paid him the $1,995 on August 30, 1967. The log shows that Ray did not have access to his deposit box between August 28, when he rented it and put something in it, and September 5. So the $2,000 with which Ray bought the car was never in his bank box. This means either that he had the money when he arrived in Birmingham and did not put it in the bank box on August 28; or that he obtained it in a robbery in or near Birmingham on August 25–29; or that, as he insists, he was handed the $2,000 in Birmingham only a few minutes before he handed it to Mr. Paisley.

A criminal fugitive like Ray takes a risk each time he meets a law-abiding citizen like Mr. Paisley. So if Ray had the $2,000 on August 29, wouldn't he have completed the deal for the car when he went to the Paisley home? Why would he have risked meeting Mr. Paisley again next day? The answer could be what Ray says: that he first had to examine the car, then describe it to Raoul, get his approval and get the money from Raoul before he could buy it.

The bank box raises other questions—why Ray rented it and what he used it for, as well as where and when he got the $2,000. A fugitive like Ray may rent a bank box for several reasons. First, to "get some I.D." Ray used the bank-box rental contract, with the name Eric S. Galt on it, to show the mail clerk that he had the right to claim mail addressed to Eric S. Galt. And the box enabled Ray to tell Mr. Paisley that he "did business" at the Birmingham Trust National Bank and thereby relieve any suspicions Mr. Paisley might have had about a man from outside the state who appeared after dark wanting to buy for cash a car he had not driven.

More important, a fugitive like Ray rents a bank box to hide in it everything he has which might cause him to be held for questioning should he be stopped by police for some minor infraction of the law. (In Toronto, after the murder of Dr. King, Ray got a ticket for jaywalking, and he suffered an anxious moment trying to think what he should tell the policeman. I will detail this incident later.) Ray told me he rented the box in Birmingham "to hide my Rayns I.D. in." While he was claiming to be Galt, and "getting I.D. for Galt," he didn't want to risk being caught with a social security card identifying him as Rayns.

But Ray, you can be sure, hid more than his Rayns I.D. in that bank box. He didn't go to the box on September 5 and 21 only to look at a social security card. Certainly he kept his Canadian currency and some of his U. S. currency in it. And he probably put his pistol in the box on August 28 and kept it there during the more vulnerable days while he was buying the car and getting his driver's license. The rooming-house operator, Mr. Cherpes, helped him transfer the car title and get the driver's license. Mr. Cherpes's reaction to Ray was standard: "You couldn't imagine a nicer guy to have around—quiet, neat, paid his bill promptly every week, talked mostly about the weather. Sure, when he asked me to go down to the courthouse and help him out, I was glad to do it. I thought he was just a good fellow temporarily out of work. I never dreamed he was a crook."

Ray's application for a driver's license was filed at the Jefferson County Courthouse, Birmingham, on September 6, 1967. Mr. Cherpes is noted as the "accompanying driver." Since this application demanded a middle name, Ray used for the first time the middle name "Starvo." Eric Starvo Galt. The application says that Eric Starvo Galt, of 2608 Highland Avenue South, Birmingham, was born on July 20, 1931; that he weighed 175 pounds, was five feet eleven inches tall, with blue eyes and brown hair; and that he was a merchant mariner by occupation, presently unemployed. The application further claims that Eric Galt had previously been licensed to drive in Louisiana, but that this license had expired in 1962. The report of the examination shows that Galt "needs training as to posture and attention," but he was passed with a score of "86 per cent." The most significant information in the report is that Galt's vision was perfect: 20/20 in each eye and in both eyes.

About his six weeks in Birmingham, Ray wrote:

> My stay in Birmingham was uneventful. Birmingham is about like St. Louis, only smaller. I think I told you I went to that dance school three times. It cost $10 total. I thought I might have to go to a Latin [American] country, and it helps socially in those countries to know a little about Latin dances. However, you have to learn the standard dance first in order to learn the Latin, if you can believe the schools. Also I had a little experience with doctors. I went to two of them and asked about my depression. They

didn't do me any good, just gave me some anti-depressant pills. I took the pills a few days, then threw them away.

Going back to Canada a minute, when I left there I brought some Canadian papers with me. I guess you saw an article which linked me with a hippie lonely hearts club? What I did was enroll in one of these international clubs while in Birmingham. The people in these clubs are not criminals, but they are not what you would call square. I still had not ruled out a Canadian passport, and I thought I might contact some woman in Canada through this club. After I got her address, I'd go to Canada and meet her through normal channels. I wouldn't tell her I was from the U. S., or that I had been writing to her. I'd just tell her I was a Canadian from another city, and after a while ask her to sign a passport form. However, I never heard from anyone, and I forgot about it till I got to California.

I bought the camera equipment for Raoul, but had to ship some of it back. I took a driver's test, passed it, and got an Alabama driver's license. I also bought new Alabama license tags after the first of October. I remember the man who later got elected mayor of Birmingham [George G. Seibels, Jr.] shook hands with me and asked me to vote for him while I was waiting in line to buy the tags. About October 5th or 6th, Raoul wrote me and told me where and when to meet him in Nuevo Laredo, Mexico.

Exactly why Ray ordered this "camera equipment" is difficult to understand. The records show that, on September 1, 1967, he mailed an order to the Superior Bulk Film Company, 442 North Wells Street, Chicago. The order was for:

1 Kodak Projector M95Z	$168.00
1 Kodak Super 8 Camera M8	160.00
1 HPI Combination 8mm. Super Splicer	4.49
1 Remote Control 20-ft Cable	4.75
Total	$337.24

On the back of this order Ray wrote:

Dear Sir:
   Would you send these items special delivery. The manual did not list the shipping weight on the items I ordered so I added $10. If it is more I will pay on receiving.
   On sending order would you send me any manuals you might have on:

1. Sound Stripers
2. Descriptive circular on LSF automatic cine printer.
3. The price of the Eumig Mark S Sound Projector.

> Thanks,
> ERIC S. GALT
> 2608 Highland Ave.,
> Birmingham, Ala. 35205

I would like this order as soon as possible. Thanks

Shipment of this equipment was delayed, and the company apparently sent Ray a Crestline camera instead of a Kodak. On October 5, 1967, he wrote this letter to the company from Birmingham:

Dear Sir:

I received your order of four items the 4th. I was well pleased with everything except the camera, which I am returning. The camera you sent has only one film speed and I wanted the Kodak M8 which has 4. As I think I told you on the phone I will have to leave for Mexico Saturday and will be unable to wait. Due to Mexico high customs I would not want it sent there. Upon my arrival in Mexico I will send you my address and you can mail whatever remittance there.

> Sincerely,
> ERIC S. GALT

On the day he wrote the above letter, October 5, Ray bought, for $245, a Polaroid 220 camera at Lollar's Camera Shop in Birmingham. He had this Polaroid with him when he was captured in London on June 8, 1968. On October 22, 1967, he wrote this letter to the film company:

Dear Sir,

I ordered four items from your company from the address below:

> 2608 Highland Ave.,
> Birmingham, Alabama
> Invoice No. 179530

I returned the Super 8 Crestline as it was unsatisfactorily in use with Kodak Proj. M95Z, and I didn't have time to wait for the

Kodak camera. You can send the refund to the below address as I will be here for awhile.

> Sincerely,
> ERIC S. GALT
> Puerto Vallarta, Jalisco, Mexico
> Hotel Rio,
> Apartado Postal No. 23

On November 20, 1967, Ray wrote this letter:

Dear Sir,

While in Birmingham, Alabama, I ordered four items from your company. I returned one for a refund, the Kodak Super 8 Crestline. I sent you my address while in Mexico but did not hear from you. However, I did not receive any mail while there, so if you wrote, the letter may have got lost. I will be at the below address for five months. Thanks.

> ERIC S. GALT
> 1535 North Serrano,
> Los Angeles, Calif. 90027

Officials of the film company report that they mailed a refund check of $140 to Eric S. Galt, first to Birmingham, then to Mexico, but that both letters came back. Ray finally received the $140 in Atlanta, a week before the murder of Dr. King. And one of his bitter remarks to me was that he had to destroy this check because by the time he received it he "couldn't take the risk of cashing it."

What did Ray, a fugitive on the run, want with camera equipment like this? Did he, or some accomplice of his, expect to use it in some sort of criminal activity, perhaps including the murder of Dr. King? At first Ray told me that he "didn't know what the stuff was." He said he ordered only what Raoul told him to order, that it was for Raoul's use, and that he (Ray) tried to get Raoul to take it when the two met in Mexico. In the weeks before I obtained copies of Ray's letters to the company, and before Ray made further disclosures to me, I was inclined to believe this explanation.

The letters, however, reveal that Ray had some knowledge of photographic equipment. And after he had been in the Memphis jail for two months, he began to tell me about a ruse he used to "confuse the FBI." Ray enjoys only one game: cops and robbers, hare and hounds, with himself the elusive robber-hare pursued by the stupid cop-hounds. In fantasy he plays this game during his endless days and nights in prison. He played it in his loneliness while he was free. He told me that "the law" had very poor pictures of him, that he looked much younger than he actually was, and that therefore, when the FBI put out a Wanted poster on him, using a poor picture and saying he was born in 1928, "nobody could recognize me from the poster." In Ray's mind, from the moment he escaped the Missouri State Penitentiary, the FBI and other law officers were furiously searching for him.

The most startling statement he ever made to me, and he made it several times, was that, while he was in Birmingham, then in Mexico, then in California, he expected the FBI "to put me in the Top Ten most any day." What makes this statement so startling is that, prior to April 4, 1968, of all the criminals at large in North America, James Earl Ray was regarded by the FBI as one of the least likely ever to be elevated to the élite list of the Ten Most Wanted Criminals. Yet Ray expected to make this list, meaning apparently that he hoped to make it, and his camera equipment is somehow related to this hope.

Ray used this equipment to photograph only himself. He told me how, on deserted beaches in Mexico and California, he spent afternoons setting up his camera, posing himself before it and snapping pictures with the remote-control cable. He planned to have plastic surgery, to make himself look even younger and more different, and this is why he joined the lonely-hearts clubs and advertised in the hippie press for companions and pen pals. He mailed out dozens of pictures he had made of himself, in what he believes was a successful effort to create confusion about his actual appearance and identity.

Before I leave Ray's letters to the film-equipment company, one other comment must be made. These letters reveal that Ray's movements were not entirely aimless and impulsive. The Leavenworth report on him says: "He apparently lacks foresight, or is afraid of the future, as he absolutely refuses to look forward." But his letters indicate that he knew where he was going and how long he would stay. Late in September he telephoned the film company and told them he had to leave Birmingham not later than Saturday, October 7, 1967. From Mexico he wrote that "I will be here for awhile." He stayed a month. And from Los Angeles on November 20, 1967, he wrote: "I will be at the below address for five months." From the date of that letter to the day Dr. King fell was 16 days less than five months.

Back to Birmingham: except for his bouts of melancholia, the word for Ray's six weeks in Alabama is "success." He had come for "capital and I.D. for Galt" and he got them. There was method in the length of his stay. New automobile license plates go on sale in Alabama each October first. On October 2, 1967, Ray got new plates for his Mustang, to go with his certificates of registration and ownership. So now he had "good I.D." Eric S. Galt didn't have a passport, or a birth certificate, or a social security card, or any record of previous employment, but he had a driver's license, a car registration certificate, a car title, and a bank-box contract, all showing him to be a taxpaying citizen of Alabama with a "permanent residence" at 2608 Highland Avenue, Birmingham. And he told me he left Birmingham with about $1,000 in Canadian and U. S. currency.

Therefore Ray, when he left Birmingham, was in the most secure position he had been in since he began his criminal career in 1949. Nobody was looking for him. His own fantasies notwithstanding, he wasn't the object of any nationwide manhunt. He wasn't on the FBI's Top Ten or Top Thousand. He was an insignificant criminal, one of thousands in America's floating criminal population. The reward for his apprehension was still $50. Nobody really cared whether or not he was ever caught. To remain free, all he had to do was stay out of trouble. But, of course, he couldn't get a job, except perhaps as a dishwasher, because he lacked the social security card and the record of previous employment.

I could find no women in Birmingham who knew anything more about him than that they had been "out with him" once or twice. The dance instructors said he was a "clumsy loner who came in here a time or two, and couldn't be taught to dance if he took a lesson every day he lives."

Did Ray see "Raoul" or some other contact in Birmingham? I don't doubt that he had one or more criminal contacts there. Maybe it was the man he met in Montreal. Maybe it was a man sent from New Orleans by the man in Montreal. Maybe it was a man who lives in Birmingham. Maybe the contact advanced the money to buy the car. What does seem doubtful is that Ray was criminally inactive all those six weks. Alabama has its share of crimes, many of them unsolved. Every week there are robberies of branch banks, loan companies and food stores. Businesses and homes are burglarized for jewelry, money, particularly for coin collections. As in other states, Alabama has citizens who live well and travel the highways in expensive cars, with no apparent means of support. There are rings of auto thieves, because Alabama is a "no title" state. To buy a license plate for a car, you don't need to show proof that you own a car; you only have to recite a motor number. You can sell a car without showing proof of ownership. So the state is nationally known as a place to dispose of stolen cars.

One reason why Mr. Cherpes found Ray to be a quiet man was that "every morning he left the house after breakfast and you'd never see him until maybe that evening at dinnertime." I find it easy to believe that sometime during September, either alone or with the accomplice who may have advanced the money for the Mustang, Ray pulled an armed robbery or two, paid back all advanced money and put his extra capital in the bank box. Of the money he was spending at Gray Rocks Inn, he told the woman: "There's more where that came from." Why should anyone believe that the holdup in Montreal was his last? He told me he came to Alabama to get "capital and I.D." He got the I.D.; why should I doubt that he got the capital?

In further explanation of why he went to Birmingham, Ray wrote to me:

> Going to Alabama from Montreal wasn't my idea. It was Raoul's. Raoul said he operated out of New Orleans, and he wanted me and him to pull two or three jobs down in that area. Raoul said for me to go to some place close to New Orleans and stay and buy the car, and he suggested Mobile. I told him I preferred Birmingham to Mobile, since I'm allergic to salt air, and Birmingham is bigger than Mobile and therefore safer. So me going to Alabama was Raoul's idea, but me going to Birmingham was my idea.

What is missing from Ray's experience in Birmingham is any solid evidence that either he or any accomplice was thinking about killing Dr. King. What sort of rich or not so rich citizen of Alabama or Louisiana would have hired James Earl Ray in September 1967 to kill Dr. King in April 1968?

In September 1968, I asked Ray when he thought he became involved in the plot to kill Dr. King. He replied:

> I suppose I became involved in the plot to kill King when I took those packages into the U. S. from Canada. I would think it had all been decided before the car was bought in Birmingham, as no one would have given me $3,000 in Birmingham just to haul narcotics across the border. But nobody told me about any planned murder of King or anyone else.

I find it difficult to believe that any accomplice of Ray's in smuggling narcotics from Windsor to Detroit in August 1967 was planning to murder Dr. King in April 1968. And what criminal would have bought a car for Ray on August 30, 1967, for him to use in fleeing a murder scene on April 4, 1968?

Before closing Ray's Birmingham chapter, one other revelation should be made.

For two months after I began communicating with Ray, he insisted to me and to Mr. Hanes that he has no strong feelings about politics or racial conflict. He convinced Mr. Hanes that this is true, and since I was not allowed to see Ray, I had to believe that it might be true.

Then I began to accumulate more evidence that Ray is a morbid Negro-hater and an emotional supporter of George Wallace. And on the evening of March 10, 1969, after Ray had pleaded guilty to killing Dr. King, his two brothers, Jerry and John, were talking in Memphis. "All his life," they agreed, "Jimmy has been wild on two subjects. He's been wild against niggers, and he's wild on politics. He's wild against any politician who's for niggers, and he's wild for any politician who's against niggers. Nobody can reason with Jimmy on the two subjects of niggers and politics."

When Ray came to Birmingham in 1967, the Wallace movement was noisily under way. This could have influenced his decision to come to Alabama. Whether it did or not, on his transistor radio he must have listened to many exhortations to "Stand Up for America." And whatever George Wallace thinks his movement is, his emotional supporters think it's a movement to "put niggers back in their place." That's what James Earl Ray thinks, and he is a Wallaceite. Later, in California, he used his Mustang to transport voters to Wallace headquarters to get them to sign petitions to put Wallace on the ballot.

I doubt that Ray decided while he was in Alabama to kill Dr. King. I believe that decision came later, and Ray may or may not have been assisted in making it. But his spending six weeks in "Wallace Country" certainly did nothing to slow the growth of an idea which may have been in Ray's mind since 1964.

Five

In every man's life, I suppose, there is a year, a season, or a month which he always remembers as his best, the time when he conquered despair and felt most like somebody. This time for James Earl Ray was the month he spent in Puerto Vallarta, in the state of Jalisco, Mexico. He told me repeatedly: "When I get out of jail again, I'm going back there to live."

But before he reached Puerto Vallarta, he said, he committed another border-crossing crime, which again raises all the unanswered questions. He wrote:

> I left Birmingham on Friday morning, October 6th. Somewhere in Louisiana [Baton Rouge] I mailed the safety deposit box key to the bank in Birmingham as I was sure I'd never see Birmingham again. I reached Nuevo Laredo about dark on Saturday, October 7th. I don't remember the name of the motel in Nuevo Laredo, but I'll draw you a map so you can find my registration record. I had been in the motel about two hours when Raoul came to my room. He told me to follow him across the border, back into Texas. He took a cab, and after we passed through U. S. customs he got out of the cab and into the Mustang with me. He directed me to a car in front of a frame house. He opened the

66

trunk of that car and transferred a tire on a car wheel to my car trunk. He rode with me as we again crossed the border into Mexico. At Mexican customs he got out and waited beside the building. Following his instructions, I asked the customs men for a tourist card, telling them I was going into the interior of Mexico, not just into Nuevo Laredo. [No tourist card is necessary to visit the border towns of Mexico; only if you are going into the interior. Mexican records show that such a tourist permit was issued to Eric S. Galt on October 7, 1967.] When the customs men started to search the car, I gave them $3 as Raoul had told me to do, and they stopped the search and put a mark on everything. Raoul and I then got in the car and drove to the motel where we had met and where I was registered. There we found the car Raoul had taken the tire out of: it had been driven there by another driver. Raoul again transferred the tire and wheel from my car back to the other car, which had a Mexican license plate. We talked a while, and Raoul said he wanted me to haul the tire through the Mexican interior customs check which is about 50 kilometers south of the border. He also told me to keep the photographic equipment for the time being.

I stayed at that motel that night, and next morning Raoul came and again transferred the tire to my car. Then I followed him and another man in the other car to the interior customs house where the officers checked both their car and mine. We drove both cars a little further, and when we were out of sight of the customs house, we again transferred the tire from my car to the other car. Then Raoul gave me $2,000, all in 20-dollar bills. He said he couldn't get the passport for me as yet, but for sure he'd have it for me the next time he saw me. He also said he'd have for me the $12,000, enough for me to go in business in a new country.

Raoul said he figured he'd need me again in about two or three months, and he suggested that I stay in Mexico. I told him I'd stay in Mexico for a while, but then I wanted to go to Los Angeles and wait there. (The main reason I wanted to go to Los Angeles was to see if I could get a job on a ship.) Raoul said okay, but for me to let him know where I was by calling the New Orleans telephone number from time to time, and that he'd write me general delivery in Los Angeles.

That scene, along a Mexican highway about 40 miles south of Nuevo Laredo, was enacted on Sunday morning, October 8, 1967.

Ray and *two* other men. This is the only time, according to Ray, that he ever met Raoul in company with a third criminal. Ray later expanded his account of this meeting. He said he got "mad as hell" when Raoul did not deliver him a passport, as Raoul had promised. And finally, to appease Ray, Raoul "coughed up another thousand, giving me a total of $3,000, which was more money than I had ever had just to live on."

Is Ray telling the truth about this border incident? There are indications that he is. Unless you insist on believing that he was retained in Montreal in August 1967 to murder Dr. King, and that he did nothing from then on but stand by, while being paid, waiting for someone to say *when,* then you must believe that Ray, a habitual thief, was practicing his trade. What Ray says he did on the Rio Grande is standard operating procedure for criminals who are running stolen goods from the United States into Mexico.

Criminals normally do not smuggle narcotics from the United States into Mexico. That traffic is one-way: from Canada and Mexico into the United States. What criminals smuggle from the United States into Mexico is jewelry and coin collections, either stolen by themselves or purchased from other robbers. Jewelry and rare coins can be "fenced" more easily in Mexico than in the United States. An automobile tire, looking like a normal spare in any car, can carry a fortune in such jewelry and coins.

I believe Ray got $2,000 or $3,000 at the border, but I feel that he has not told the whole truth about why Raoul and the other criminal paid him this money. I don't believe they would have paid him $2,000 or $3,000 for nothing more than his transporting the tire past two customs check points. If Raoul paid Ray only $750 for two trips across the border at Detroit with heroin, why would he have paid $2,000 or $3,000 for one trip with jewelry at Laredo? I believe that Ray himself had stolen, or helped to steal, some of the jewelry or rare coins, and that the money he received was payment both for his part of the stolen goods and for his taking the border risks.

In any case, on October 8, 1967, as he drove into Mexico, Ray was richer than he had ever been before. He told me:

> I had $1,500 when I got to Birmingham. There I was given $3,000. That made $4,500. I spent $2,500 for the car and the

photo equipment, and another $1,000 for living expenses. So I left Birmingham with the car and $1,000. Then I got all that money at the border. So I was a lot better off than I had ever been when I got to Mexico.

Ray's travels during his first ten days in Mexico proved revealing to me. He wrote:

I decided to go to Acapulco, and I drove directly there after leaving Raoul and the other man. In Acapulco I checked in at the San Francisco Motel, where I had stayed in early 1959. But next day I moved to another motel and stayed three days, before I decided to go to Puerto Vallarta. The reason I left Acapulco was that it had changed in the eight years since I had been there. Now everything was money, money, money. You couldn't park or go to the beach without somebody wanting pesos. I had read about Puerto Vallarta in *True*. On the way there I stayed three days at the Pancho Villa Motel in Guadalajara. I had an infected tooth, and the manager referred me to a dentist.

The fact that Ray was in Acapulco in 1959 indicates that between 1958, when he was released from Leavenworth, and 1960, when he was sent to Jefferson City, some of his robberies were successful. He was not always inept. Even then he was learning his trade and becoming crafty. And he had more highway mileage on him than Bonnie and Clyde.

One of my strangest discoveries was in Acapulco. There Ray spent the night of October 10, 1967, at the San Francisco Motel. On the morning of Monday, December 16, 1968, I walked into that motel with the chief of police of Acapulco. We told the manager we wanted to examine the registration of Eric S. Galt, and we thought the date was "around" October 10, 1967. The motel does not use registration cards: guests sign their names in a book. The manager found that the space in which Galt had registered had been scissored out; and, in accordance with police regulations, further down on the page an explanation had been written and signed. According to this explanation, on October 14, 1967, only four days after Ray arrived in Acapulco, and only seven days after he crossed the border at Nuevo Laredo and was given a tourist permit, his registration at the San Francisco Motel in Acapulco had been sought, examined and taken by Ramon del Rio, a Mexican federal police officer from Mexico City.

This can only mean that the border-crossing activities of Eric S. Galt had caused somebody to suspect him of criminal intent; and he was being trailed, perhaps watched, by Mexican police. In short, he was a criminal suspect in Mexico six months before the murder of Dr. King. And had the Mexican police only suspected him enough to question him, Dr. King might still be alive.

Ray didn't remember the name of the motel where he spent the nights of October 11, 12 and 13 in Acapulco. But he drew me another of his incredibly accurate maps, and I found it, and scissored his registration out of the book. The motel is the Marvel Inn, at 16 Costera Miguel Alemán, several blocks north of the San Francisco. In giving his address, Ray carelessly omitted the "Highland Avenue" and wrote only "2608 Birmingham, Alabama."

Ray continued:

> After having my tooth trouble in Guadalajara, I drove through Tepic toward Puerto Vallarta. The road between Tepic and Puerto Vallarta was bad. The rainy season was just ending. About 30 kilometers from Puerto Vallarta I got stuck. But since the road is just one lane wide, some Mexicans in a truck pulled me out so they could get through. I spent a month in Puerto Vallarta. The first three weeks I stayed at the Hotel Rio; the last week at the Tropicana which is right on the beach. This is the best town in Mexico. When I get out of jail again, I'm going back there permanently. Quite a few businesses there are owned by English-speaking persons.
>
> I spent most of my time on the beach. I was in one brothel in town several times, plus twice during the day on business. A male waiter there had a small lot he wanted to trade for my car. I went out and looked at the lot. The main reason I didn't trade for it is that it's illegal to trade or sell your car while in Mexico; and I was afraid if I traded, the police would find out and I'd be out both the car and the lot. For a time I thought about going back to the U. S., stealing a Mustang, and bringing it to Puerto Vallarta and trading it for the lot.
>
> On one occasion a man came to my hotel room late at night and said he had seen my Alabama tag and that he was from Alabama. He wanted to talk about Alabama. I guess he thought I was

crazy since I didn't say much as I didn't know much about the state. Several times people have said things to me about Alabama, both pro and con. In Los Angeles I once almost got arrested when people in a bar were razzing me about Wallace and Alabama. If I'm ever a fugitive again, I won't buy a car tag in Alabama. I'll pick some state that people don't want to talk so much about.

I spent three days in Puerto Vallarta, December 17–19, 1968, reconstructing the month which Ray spent there 13 months earlier. It's easy to understand why Ray found his month there so satisfying. Like Acapulco, Puerto Vallarta is on a Pacific Ocean bay, Bahía de Banderas, about 300 miles north of Acapulco. But unlike Acapulco, Puerto Vallarta is still primitive and cheap, though it has been discovered by American tourists, so it is "developing" rapidly and losing some of its primitiveness. Just how rapidly it is developing struck me when I reached my hotel, Posada Vallarta, and saw on a blackboard: "WELCOME PFIZER PEOPLE FROM ALABAMA AND MISSISSIPPI!" A hundred or more druggists and their families from these states were enjoying primitive, exotic sights as their reward for having "pushed" Pfizer pharmaceuticals.

In a place where donkeys still carry cinder blocks to build new motels, where the streets are rough cobblestones, and where the cars are jeeps and jalopies, Ray's Mustang gave him the status that a Rolls-Royce merits in Abilene, Kansas. Bartenders and whores alike yearned for rides in the Mustang and made it a conversation piece. Ray told them that he traded cars often, and that the reason why he hadn't traded this 1966 Mustang for the new 1968 model was that he particularly liked the 1966 model.

Ray achieved even higher status by changing his line of work. No longer was he an unemployed ship's cook or merchant mariner or shipyard worker; now he was a writer, employed by a publisher, and equipped with typewriter, notebooks and cameras. This won him attention because another writer, Tennessee Williams, started Puerto Vallarta on its road to development when his play *Night of the Iguana* was filmed there. Richard Burton and Elizabeth Taylor still own a home there.

Ray registered as Eric S. Galt at the Hotel Rio on October 19, 1967. He listed Alabama as his native state, and 2608 Highland

Avenue, Birmingham, as his permanent address. On the line asking his profession he wrote: "Employed by Publisher." He took a single room, European plan, and paid 60 pesos, or $4.80, a day. On November 6 he checked out of the Hotel Rio and into the Hotel Tropicana. Here he gave the same information about himself, but he took a *double* room, at 110 pesos, or $8.80, a day. This was unusually expensive for Ray, and the only time in his travels that I found him taking a double room.

Does this double room indicate that he was visited by a criminal accomplice? I thought it might, but Ray said no, it meant nothing more than that he had decided to spend his last week in Puerto Vallarta in a more expensive hotel which is directly on the beach. When a man traveling alone engages a double room, he often does it to secure the right to take women to the room; and this may be the explanation in this case. In Puerto Vallarta, as an author with a Mustang, Ray was more active sexually than at any other time or place in his life. He had at least two women, one named Irma and the other, Nina, and I found them both.

Irma was an attraction at one of Puerto Vallarta's two whorehouses, Casa Susanna, or the Blue House, which is not far from the Burton-Taylor home. I went there one evening. To me all whorehouses are sad places, and Mexican whorehouses seem sadder than most. At Casa Susanna the ground floor is for drinking and some dancing to jukebox music, and it's like a primitive bar or community center. The whores sit around the walls, waiting, while the men sit in the center of the room drinking and talking. Children wander in, then perhaps a goat or a pig, making the atmosphere earthy and elemental. Irma, of course, got her name from *Irma La Douce,* and since that musical was popular a decade ago, Irma is a decade past her prime. But she is not yet fat, and she still gets her share of attention.

Irma knows only those English words commonly used in her profession, but in Spanish she said she remembered Eric, that he liked to take her to the beaches, where he made pictures, that he was quiet and never laughed, that he had an English-Spanish phrase book and was trying to learn Spanish words, that he also wanted to learn Spanish dances, that he was not generous with her but was all right, and that she was surprised to learn that he could be a big killer.

The waiter at Casa Susanna who wanted to trade his land for Ray's Mustang is named Oscar Mendiola, a skinny little man with bad teeth. He said "Galt" came to Casa Susanna many nights to drink two screwdrivers, and that he usually sat alone or with Irma and said little.

The spot where *Night of the Iguana* was filmed, Mismaloya Beach, is 12 miles west of Puerto Vallarta. You can now go there on a bumpy gravel road, and on the beach is an open-air cantina which serves food and drink to patrons, who sit under palm trees. The manager of this cantina told me that Ray sometimes came there with Irma and Oscar, and the three always sat under the most remote palm tree.

Nina, younger than Irma, was a photographer at the largest and most expensive hotel, Posada Vallarta. Ray apparently had two interests in her: he also wanted her to help him with photography. She said she went out with him several times, and some of these trips were to a hidden, deserted beach where Ray made pictures of himself and also had her make pictures of him. Ray gave her the largest amount of money he ever gave any woman at one time: 500 pesos, or $40, and I couldn't learn from either Ray or Nina whether this was for sexual favors or photographic assistance.

Ray described for me an ingenious place maintained by Mexicans for "men and girls." I visited it with interest. It seems to be the Mexican answer to the American "hot bed" motel; and it's cheaper and more fun. At first sight it reminded me of the cribs which once graced Rampart Street in New Orleans; and, watching it being enjoyed, I thought of long-past orgies aboard ancient Pullmans on college football special trains.

To achieve this Mexican design, you first build a dozen or more cubicles, each a little roomier than a telephone booth. Then you stack these cubicles like cordwood, leaving the ends open and curtained. The only furniture is a blanket or pallet on what becomes the floor of each cubicle. Then you rent the cubicles to couples at 20 pesos ($1.60) an hour; and they climb up and in, using ladders, somewhat like climbing into an upper berth in an old Pullman.

The most appreciated advantage of this sort of honeycomb sex is the sound effects. Each couple is stimulated by the ecstasy voiced by their fellows, much, I suppose, as San Fernando Valley couples are said by *Playboy* magazine to enjoy communal intercourse on wall-to-wall carpets during Saturday nights of wife-swapping.

Twenty years ago, in *The Revolt of Mamie Stover,* I described how Mamie, in wartime Honolulu, constructed a "bull ring" of similar cubicles, around which she could walk, while quickly darting into a succession of openings to service a ready-and-waiting sailor or marine. So, after watching this Mexican variation, I suggested to the operator that he and I should incorporate and sell franchises in the United States.

For 20 pesos James Earl Ray could enjoy such pleasures in Puerto Vallarta. They would have cost him much more in Acapulco, where, as he says, everything is now "money, money, money."

To learn about what he called his "illegal activities" in Puerto Vallarta, Ray advised me to talk with "a fat bartender" at a hotel the name of which he had forgotten. He drew me a map showing how to find the hotel, and I found it. It is the Hotel Oceano; and the fat bartender's name is Louis Garcia, and he is an Indian-Mexican rather than a Spanish-Mexican. Louis speaks almost no English, but he said he saw Ray frequently, that Ray sometimes drank at his bar, and that Ray allowed him to drive the Mustang two or three times. He said Ray told him that he came to Mexico after serving 20 years in the U. S. Army. (Several hundred retired American service people have settled in Jalisco, most of them in and around Guadalajara.) And Louis Garcia described for me an evening he said he spent as Ray's guest at the Posada Vallarta when Ray was "after the photographer."

Ray and Louis drove to the Posada Vallarta in the Mustang and went into the bar area to be served drinks. When Louis ordered Scotch, Ray said: "That costs too much. If you drink Scotch, you'll have to pay for it yourself." Louis drank Scotch through the evening and paid for it himself. He said that Ray, when he came to the Oceano bar, never tipped anybody.

As an Indian, Louis Garcia came to Puerto Vallarta from "back in the hills." From time to time he returns to those hills. And it is "back in the hills" where marijuana is grown. When Ray left Puerto Vallarta to go to Los Angeles, he said he had a "large quantity" of marijuana in the Mustang. But he said he "got rid of it" before he reached the border.

At Hotel Rio, where Ray spent 19 days, I obtained his complete hotel record. It shows not a single charge against him, other than the room rent, for the entire 19 days. Not one telephone call or postage stamp. At the Hotel Tropicana, where he spent his last seven days, I was told that the charge record had been taken by Mexican police because there was one telephone call on it: a call from Ray to someone in Corpus Christi, Texas, made the day before Ray left. Ray told me he didn't make any such call, and I was never able to get any information from either the Mexican police or the FBI.

I visited the hidden beach where Ray told me he spent many hours alone, studying his features in a mirror and photographing himself. I tried to imagine him being there, and I tried to recreate his fantasies. Most certainly he was obsessed with the idea that the FBI would soon put him in the Top Ten and give him his yearned-for status as a criminal. Since the FBI couldn't confer such status on him until he committed a shocking crime, Ray might have been trying to think of a crime to commit which would qualify him for the Top Ten. As part of the game he thought he was playing with the FBI, he was trying to make pictures of himself in which he looked younger than in the pictures of him which the FBI would circulate. By the hour he studied the two "prominent features" of his face which he intended to have altered. These were his "prominent nasal tip" and the right ear lobe, which stood out too far from his head. (He explained to me how a criminal cannot afford easily described and easily recognized features. He said a criminal must have a face which "nobody can describe.") His plan was continuously to change his face and continuously to photograph it, while mailing out pictures of himself to correspondents in lonely-hearts clubs. Apparently he thought that, when he became a notorious criminal and the FBI published its pictures of him, then some of his correspondents would give their pictures of him to newspapers, the differences in the pictures would be noted, and this would spread the confusing impression that the man being sought by the FBI was not, in fact, the *real* James Earl Ray.

As I sat on that deserted beach, I couldn't believe that Ray, when he was there, already had been hired to kill Dr. King. Nor had he yet decided to kill Dr. King or anyone else. He was a self-obsessed criminal fugitive, determined to become notorious, but he hadn't chosen the crime he thought would make him notorious. At a cost of about $25 a day he was sleeping, eating, drinking, fucking, driving a Mustang, lying on beaches, following a routine he could support by criminal activity which might or might not involve using the pistol he carried. Yet he was dissatisfied and depressed. He thought notoriety would make him feel better. So he was trying to decide how to achieve notoriety.

On Tuesday, November 14, 1967, his Mustang loaded with marijuana, Ray left Puerto Vallarta, heading up the Pacific Coast. He crossed the border again, and on Sunday, November 19, as Eric S. Galt, he rented, for $100 a month, apartment 6 at 1535 North Serrano Avenue, Los Angeles, California.

Hollywood Boulevard is about four miles long, and it runs east and west through the Hollywood District of the City of Los Angeles. Once, when "Hollywood" meant motion pictures, this boulevard was thought to be glamorous, and the intersection of Hollywood Boulevard and Vine Street was almost as famous as that of Broadway and 42nd Street. Now the glamor is long-gone. Much of the boulevard has been claimed by hippies and other rootless, aimless people; and the shops, bars and rooming houses are relatively cheap.

About a mile east of the Hollywood and Vine intersection, and a mile south of Griffith Park, Hollywood Boulevard intersects Western Avenue. And it was in this neighborhood—Hollywood and Western—that Ray lived during the four months immediately preceding the murder of Dr. King. Serrano Avenue parallels Western and is a block east of Western; and Ray lived at 1535 North Serrano, a few doors south of Hollywood Boulevard, from November 19, 1967, to January 17, 1968. He then moved about three blocks, to the St. Francis Hotel, at 5533 Hollywood Boulevard, and lived there from January 17 to March 17, when he left Los Angeles to murder Dr. King in Memphis on April 4, 1968.

The St. Francis is a narrow, four-story yellow-brick hotel. Most of its rooms are occupied by retired men and women. On its ground floor is a bar, the Sultan Room; and a block west, at 5623 Hollywood Boulevard, is another bar, the Rabbit's Foot Club. Both these bars open at 6:30 A.M. to offer pick-me-ups to their patrons; so each provides 20 hours a day of convivial seclusion, in murky, jukebox-riven atmosphere, to lonely people with modest means. Ray was a patron of these bars during his four months in this neighborhood.

He made no friends or close acquaintances, and he found no sexual partners he can remember. The several employes of the bars who remember him say that he told them that he was "from Alabama" but that he had been living in Mexico, where he owned a tavern. He affected several Spanish words and phrases. So in the seven months since he escaped from the Missouri State Penitentiary, he had traveled 7,000 miles and progressed from being a dishwasher to being a merchant mariner, then a shipyard worker, then an author employed by a publisher, and now he was an Alabama-born owner of a tavern in Mexico and he was in Los Angeles "looking around for another tavern to buy."

The woman he says he knew best worked as a cocktail waitress in the Sultan Room. He says her name is Marie Deninno, but she says she changed her name to Marie Martin during the years when she was an "exotic dancer." In 1968 she said she was thirty-five. Soon after he reached Los Angeles from Mexico, Ray bought a console TV set; and before he left Los Angeles for Atlanta, he traded his console set to Marie Martin for her portable set. (He left this portable set in Atlanta when he fled to Canada after the murder.) Marie Martin has two cousins: Rita Stein and Rita's brother, Charles Stein, who is a bearded, thirty-eight-year-old writer of songs. In a casual way, Ray became involved with all three of these people.

About two weeks after he began coming to the Sultan Room, Ray mentioned to Marie Martin that he'd soon be making a "quick trip" to New Orleans. Marie Martin then explained to him that Rita Stein had two children, about eight and ten years old, who

were visiting Rita's sister in New Orleans; and Marie Martin asked
Ray to take Charles Stein with him on the round trip to New Orleans and to bring the two children back on the return trip. Ray
agreed on one condition. George Wallace was then campaigning
to get on the California ballot as a Presidential candidate, and Ray
told Marie Martin that he'd "help her out" if, first, she and Rita
Stein and Charles Stein would go with him to Wallace headquarters
in the Hollywood District and sign a petition to get Wallace on the
ballot. The three agreed, and Ray drove them in the Mustang to
Wallace headquarters on Lankershim Boulevard, where they
signed the petition. Charles Stein then made the round trip to New
Orleans with Ray, and the children rode with them from New Orleans to Los Angeles.

This means that only four months before the murder, and on a
trip which might have been connected with the murder, Charles
Stein spent 50 hours at Ray's side in the Mustang. So FBI agents
questioned Mr. Stein as to Ray's conversation and conduct. But
Mr. Stein could add little to the general report on Ray. He said
that Ray's few Spanish words struck him as being "touristy" so he
didn't believe Ray's claim that he owned and had operated a bar
in Mexico. The two men separated when they reached New Orleans, and Mr. Stein said he had no knowledge of what Ray did
during the 36 hours they spent there. Mr. Stein said that Ray made
several telephone calls during the trip.

Ray told me that he told Mr. Stein nothing, that during the trip
Mr. Stein busied himself looking for flying saucers, and that he
(Ray) made only one telephone call—to his brother Jerry at the
Sportsman's Country Club in Wheeling, Illinois. (Jerry was work-
ing as a "maintenance man" at this club.) Ray wrote:

> In the bar of the St. Francis I mentioned I was making a quick
> trip to New Orleans, and a waitress asked me to give her cousin
> a ride and to bring two children back. I didn't mind helping them
> out. I was just going for a conference with Raoul, and I was com-
> ing right back to L. A. Stein and I took turns driving and drove
> day and night.
> The day after I got to New Orleans I was ready to leave. I just
> talked to Raoul about some activities. Raoul was interested in a
> job he wanted us to do in about two or three months. Then he

said we'd be finished, and, for sure, he'd give me complete travel papers and $12,000 and help me go anywhere in the world I wanted to go. He wanted me to be careful, and not get in any trouble, and he'd keep in touch. When I asked him what the next job was, he said not to worry about it and not to ask questions. Then he gave me another $500, all in 20-dollar bills. I wanted to leave for Los Angeles next day, but Stein was picking up the children and wanted to visit some more relatives, so I agreed to wait one more day for him.

Ray told me that he didn't remember the name or exact address of the tavern in New Orleans where he met his criminal contact, but again he drew me a diagram. He placed the tavern on Canal Street and showed me its location in relation to the intersections of Canal Street and St. Charles Avenue and of Canal Street and Chartres Street. He said that the tavern "backed up" to the French Quarter and that, when I got inside, I'd find that the bar was not "straight but had bulging waves in it."

On the night of Saturday, December 14, 1968, almost exactly a year after Ray was there, I was in New Orleans retracing his movements. The temperature was near freezing and the wind cut through my topcoat. I have known New Orleans since my university days and as a journalist I have been there many times. It was there in 1954 that I found the doctor who, in the Vosges Mountains in France on January 31, 1945, pronounced Eddie Slovik dead from a firing-squad volley (*The Execution of Private Slovik*). And it was there in 1963 that I investigated Claude Eatherly's role in a 1947 plot to invade Cuba. (*The Hiroshima Pilot*). I don't know all the taverns in New Orleans, but I know my share of them.

The tavern Ray described was easy to find. It is called Le Bunny Lounge and is at 611 Canal Street. In the shadow of the Monteleone Hotel, it is within a few feet of where Exchange Place intersects Canal. Lee Harvey Oswald lived on or in Exchange Place, which is also called Exchange Alley. So the assassin of Dr. King met a criminal contact in New Orleans within a few hundred feet of where the assassin of President Kennedy once sat in his doorway and whistled at passing women.

On the two nights which Ray spent in New Orleans on that trip, he slept ten blocks from Le Bunny Lounge, at the Provincial Motel, in the French Quarter, 1024 Chartres Street. The Provincial is one of several motels which have been built recently in the Quarter. Its postcards furnish this information: "Virtually all the rooms in this handsome, two story, red brick, award-winning motel overlook a charming patio. The Provincial is the only motel in the heart of the French Quarter that has self-service parking near rooms. It combines the elegance of the centuries old French buildings that surround it with swimming pool and all modern conveniences."

In the lobby of the Provincial I examined the registration of Eric S. Galt, of Birmingham; and a friendly, white-haired woman spoke guardedly to me. "I wonder," she said, "when you investigators are going to uncover the man who is behind all these assassinations? I think I know who he is. I worked at the Monteleone for years. I used to walk down Exchange Alley every day to work, and that crazy Oswald used to whistle at me, though obviously I'm not a young woman. I watched some of the survivors of the Cuban Brigade parade in New Orleans after they had been ransomed from Castro. They were captured by Castro at the Bay of Pigs when the Kennedys double-crossed them and failed to give them air support. Many people in this city had hopes and money bet on the Bay of Pigs, and they hate everybody they blame for our failure there. They hated Dr. King because he supported Castro. Now they want Wallace for President. I think Bay of Pigs hate is behind all the assassinations, and I think one or two men have put up all the money." She whispered to me the name of a prominent citizen of New Orleans whom she suspects of "paying for the assassinations."

That woman voiced an opinion held by many Americans. She honestly believes that one or two men in New Orleans planned and paid for the murders of President Kennedy, Dr. King, and Senator Kennedy. She can never be convinced that these three murders are not "connected together in some way." She believes that they all resulted from some high-level conspiracy.

If you are in New Orleans on a cold Saturday night, walking through the French Quarter with the ghosts of assassins, you find it easy to believe in conspiracy. You feel surrounded by criminal intent. You suspect every fellow who approaches you through the shadows of being either a kook or a convict. Evil seems to lurk behind every lattice, and wherever you see two heads together, you imagine they are plotting treason, murder or highway robbery.

As I walked from the Provincial Motel back to the St. Charles Hotel, I felt this old urge to believe in conspiracy. I thought: "When James Earl Ray was walking here, along Chartres, Bourbon and Royal Streets on the nights of December 17 and 18, 1967, goddam it, he *might* have been plotting to murder Martin Luther King on April 4, 1968! He *might* have made that trip from Los Angeles because he was summoned here by men who had retained him to murder Dr. King at what they thought would be the most opportune moment to trigger racial rioting which would aid the Presidential candidacy of George Wallace!" Ray wanted me to believe this. He wanted his lawyers to believe it. He wants everybody to believe it. And for *Look* magazine in September and early October 1968, I had written that I believed it would prove to be true.

But it didn't prove to be true. The Retainer Thesis—that James Earl Ray was retained by somebody, either with or without his own knowledge when the first payment was made, to stand by for months and then murder Dr. King on cue—this thesis will not survive daylight and reason. I began to reject it by late October 1968. Ray's subsequent behavior belies it.

Ray didn't make this trip to New Orleans because he was summoned there by men who had retained him to kill Dr. King at a time and place to be decided. Ray later insisted to me that he traveled to New Orleans on his own initiative, that he was never *summoned*. He made this trip because he was a burglar, a thief, an armed robber, a smuggler, a forger, and a dealer in marijuana and other drugs. He came to New Orleans to dispose of stolen goods. Or to receive stolen goods he was to dispose of. Or to deliver or receive drugs. And to discuss more such criminal activity. For three months he had been taking a correspondence course in locksmithing. Since he didn't plan to serve the public as a locksmith, he could only have been trying to improve himself as a burglar. Later he told me that, while he was in New Orleans on this trip, "another trip to Mexico was discussed." He met criminal contacts in New Orleans for the same reason he had met them in Montreal and Windsor and Birmingham and Nuevo Laredo.

Had Fidel Castro wanted to murder Dr. King to intensify racial conflict in the United States, Castro's agents in New Orleans would have hired an experienced killer, not James Earl Ray. Had some wealthy citizen of New Orleans wanted to murder Dr. King for a similar reason, he could have hired the job done for $3,000 or less. Killing Dr. King was an easy criminal chore. He was an unarmed citizen who entered and left his home each day without armed escort. Anyone wanting to murder him didn't have to retain James Earl Ray nine months or even four months in advance.

All this was to become clear to me. But on the night of December 14, 1968, as I roamed through the French Quarter listening to whispered convictions of conspiracy, I was tempted again to concede that *somebody* other than Ray had planned the death of Dr. King.

I reminded Ray that Christmas 1967 was the first Christmas in eight years he had spent outside prison. "So it must have been a memorable day for you," I wrote. "You had returned to Los Angeles from New Orleans. You say your cash balance was then $2,800. What do you remember doing that Christmas?"

He replied:

> I don't remember anything about that Christmas. You ought to know that Christmas is for family people. It don't mean anything to a loner like me. It's just another day and another night to go to a bar or sit in your room and look at the paper and drink a beer or two and maybe switch on the TV. No, I don't remember anything about Christmas. But I do remember New Year's Eve and New Year's Day. I drove up to Las Vegas. Nobody went with me. I didn't do any gambling. I just drove up there and looked around and watched people poking money into slot machines. I slept a while in my car, then drove back to L. A.

That was two and a half months before he left Los Angeles for New Orleans, Selma, Birmingham, Atlanta and Memphis to murder Dr. King.

Six

The answer to why Ray killed Dr. King begins to become apparent, I believe, when you study his position and conduct in Los Angeles during the two and a half months between January 2 and March 17, 1968. His position was hopeless, yet he tried to hope. He couldn't work at any lawful job because he couldn't furnish a social security number or any record of past employment. Yet he sought jobs. Twice he advertised in *The Los Angeles Times* for employment as a "culinary," which means kitchen work. He received offers which he couldn't accept, because each prospective employer asked for his social security card. He took a course in bartending, did well in it, completed it and was offered jobs. But there was an additional reason why he couldn't work as a bartender. In addition to wanting to see every employe's social security card, most employers of bartenders in California insist that their prospective employes be "passed" by the police. And there is a bartenders' union to consider.

Ray took a course in dancing, still, in fantasy, seeing himself doing the rhumba in some Latin American country from which he could never be extradited to the United States. And while he was trying to get a job, and to learn to dance, and to tend bar, he consulted no fewer than eight different psychiatrists, hypnotists and Scientologists, trying to find relief from his depressions and feelings of inadequacy. He planned, then had plastic surgery, and all the while he was mailing photographs of himself to women in lonely-hearts clubs. He was a habitual criminal, at war with society, hopelessly alone, obviously doomed to death in some institution, yet he still yearned to be something he could never be. And he continued to search for someone who could tell him how he could feel like somebody.

During his eight months in jail in Memphis Ray wrote three separate accounts of this California period. In February 1969, after Percy Foreman had become his attorney, he wrote the following account. And I will reproduce this account exactly as he wrote it.

> Upon my arrival in California from Mexico I moved into an apartment at 1535 Serrano. (Rent $100.00 a month) After I was in L. A. about 10 days I went to the post office and inquired if I had any mail (Gen Dil.) I was told no, then I called Raoul in N. O. Someone else answered and ask me if I could come down around Xmas, I agreed. I also had a phone instaled as I wanted to inquire about jobs. During this time I made the following efforts to obtain employment.
> 1. Attempt to get job (filled out form) with internal revenue. This job consisted of filling out peoples income tax forms. This add was in the *L. A. Times*.
> 2. Ran two adds in the *L. A. Times* but all wanted S. S. cards or references.
> 3. Took bartending course, $125.00.
> 4. Made long distance call to Big Bear Ski Lodge.
> Also took dance course but complete only half of it, price $466.00. The add in the paper said it would cost $32.00, but they coned the country boy. The reason I took this was that I thought I mite stay in Mexico if I went their again, also about this time I found out you could go to Columbia S. A. without a passport.
> While I was in Canada an escaped convict named Benny Edmondson was arrested working in Montreal at Expo. He had escaped from the same pen as me. I knew him, and he had been out about a year when the FBI put him on the Top 10. There Fore when I got to Calif I thought there was a good chance I would

be added to the list in the not to distance future. It was while in Mexico I thought of a way which I mite beat a chance identification. And that was to have plastic surgery. Also I had took a picture of myself in Mexico, the only one I ever had taken outside of prison, I saw it made me look younger than I was. I had also read that in a photograph your nose and ears or prominent features show up, so I desided to have them altered. I had also read some people are not photogenic, which I am not. Therefore I made an appointment with Dr. Russell Hadley for plastic surgery on my nose. I told the doctor I was going to get a job during T. V. commercials was why I wanted plastic surgery. Before I had the surgery I took more pictures of myself with the camera. I then ran an add in one of the underground newspapers asking to exchange photographs with women. I thing most of these are hippie types as hippes sell the papers. I didn't give my address in the add as I didn't want the police or any of the hippies coming around. I instead rented a mail drop in Alhambra, Calif. I then sent $2.00 to this same paper for a list of these women advertisers.

When I got the list of women who wanted to exchange pictures, I sent out pictures I had took of me all over the U. S. They were all the same, a kind of profile view. I then had the plastic surgery.

When your operated on for plastic surgery they freeze the area, my case the nose, then they tear down the cartliage and mold it any way they want to. My nose was straight and pointed before operation and to one side. After he had finished I went back to the hotel room and while the nose was still numb I removed the tape and pushed the nose to the other side and down to change the way the doctor had shaped it in case he remembered me. I was supposed to go back for pictures later but naturlly never did. I was then going to another plastic surgeon to have my left ear set back but never did as I had to meet Raoul and never had time.

During this time I had wrote Coast Guard about procedure for getting job on ship. Coast Guard may have record or letter may have been left in Atlanta. This was one reason I wanted plastic surgery, for the picture on seamans papers (U. S. or Canada) or for passport. During this time I saw an article about the South African Regional Concil. This concil was supposed to have info. about English-speaking countrys in Africa, but it didn't give the address. I then called several org. asking info. about this concil, one of them was the John Birch Society. They said they had the address and would send it to me which they did along with a pamphlet. This pamplet and the under ground newspaper are the only publications which could be called controversial. (When I left Atlanta I left these two publications on a table and threw the other books away, that might be why the hunt centered in L. A. right after the shooting, both publications were from Calif. and they mite of thought I was involved with them. I also went to Las Vegas New Years.)

I also took a course in hypnosis while in L. A. I had read a lot about it in prison on how it was used in dintistry and medicine. The first person I went to wasn't a hypnosis but I gave him my right name (Ray) as I thought I might tell him under hypnosis influence. The other one I went to was a hypnosis and also a preacher and he ran a business consultant school on the side. Most of his clients were salesmen and people who were trying to stop smoking or drinking, and I don't think he had any doctors license. In this part of the country (Memphis) hypnotism is kind of frown upon I guess but in Calif. their are many of these schools. (All of this cost about $65.00)

Their was also an article in *Life* which said I made an anti Negro statement in a L. A. bar. It quoated the bartender as saying that I made the statements on my last appearance in that bar.

This is my version. I did go in that bar several times. The only reason I went in their was to watch the floor show. On this particular nite they was someone sitting next to me who talked about 30 minutes without stopping about the state of the world. Their was also a young girl sitting on the other side of me. I mite of told the guy who was talking to me where I was from as I think he ask me, or she mite have seen my car with the Alabama licence on it. Anyhow when the conversationlist left she started by asking me how come they deny colors their rights in Alabama. I think I ask her if she had ever been there or something like that and walked out. Their was two guys next to her and when I went out they must of followed me. (The story in *Life* don't mention this part) Anyhow the big one grab me from behind and pulled my coat over my arms (I had a suit on) the shorter one started hitting and asking for my money. He pulled my watch off I jerked away (as I was scared police would show up) but he held on to my coat and guess he still has it. I ran across the street to the car but couldn't get in as the keys were in my coat. I had a 38 under the seat so maybe it was just as well. I then ran through a church yard and circled around and got back to apartment. The next day

I went to a locksmith on Hollywood Blvd and had him make me
a set of keys as I only had one. I also bought another watch on
Hollywood Blvd. The locksmith guy ask me what happened and
I told him I lost them outside the tavern. I didn't want to tell him
I was robbed as he mite of went to police. He also told me he
was from Tennessee. (I know the app. address of both the locksmith and the store I bought the watch at) Also the pants of this
suit coat they took from me is in my personal here. The next day I
went back to the tavern and asked if my coat was their as someone
might of found it on the street. The bartender said no, and the
girl was also in their. The place wasn't a hippie joint but the client
were not average people.

This account is important in understanding Ray: important for
what it doesn't say as well as for what it says. The altercation and
robbery he describes occurred in and outside the Rabbit's Foot
Club. I found five employes or habitués who say they remember
Ray, and clearly remember the evening of the hot dispute "when
a Negro got hit on the head with a rock in the nearby parking lot."
They all describe Ray as a "quiet, moody fellow from Alabama who
said he owned a bar in Mexico and who preached Wallace for
President." They say he was neat, always tried to sit on a barstool
near the door, and usually just sat there alone, staring at his drink
(vodka and orange juice) and maybe pulling on his ear. To none
of them did Ray say what his name was, and they learned his real
name and some of his aliases when, after the murder, FBI agents
showed them pictures which they identified.

In their version of the dispute, the white girl sitting next to Ray
was indeed needling him for "the way you treat Negroes in Alabama." She asked him: "Why don't you give them their rights?"
Ray, quite angry, jumped off his stool, grabbed the girl by the hand
and pulled her off, and said loud enough for everybody to hear:
"Since you love niggers so much, I'll just take you right down to
Watts [a Negro district in which there had been a highly publicized
riot] and drop you off down there and see how much you like it!"

When Ray stalked out, two men, one white and one black, followed him. I couldn't learn their names, but Ray's account of
what happened outside is apparently correct. He says they jumped
on him and stole his watch and his coat, in which were his wallet

and his car keys. Ray told me that, "to get away from them, I picked up a brick and hit that nigger in the head."

After this fight Ray was gravely worried. His brothers say he has always had a high temper. But, as a fugitive, he knew he couldn't afford a barroom brawl. So this is the only occasion I can find where, after his escape from the Missouri State Penitentiary, he did any yelling or fighting. Hiding in darkness outside the Rabbit's Foot Club, he figured the police might be notified and that they might watch the Mustang and arrest him when he approached it. He was also afraid that his assailants, since they had his keys, might steal the car. So he spent the night hiding and watching the car. By 9 A.M. next day he decided that the police had not been notified, that they were not watching the car, so he then engaged the locksmith, who went with him to the car, opened it and made him a new set of keys.

The wallet stolen from Ray contained about $60; it also contained his precious driver's license. So here I can clear up a mystery which has puzzled FBI agents and other students of this case. On March 1, 1968, about a month before the murder, Alabama traffic authorities issued a duplicate driver's license to Eric Starvo Galt and mailed it to 2608 Highland Avenue, Birmingham. This fact has been interpreted to mean either that Ray was in Birmingham at this time or that "someone else" got this duplicate driver's license. The truth is that, from California, Ray telephoned the Alabama authorities, told them he had lost his license, and was instructed to send 25 cents and make application for a duplicate. He did this; the duplicate was mailed to him in Birmingham, where it was forwarded to him at general delivery, Los Angeles. Ray received this duplicate license about March 10, a week before he left Los Angeles to murder Dr. King. He carried it until he reached Toronto, after the murder, where he destroyed it. (By then he had assumed another name, and a license in the name of Eric Starvo Galt in his possession was a threat to him.)

Ray's story of the car keys, however, does provide evidence of "someone else." The man in Birmingham who sold Ray the Mustang, Mr. Paisley, distinctly remembers giving Ray two sets of keys. Ray told me that in Birmingham he delivered one set of these keys to Raoul, the man who, Ray says, put up the money to buy the car.

The fact that, after one set of keys was stolen from him, Ray was compelled to engage a locksmith to make a new set for him, indicates to me that Ray is telling the truth when he says he delivered to someone else the second set of keys given to Ray by Mr. Paisley.

I believe that on April 4, 1968, when Dr. King was murdered, somewhere else, perhaps in Birmingham or New Orleans but possibly in Memphis, there was another man who had keys to the Mustang in which Ray fled the murder scene. And this other man may still have that set of keys.

Ray's reference to a criminal named Benny Edmondson needs careful explanation and understanding. First, you must know that there is a television show called *The FBI*. It is shown on the ABC network each Sunday at 8 P.M. Eastern time. This weekly TV drama is Ray's favorite entertainment. In prison or out, he never likes to miss it. Invariably it shows FBI agents in clever and successful pursuit of clever criminals. Frequently, near the end of the show, the FBI presents its gallery of Ten Most Wanted Criminals—what Ray calls "the Top Ten." Ray regards the criminals in the Top Ten the way people in show business regard Academy Award winners. Or the way fashionable women regard the annual list of Ten Best-Dressed Women. Criminals, too, want status—as criminals.

The FBI's Top Ten changes, of course, when one on the list is caught or killed and another is elevated to the tenth position. On the television show, the newest member of the Top Ten is given special attention. His features, habitats and modes of operation are described; and TV viewers are asked to look for him and, if they see someone they think may be him, to telephone the FBI. It is very dramatic: a nationwide game of hide and seek.

During some of the years Ray spent at the Missouri State Penitentiary, Benny Edmondson was also a prisoner there. He was a much higher-status criminal than Ray: he was better educated, more dangerous, had pulled off bigger robberies, and was therefore more respected among prisoners. Late in 1966 Edmondson escaped, reached Canada, and, using the alias Alex Borman, he worked himself into a responsible position with the Canadian Centennial Exposition, called "Expo." After the FBI "put him on the Top Ten" and publicized him on the TV show, he was recognized and arrested in Canada. He fought extradition, but he was returned to the Missouri State Penitentiary.

Ray escaped from the Missouri State Penitentiary while Edmondson was in Canada, while Edmondson was on the Top Ten, and before Edmondson had been arrested. So when Ray began writing to me about his knowing Edmondson and about Edmondson's having been arrested at Expo, I suspected that Ray, in July 1967, might have gone to Canada to meet Edmondson and that Edmondson might have been the brain behind the murder of Dr. King.

Accordingly, when on December 27, 1968, I visited the Missouri State Penitentiary, I had with me Ray's written references to Edmondson, and I wanted to show them to Edmondson and ask him if he ever had any conversations with Ray. I particularly wanted to ask Edmondson if he had met Ray in Canada.

The Missouri prison system is headed by three remarkable men. They are not the political hacks who often head such systems. All three are veterans of the Federal Bureau of Prisons, and they were persuaded to come to Missouri and try to upgrade and modernize that state's system. The highest ranking officer is Fred T. Wilkinson, head of the Missouri Department of Corrections. His deputy is Ward G. Kern; and the warden of the Missouri State Penitentiary at Jefferson City is Harold Swenson. Mr. Wilkinson is a former deputy director of the Federal Bureau of Prisons, and a former warden of the federal prisons at McNeil Island and at Atlanta. Mr. Kern was at Leavenworth, Alcatraz and McNeil Island; and Mr. Swenson was at Leavenworth, Terre Haute and Texarkana. So these men are capable professionals.

Mr. Swenson showed me that Edmondson was arrested at Shawville, Quebec, Canada, on June 29, 1967. That was five days after Ray left the Indian Trail Restaurant in Chicago. It seems unlikely that Ray could have met Edmondson in Canada because, by the time Ray is known to have reached Canada, Edmondson had been in custody almost a month.

I then suggested that I be allowed to talk with Edmondson, to show him what Ray had written and to question him about any conversations he may have had with Ray while they both were in the Missouri prison. To that suggestion Mr. Swenson's reaction was revealing.

"Well," he said, "if you insist, I suppose we can let you talk with Edmondson. But I had rather you didn't. Edmondson is a big shot among prisoners. It has taken us months to get him quieted down after his escapade in Canada. If you show him that Ray was influenced by him, hell, Edmondson will get all excited and probably start taking credit for the King murder. And you can be certain on one point. Benny Edmondson never talked with James Earl Ray. Edmondson wouldn't give Ray the time of day. Edmondson is a big shot; Ray, while he was here, was a nobody. Nobody ever paid any attention to Ray. The only reason I remember Ray is because he was always trying to escape."

There, I'm convinced, is a large part of the explanation why Ray killed Dr. King. Ray wanted to be like Benny Edmondson. Ray didn't want to remain a nobody among prisoners all his life. Ray wanted to make the Top Ten as Edmondson had. Ray wanted to see his own face in full color on his favorite TV show. Ray thought that attention and recognition would relieve his feelings of inadequacy and make him feel like somebody.

On January 4, 1968, exactly four months before he killed Dr. King, Ray kept an appointment he had made with the head of the International Society of Hypnosis, the Reverend Xavier von Koss, at his office at 16010 Crenshaw Boulevard, in the South Bay area of Los Angeles.

Nine months later, on September 27, I talked with the Reverend von Koss, a well-educated, middle-aged man who conducts self-improvement seminars and, among other things, tries to help salesmen find more self-confidence. Ray had forgotten his name and exact address, but again Ray's diagram showing me how to find the office was accurate. The office is almost directly across Crenshaw Boulevard from El Camino College. The Reverend von Koss describes himself as "an internationally recognized authority on hypnosis and self-hypnosis in the field of self-improvement."

"Yes," said the Reverend von Koss, "according to my record and my notes, Eric Galt telephoned me and came here for an interview at 2 P.M. on Thursday, January 4, 1968. We talked for an hour. I remember him clearly. He seemed very much interested in self-improvement. He wanted to find a way to improve himself and his life. He had read several books on the subject and was impressed with the degree of mind concentration which one can obtain by the use of hypnosis. He wanted to use this for self-improvement. He mentioned that people who use hypnosis often can solve problems in 30 seconds which normally would require 30 minutes at the conscious level. He also seemed to be aware of self-image and its importance to a person. So he had studied hypnosis and self-hypnosis, and he came to me seeking further information.

"I questioned him about his goals in life, and he told me he was considering taking a course in bartending. I explained carefully that, to reach a better and more satisfying life, one must clearly see in one's mind what one wants to achieve. He seemed in full agreement. But when I emphasized that he must complete his course in bartending, that he must work hard, that he must go to night school, that he must construct a settled-down life, I could feel a wall rising between us. I lost him. His mind moved far away from what I was saying to him. I, of course, did not then know of his desperate situation. But I could clearly feel whatever it was in him which prevented his moving toward a way of life that would satisfy him."

"Did you reach any conclusions about him?" I asked. "His capabilities? His fantasies?"

"Yes. All persons, like myself, who work in the profession of mind power can readily discern the main motivational drive of any person. Ray belongs to the *recognition* type. He desires recognition from his group, from himself. He yearns to feel that he is somebody. The desire for recognition for him is superior to sex, superior to money, superior to self-preservation."

"Did you offer him any advice?"

"Well," said the Reverend von Koss, "I tried to paint a picture of a future in which he would have recognition as a worthwhile member of society. I noticed how he went along with me and then seemed to collapse."

"Of course," I said. "He was a fugitive. He couldn't hold a job in a society where every member is numbered. The way of life you pictured was impossible for him."

"I know that now," the Reverend von Koss replied. "I learned it when Eric Galt was revealed to be an accused assassin. He had given my name as a reference somewhere, so FBI agents came and I gave them my record."

"Did you hypnotize him?"

"I tested him for hypnosis. But I quickly encountered very strong subconscious resistance. He could not cooperate. This, of course, is always the case when a person fears that under hypnosis he may reveal something he wishes to conceal. So I didn't press further with Ray. I felt sorry for him. I wished I could help him. But there was nothing I could do except recommend a few books for him to study."

"What books did you recommend?"

"Well, the list is here in my notes. I recommended three books: *How to Cash in on Your Hidden Memory Power* by William D. Hersey. *Self Hypnotism: The Technique and Its Use in Daily Living* by Leslie M. LeCron. And *Psycho-Cybernetics* by Maxwell Maltz."

When Ray was arrested at the London airport, in his luggage officers of Scotland Yard found well-worn copies of all three of these books. I read them. All of them are addressed to individuals who feel inadequate and who yearn for self-improvement. All of them emphasize that one must first envision a goal in life and then seek it. The definition of psycho-cybernetics seems to be "goal seeking." Since I am a golfer, concerned with sinking putts and depressed when I miss a short one, I noted Dr. Maltz's advice on how to sink a putt. The doctor says that, as you survey the putt, you must convince yourself that you can sink it. Using your mind power, you must compel yourself to "see" the putt rolling along your selected line and falling into the cup. In your mind you must never "see" the ball hanging on the lip, or rimming the cup, or missing in any other manner. This is good advice, but I still miss putts which I have "seen" drop into the cup.

Ray attended the International School of Bartending, 2125 Sunset Boulevard, from January 15 to March 2, 1968. The manager, Tomas R. Lau, said that the tuition was $220. He also said that Ray was a "nice fellow with a slight Southern accent, very intelligent, with ability to develop in this type of service." When Ray first talked with him, Mr. Lau said, "he was desperate to get a job and wanted to go to work as soon as possible." However, upon graduation, when Mr. Lau obtained a job for him, Ray turned it down, saying: "I have to leave to see my brother. What good would it do for me to work only two or three weeks? I'll wait till I get back here, then I can take a permanent job."

This means that a month before he killed Dr. King, and two weeks before he left Los Angeles to commit the murder, Ray told Mr. Lau that "I have to leave to see my brother."

When Ray graduated from the bartending school, on Saturday morning, March 2, 1968, he was photographed in a group with other graduates. He had arrived at the school that morning without a coat or a necktie. For the photograph, Mr. Lau loaned Ray a black coat and a black bow tie. Ray didn't want to be in the picture, but felt he couldn't refuse. So he put on the coat and bow tie, and he told me that, as the picture was snapped, he deliberately closed his eyes. He also told me that this was the first time in his life he had ever worn a bow tie.

FBI agents visited Mr. Lau and his school on Tuesday, April 16, 12 days after the murder. "I was really surprised when the FBI came here and asked about him," Mr. Lau said. "I could believe it was almost anyone but him." The agents seized Ray's application to attend the school, along with his graduation photograph. This picture of Ray, with the bow tie and his eyes closed, is the last known picture to be made of him before the murder. So FBI agents used it in tracking Ray and released it for publication. An FBI artist painted eyes on it, after which the agents used two pictures: one with the eyes closed, and another with the artificial eyes painted on. Use of this photograph, with the painted-on eyes and the bow tie, which no one had ever seen Ray wear, was, to a degree, unfortunate. Ray was recognized, but there was some confusion, and recognition was not so instant and positive as it could have been. In short, Ray's trick of closing his eyes was at least partially successful.

When you examine Ray's application for admission to the bartending school, you wonder how Mr. Lau could have admitted him on it. He gave his name as Eric S. Galt, but he declined to give his social security number. He gave his age as thirty-six when he was nearly forty. He listed only one former employer: a "Mr. Willer, 751 S. Figeroa," who apparently did not exist, and Ray gave no date of employment by Mr. Willer. He listed his salary as "50.00." His three character references were the three he had befriended on the trip to New Orleans, but he got their names wrong: "Marie Deninno, Rita Steen, Charly Deninno." Ray paid so little attention to names that he didn't remember the name of Charles Stein, with whom he had ridden to New Orleans and back.

The school where Ray tried to learn to rhumba, National Dance Studios, is in Long Beach, at 2026 Pacific Avenue. Its manager, Ron Arvidson, said that Ray attended classes there from mid-December 1967 to February 12, 1968. "He seemed to be a Southern gentleman," Mr. Arvidson said. "He had money. He peeled off five $20 bills for the $100 deposit on his lessons, then on his next visit he peeled off $465. He was neatly dressed, but not sharply dressed, except for the alligator shoes he wore all the time. He was the shy, withdrawn type of individual, the type that often wants and needs to learn to dance."

A miniskirted instructor at the studio, the one Ray says "coned [conned] the country boy," said: "He told me he had a restaurant or a bar along the coast of Mexico somewhere. He told me the name, but I've forgotten." Another instructor said: "One time I talked with him for an hour and tried to break him down. Every time the conversation got personal he became quiet. He was a clam. I saw him drive away several times in his white car."

Mr. Arvidson said that "Galt" left before completing all the 50 hours of instruction that were due him. "He said he planned to open a bar in the Los Angeles area," Mr. Arvidson continued. "That was the reason he gave us for leaving before the course was completed. He wanted to concentrate on his bartending course."

I spent as little time as possible at the dance studio. It seemed like a sadder place to me than the whorehouse at Puerto Vallarta.

On Wednesday, September 25, 1968, I walked into the busy offices of Dr. Russel C. Hadley, in the new Muir Medical Center, at Hollywood and La Brea, 7080 Hollywood Boulevard. I pretended to be a prospective patient. I filled out a form, paid a $10 consultation fee and waited, along with a Mexican-American boy with a scar on his lip and a woman who had always wanted her nose made smaller.

Dr. Hadley has impressive credentials. He is on the teaching staff of the University of Southern California Medical School, where he got his MD. He is on the staff of the Children's Hospital of Los Angeles, a member of the Los Angeles Surgical Society, and one of his duty assignments during the Second World War was with the 7th Infantry Division in the Aleutians, where the chief medical problem was frozen feet. He is a big, gruff, no-nonsense man, balding, with reddish hair. Because he does much of his operating in his own suite of offices, he wears his skull cap and green surgical suit while he receives prospective patients.

When I was alone with him, I closed the door and said: "Doctor, I'm not really a prospective patient. I signed one of these forms for your secretary so I could reach you in confidence. I came here at the request of a former patient, a man you knew as Eric S. Galt and whose real name is James Earl Ray."

"Who's he?" the doctor asked. "And who are you? I don't get the connection."

"I'm only a writer," I said. "But I thought you might remember operating on James Earl Ray, alias Eric Galt. He is a man of some prominence. Hasn't anyone been here in the last few weeks to refresh your memory?"

"I'm still in the dark," Dr. Hadley said. "I don't remember any Galt or Ray. I'm a busy man. And nobody has refreshed my memory."

"Well, Ray, alias Galt," I said, "is charged with the murder of Martin Luther King. And he told me you operated on him earlier this year."

With that, I got the doctor's undivided attention. "What!" he said. "You mean I operated on this fellow who's accused of killing King?"

"He told me that you did," I said.

"And what was the name he says he came here under?"

"Galt. Eric S. Galt."

Abruptly, the doctor left the room, and I knew he was looking at his files. When he returned, he was on guard. He was also shaking his head in disbelief.

"Do you have his medical authority?" he asked.

"No, sir," I said. "I don't have it at this moment. Ray is in jail in Memphis, and his lawyer will have to take the authority into his cell for him to sign. I'll have the authority, signed by Ray, in 36 hours."

"Well, let's get this straight," the doctor emphasized. "I will not tell you anything. You bring me proper medical authority, and I'll proceed in the legally prescribed manner."

On Friday morning, September 27, 1968, I telephoned Dr. Hadley and told him I had the authority. He invited me to come to his office at 5:30 P.M. When I arrived, his nurses were gone. Only the doctor, his lawyer and his wife were present. After the lawyer examined and approved the authority I presented, Dr. Hadley was friendly and cooperative. But he was still stunned at the realization that during all the publicity he had never remembered that, less than a month before the murder of Dr. King, he had altered the appearance of Eric S. Galt.

The doctor's records show that Ray first came to his office on February 19, 1968. Ray did his usual cheating on his age, giving his birth date as July 20, 1931. He gave his address as the St. Francis Hotel and listed his nearest relative as Carl L. Galt, 2608 Highland Avenue, Birmingham. (He had used the same name before, with a different spelling of the first name and a St. Louis address.)

Ray's surgery was for "Reduction of Prominent Nasal Tip." On the record are these entries:

3/5   Nasal tip reconstruction for pointed tip.
      Under local anesthesia in office.
      Ret. Thurs.

3/7   Nasal pack removed. Doing well.
      Ret. Mon.

3/11 Sutures removed. Healing well.
      Ret. 6 wks.

Ray, of course, did not return in six weeks. (He killed Dr. King three weeks later.) And this meant that Dr. Hadley did not have before-and-after photos of this patient. Normally, the doctor makes before-and-after photos of every patient. He made *before* photos of

Ray, but, for some reason, the camera wasn't working properly, and Ray's *before* photos were spoiled, along with those of several other patients. The *after* photos are not made until about six weeks after the operation, when healing is complete; and even had Ray remained in Los Angeles, he would not have returned for *after* photos. He didn't want the doctor to have a record of how he looked after the operation.

The fee for Ray's operation was $200, paid in cash.

"I suppose I'm a fairly observant person," Dr. Hadley said. "Faces are my business. And what amazes me is that, try as I might, I cannot remember anything at all about Eric S. Galt. I guess nobody will believe it, but it's the truth."

"I can believe it," I said. "Ray worked at making himself hard to remember."

I advised Dr. Hadley to notify the FBI, which he promptly did. He also notified the Los Angeles Medical Association.

The week between Monday, March 11, and Monday, March 18, 1968, was Ray's last week in Los Angeles. On March 11 he visited Dr. Hadley's office, and on March 18 he left Los Angeles for New Orleans, Selma, Birmingham, Atlanta and Memphis. What caused him to leave Los Angeles? Did he make the decision to leave or did someone else make it? Consider first one of his brief, fast accounts of his movements:

> After I got to New Orleans [in December] I called the New Orleans [telephone] number. I was asked where I was staying, then told where Raoul would meet me. The gist of the conversation [between Ray and Raoul] was that he had a good deal for me. He wanted me to help take some guns into Mexico and there would be 10 or 12 grand in it for me plus the usual promise of travel documents. During the conversation he said after I got to Cuba I could go any place in the world. I told him I wasn't interested in going to Cuba and I wanted the travel documents and part of the money before I went into Mexico again. He said all right I would get half the money plus the ID. I told him I was getting short of money and he gave me $500. He also told me he would contact me the latter part of April as the project would start about the 1st of May, and that he would write me the specific date later on

to meet him. I told him I would probably move but would leave a change of address.

Sometime, I think it was late in February, he wrote and ask me to meet him at the bar we had met in before in New Orleans, that we would go from there to Atlanta, Georgia. He gave me a date [March 20th] and ask me to call acknowledging the letter and also telling him if I could meet him on that date. I called and said I would be there but would call him back if something happened that I couldn't make it.

This left me pressed for time as I was due for operation and was taking a couple courses. I wrote to the locksmith school saying I was going to Atlanta and not to send any more courses. Upon my arrival in New Orleans I called Raoul and was informed that he had went on ahead to Birmingham and to meet him at the usual place in two days. I had some packages for some people [in New Orleans] and I dropped them off. I stayed close to New Orleans that day as I had two days to get to Birmingham. Upon my arrival in Birmingham I went to the Starlite. Raoul was there and ready to go, so we drove on to Atlanta. I was late getting to Birmingham as I got on the wrong road and went to Montgomery.

Now consider these points:

1. Ray, in some ways, was a penny-pincher. In Los Angeles he paid his rent in advance by the month. His month ended on March 17. So, if he was going to leave, March 18 was the normal day for him to leave.

2. In November Ray had written that he expected to be in Los Angeles five months. Every fugitive knows that he must move often. The longer he stays in one place, the more likely he is to be identified and captured. Many criminals spend the winter in and around Los Angeles. When spring comes, they leave. The time had come for Ray to move.

3. Dr. King was in Los Angeles on March 16 and 17. His movements and statements were reported by newspapers, radio and television. On Saturday, March 16, he addressed the California Democratic Council in convention at Anaheim and "called for the defeat of President Johnson." On Sunday, March 17, he spoke at the Second Baptist Church in Los Angeles. His subject: "The Meaning of Hope." He said that hate had become

the national malady, that he had seen hate on too many faces, "on the faces of sheriffs in the South and on the faces of John Birch Society members in California." He closed by saying: "Hate is too great a burden to bear. I can't hate."

4. Literally while Dr. King was delivering that sermon, at a post office three miles away Ray was filing a card changing his mailing address from the St. Francis Hotel, Los Angeles, to General Delivery, Atlanta. In addition, in his letter to the correspondence school, Ray advised the school not only to stop mailing his assignments to Los Angeles, but to begin mailing them to General Delivery, Atlanta. This certainly seems to indicate that Ray expected to spend several weeks, perhaps several months, in Atlanta. It also indicates that Ray was making no secret of his going to Atlanta.

5. Ray told Marie Martin that he was traveling again to New Orleans and then on to Atlanta. She asked him to carry a package of clothing to her daughter in New Orleans. Ray carried this package and on March 21 delivered it in New Orleans. Is this an action that a crafty criminal would take if he knew that he was traveling to New Orleans and Atlanta to commit a sensational murder?

The answer to this last question is not necessarily no. A crafty criminal intending to commit a sensational murder might not hide his movements if, after the murder, *he expected to escape!* I once believed that Ray did not decide to kill Dr. King, or did not know he was to kill Dr. King, until he reached New Orleans on the evening of March 20. But I subsequently came to believe, and I am now convinced, that Ray, in Los Angeles, finally set a goal for his life. He decided to "make the Top Ten" by killing Dr. King. He decided that, while committing this murder, he would deliberately leave evidence to identify him as the murderer. He could hardly risk not being identified as this would defeat his purpose. Only by being identified could he attain the Top Ten. He also convinced himself that he could escape to Portuguese West Africa, from where he would never be extradited and brought to trial.

Subsequent developments convinced me of this, and I believe they will convince most of my readers.

Seven

From July 1968 to February 1969, Ray wrote and orally recounted several versions of his movements during the 14 days immediately preceding the murder—from March 22 to April 4, 1968. Disagreements developed between me and Ray, between Ray and his first attorney, Arthur Hanes, then between Ray and his second attorney, Percy Foreman. Here is a general account which Ray wrote in February 1969, when Mr. Foreman was his attorney:

> Because I had got lost and got on the wrong road between New Orleans and Birmingham I had to spend the night of March 22nd in Selma, Alabama. I left Selma on the 23rd and drove through Montgomery and on to Birmingham. Raoul was there and ready to go to Atlanta. When we got to Atlanta we started looking around for a place for me to stay. We finally found a place but the landlord was too drunk to make it next door where he had the room to rent, but he said I could stay in another roomer's room for the night as he was out of town for the weekend. I had been talking to the landlord a long time and Raoul came in to see what was going on. I explained to him about the room next door. We then went to a restaurant on Peachtree Street as I hadn't eaten since breakfast.

Up until Raoul and I arrived in Atlanta he hadn't said what he wanted me to do. He told me while we were eating that he would come back the next day about 12 o'clock as the landlord would probably be sober by then and he could find out what room I had, if any. He came there the next day at about that hour. I had moved in and I don't know if he went next door or not, but he had trouble getting in as he didn't have no key. There was a lot of extra keys in the house (this place was practically deserted and I had the run of it including the room where they kept all the spare keys) and I made a key for Raoul but it didn't work too good. I was taking a locksmith course. We decided to leave the side door open in the event he came to see me and the key I had made him didn't work. I guess the landlord was always wondering why the side door was always unlocked as he or somebody was always locking it.

Raoul then explained to me what he wanted me to do and that was to get a large bore deer rifle fitted with scope, plus ammo, also to inquire about the price of cheap foreign rifles. After I had bought the rifle we would take it to the buyers and if it was O. K. I would then buy 10 of them, the scoped ones, and about two hundred of the cheap foreign ones. The scoped ones would have to be new, the others they were not too particular about. He wanted me to buy the gun there [Atlanta] and he would come to Atlanta when he got word that the buyers were ready to look at the gun. Then me and him would take the gun and show it to the buyers to get it Okayed. I then explained to him that I had Alabama ID and might have trouble getting a gun in Atlanta especially if I had to buy many of them. He said allright, maybe I was right and we would get the gun in Birmingham. He said also that he wasn't sure what date he wanted to make the purchase in Birmingham but that he would contact me probably by mail. I also asked him for some money but he said he didn't have any right then but would have the next time we met. Before he left he said he would like for me to take him to Miami in a couple of days, but he never did show up for the trip.

While in Atlanta I got low on money and went to two different banks and exchanged Canadian currency for U. S. currency. I also resumed the locksmith course as I didn't know how long I would be there. Raoul never did write but come to the house personally for me. When we got to Birmingham he had me drop him off at the post office. He said after I got a room to meet him at the Starlite Lounge. After I checked into a motel I picked him up and we bought a paper. We got the address of the Aeromarine Supply out of the want-ad section. I called the Aeromarine and they said they had a large supply of rifles. Raoul told me again after we got there to get a large bore deer rifle and gave me over $700. I asked the salesman for a deer rifle and he showed me one which I bought. I also inquired about some foreign guns on display. After the purchase me and Raoul went back to the motel. He looked at the rifle and said it was the wrong kind. I had a catalog they had given me at Aeromarine, and he showed me what kind he wanted. I then called the Aeromarine and told them it was the wrong kind of rifle. I think I told them my brother-in-law told me this. The salesman said he would exchange it but couldn't fit the scope on until the next day. I said allright and took the rifle back.

I told the salesman it wasn't a deer rifle and showed him what I wanted from the catalog. I don't think they had the exact kind, but they had one almost like the one Raoul wanted. The salesman told me he had thought I was talking about Alabama deer when he sold me the first rifle. I went back to the motel and told Raoul that I had ordered the kind of rifle he wanted and it would be ready tomorrow. He said allright, and then told me what he wanted me to do, and that was to go to Memphis and check into the new Rebel Motel, I guess it was April 3rd that he said he would meet me there at 8 or 9 o'clock at night. He then said that he had to go to New Orleans for a couple of days and left. The next day I started for Memphis. I had app. 4 days to get to Memphis so I drove slow and stopped at about 3 motels on the way there. I checked into the new Rebel upon my arrival in Memphis. Raoul showed up that night as he said about 8 or 9. He had a raincoat on as it was raining out. He told me he would have to rent a room as we might be in Memphis for 3 or 4 days. He told me he knew a place on the waterfront and that he would rent it in my name. I told him no that I didn't think he should use my name if he was going to have any guns up there. I then gave him a name that I had used indirectly before [Willard] and one that I wouldn't forget. He said allright and told me that if everything went allright, which he was sure it would, that me and him would go back to Birmingham and buy about 10 of the scoped rifles plus a large supply of the foreign made ones. He mentioned something about shipping them down the river to New Orleans.

When he got ready to leave he told me to meet him at the address at about 4 o'clock. He then wrote the address down on a piece of paper. I wrote him the name to use to rent the room under. He also said that if he wasn't in the room he would be in the tavern underneath. The next day I stalled around a lot after checking out of the motel, I then went to a downtown parking lot and started looking for the address. I think I asked the parking attendant about the address plus a couple of bartenders. (I saw one guy twice in both taverns on Main and he looked at me kind of funny.) After I had found what I was sure was the address I went and got the car and parked it near the tavern. Then I went in the tavern with the intention of asking the address but Raoul was in there, he wasn't in their the first time. He got up as I come in, I told him I had had a little trouble finding the place. He asked me if I had brought the car with me. I pointed to it and said there it is.

After we had got up to the room he told me I might as well bring my things up as we would be there 3 or 4 days. Also to go down to a store (which he directed me to) and get a pair of infra-red binoculars as the people wanted some of them too. I went to the store and asked for a set of infra-red glasses but the salesman told me you had to get them at Army surplus as you couldn't buy that type of lens at civilians stores. I then bought a set of regular binoculars thinking I could get the lens at a surplus store. On the way back I got my suitcase out of the back of the car. I also put a bedspread in the case as I didn't want to sleep on the one they had there if I had to stay there.

When, in September 1968, Ray first told me that he spent a night in Selma because he "got lost" between New Orleans and Birmingham, I wrote to him:

I can't believe that you were in Selma because you "got lost." Your record doesn't indicate that you get lost easily on highways. The night you spent in Selma was March 22nd, two weeks before Dr. King was murdered. You had left New Orleans that morning. Selma is a city made world-famous by Dr. King. During the day of March 22nd Dr. King was within a few miles of Selma recruiting for the Poor People's March, and that he was to be there was reported in the New Orleans news media of March 21st. You spent the entire day of the 21st in New Orleans. So any claim by you that you were in Selma because you got lost seems to me to be false, and I can't report it as possible truth.

Until now you have told me much that I have been able to verify and believe. When you have told me lies, like when you went over the wall at Jeff City or how you held up the whore-house in Montreal, you have admitted the lies, and after your trial I shall publish the fact that you admitted these lies and I shall correct them. So tell me the truth now about why you were in Selma.

I suggest that you were in Selma on the night of March 22nd because you were stalking Dr. King. By then you were involved in a plan to murder Dr. King. You certainly knew of this involvement on the morning of March 22nd when you left New Orleans; and you probably knew of this involvement on March 18th when you left Los Angeles. And this involvement dictated your every movement from March 22nd to 6:01 P.M. on April 4th when Dr. King was hit in Memphis.

Sure, there are questions yet to be answered. Did you make the decision to kill Dr. King or did someone else make it? Did you fire the shot or did you only aid and abet the man who did? And what was your motive and the motives of others who may have been involved? But there is no question in my mind, and you have so informed me, that by March 22nd you were involved in the plan to murder Dr. King. You knew you were involved, and you know that I am going to report this in *Look* on November 11th, the day your trial is set to begin. I am now informing you, and I have so informed Mr. Hanes, that *unless you inform us that it isn't true,* I am going to report that you spent the night in Selma, not because you got lost but because you were stalking Dr. King.

And again I remind you of this understanding between you and me: Until your trial is over and you have been sentenced I will report your movements and conduct only up to the morning of March 23rd when you left Selma for Birmingham and Atlanta. Then, after your trial and after you have been sentenced, I will publish what I believe to be the truth about your movements, conduct and motives from March 23rd to June 8th, 1968.

Ray read that letter and accepted my suggestion as to why he was in Selma. Then, in the *Look* article published November 11, 1968, I wrote:

On Friday, March 22, 1968, Ray registered at the Flamingo Motel in Selma [as Eric S. Galt, 2608 Highland Avenue, Birmingham]. The motel is near the Edmund Pettus Bridge, which many Americans will remember. This was the bridge that became famous when Alabama State Troopers and the mounted deputies of Sheriff Jim Clark tear-gassed, beat down, rode down, and dispersed the first column of whites and Negroes that attempted to march from Selma to Montgomery. The television films of these incidents, which enraged many, are believed to have assured passage of the Voting Rights Act of 1965.

The Flamingo Motel faces Highway 80, route of the Selma-to-Montgomery March, the high-water mark of the old Movement in which whites and blacks walked and hoped together. The man who led the march was Dr. Martin Luther King, Jr.

On February 16, 1968, Dr. King had spoken in Selma, and the *Times-Journal,* under a three-column picture of him on page one, reported: "Dr. King brought his drive for a planned spring poor people's march on the nation's capital to Selma Friday in an appearance before a capacity crowd at the Tabernacle Baptist Church. During the appearance he solicited both physical and financial support for the proposed march on Washington to protest against the economic plight of the nation's Negroes. He said that just like the plagues of Pharaoh's time they are planning to send waves of some 3,000 persons each to the capital city until Congress takes some action toward eliminating economic depression among Negroes."

On Thursday afternoon, March 21, 1968, the *Selma Times-Journal* published this Associated Press dispatch: "Birmingham, Ala.(AP)—Dr. Martin Luther King Jr. takes his recruiting drive for his poor people's march on Washington back into South Alabama today after spending the night in Birmingham. King and his followers moved into Alabama late Wednesday after a two-day swing through Mississippi." The story also said: "He planned to drive to Linden and Camden today, then fly to Atlanta." Camden is 33 miles from Selma.

On the morning of March 23rd Ray left Selma for Birmingham and Atlanta.

Ray read that article before publication and approved every line of it. His brother Jerry read it, Jerry visited James Earl and the two discussed it, after which Jerry told me how much James Earl and he (Jerry) liked everything I had written and how James Earl regarded me as "his only real friend." So by November 12, 1968, when Ray's trial would have begun had he not taken the only step by which he could delay it (he discharged his lawyer), I had published, with Ray's approval in advance, that Ray admitted "involvement" in the murder, and that the three questions remaining to be answered, either during or after the trial, were:

1. Did Ray initiate the successful effort to kill Dr. King, or did someone else initiate it?
2. Did Ray fire the fatal shot, or did Ray only aid and abet the man who did?
3. What was Ray's motive, and the motive of others, if others were involved?

Ray had assured me, orally and in writing, that after his trial, after he had been sentenced, he would assist me in establishing complete answers to these three questions. At the conclusion of my article in the issue of *Look* which went on sale November 11, 1968, there was this note:

> In a future issue William Bradford Huie plans to tell in detail the personal story that may not be developed at the trial—the activities of James Earl Ray between March 23, 1968, and the day that he was arrested in London.

Ray read that note; his brothers read it; they all approved it. So as of November 11, 1968, every argument between me and James Earl Ray had been resolved. I had paid him a total of $30,000, which he had assigned to Mr. Hanes. For this money, he had contracted to continue assisting me, both during and after his trial, toward one clearly understood objective: publication of the truth about the murder of Dr. King.

As to Ray's movements and actions from Saturday, March 23, to Saturday, March 30, there was, and remains, little argument between Ray and me. For $10.50 a week Ray rented a room in Atlanta at 113 14th Street, Northeast, in a rooming house located about 50 yards from the corner of Peachtree and 14th Streets. This corner is the identifying location for Atlanta's small hippie district, which includes parts of two or three blocks in any direction from Peachtree and 14th, Northeast. The two-story house has dirty white asbestos siding; it caters to male transients, such as construction workers; and the turnover is 300–500 roomers a year. The house has a tiny front yard, with a dead ivy vine up one side, faded green exterior trim, and at the rear is a graveled parking lot with an old elm tree. Ray's room, eight by ten feet, floored with worn black and gray tile, was on the first floor, west side, with a window facing a similar rooming house next door. The room contained a single bed, a small table, a small chest of drawers, mahogany-colored, faded and scratched, a metal clothes rack, venetian blinds, and a washbasin.

The manager of the rooming house, James Garner, said:

> I saw Ray three times in all. As Eric Galt he rented the room and paid $10.50 rent on March 24th. He paid another $10.50 on March 31st. I never saw anybody else with him. The third time I saw him was when I walked past his room once. The door was open, he was in there, and we just said hello. He was always dressed in a dark suit and made a good impression. There was nothing suspicious about him. I remember asking him what he did for a living. He said he was a jack of all trades and never did really answer. I didn't ask any further questions because he seemed like a nice, well-mannered person. I had never seen him before, and I never saw him after he left. There was nothing whatever about this man that was unusual. I would have never thought about him again if they [the FBI] hadn't come and asked me those questions. When they showed me a picture and asked me if he was the man, I told them that that was certainly the man who stayed in the room and there was no doubt about it.

Ray slept in that room on Sunday, Monday, Tuesday, Wednesday and Thursday nights, March 24 to 28. He used these days to locate and observe Dr. King's home, his office at Southern Christian Leadership Conference headquarters, and his church, Ebenezer Baptist. On a map found in that room by the FBI after the murder, all three of these locations are circled. Ray's fingerprints are on the map. But Ray did not see Dr. King because, during the first four of these days, Dr. King was in the New York area and on March 28 he was in Memphis.

What else did Ray do during these days? He was worried about money. In the accounting he made for me, he says that, when he left California on March 18, he had $900. Some of this was in U. S. currency, some in Canadian currency. He spent money traveling to New Orleans and Atlanta, and he says that, when, in Atlanta, he asked his criminal contact for money, he was put off. He further says that twice he went to Atlanta banks and exchanged Canadian dollars for U. S. dollars. This exchange cost him about ten percent in dollar value.

There is physical evidence to support his assertion that he was short of money. In that room FBI agents also found a used four-inch by nine-inch mailing envelope. This envelope once belonged to the Republican party of Georgia, State Finance Committee, Suite 605, 1430 West Peachtree Street, Northwest, Atlanta, Georgia 30309. According to its postmark, on March 8, 1967, it was mailed to a doctor who, until 1964, had his office in the house which was converted into the rooming house where Ray was staying. Despite the doctor's having changed his address in 1964, the envelope apparently was delivered to 113 14th Street, Northeast, in 1967. Apparently it was not forwarded, it survived at the rooming house for a year, and Ray somehow found it and used it to scribble on.

He wrote his name in printed capitals: "ERIC S. GALT." He wrote "Room #2," which was his room number in Atlanta. Then he wrote this column of figures:

3-24-68	
3-31-68	$10.50
4-7	10.50

Underneath these figures he wrote the words: "could do several different kinds of work."

The $10.50 is the room rent, and the dates are when it would be due. So evidently, when Ray made these notes, he already had paid the $10.50 on March 24 and had not yet paid the $10.50 which would be due on March 31. He, of course, never paid the $10.50 on April 7. These notes provide additional evidence that Ray, on March 24, had no firm idea how long he would be in Atlanta. The notes indicate, however, as does his having notified the locksmithing school to mail assignments to him in Atlanta, that he thought he might be in Atlanta a month or more. The notes further indicate that Ray doubted that he would get any more money from his criminal contact because he was considering the possibility of trying to work at some job. Most important: these notes indicate that ten days before the murder, and after he had begun stalking Dr. King, Ray had received no considerable sum of money and he did not anticipate receiving any such sum.

There is a widespread, persistent belief that Ray had "lots of money" at the time of and after the murder of Dr. King. The truth is that he had very little money; and if he had had as much as $2,000 after the murder, he probably would have reached Africa and might have escaped arrest and trial.

Ray's writing that on the evening of March 23 he and his criminal contact "went to a restaurant on Peachtree Street as I hadn't eaten since breakfast" provides an example of how he worked with me and his lawyers over a period of eight months. In his first account of his activities in Atlanta, he did not mention any such meal in any restaurant. Then, in September 1968, when his first lawyer, Arthur Hanes, was permitted to examine the physical evidence collected by the state against Ray, Mr. Hanes noticed a restaurant check or bill. This bill gives no information other than that on an unspecified date food was served to two guests at a well-known Atlanta restaurant called Mammy's Shanty, which is on Peachtree Street about five long blocks from the rooming house where Ray stayed. The bill is for $1.85 for London broil. When Ray was told about this bit of physical evidence, he said he knew nothing of it. But months later, after he had fired Mr. Hanes and engaged Percy Foreman, Ray wrote another account of his Atlanta activities and included the line about him and Raoul going "to a restaurant on Peachtree Street as I hadn't eaten since breakfast."

For a criminal, this is one advantage of having one lawyer for a while, then firing the first lawyer and engaging a second. The criminal can use the first lawyer to inform him of the evidence against him, then he can fire the first lawyer and tell his second lawyer a story to fit the evidence reported to him by the first lawyer.

I couldn't find any official or employe at Mammy's Shanty who had ever been asked about Ray or about the bill for London broil. When Ray was asked if ever in his life he had ordered London broil in a restaurant, he didn't know what it was.

On Thursday, March 28, Dr. King led striking garbage workers in Memphis on a march which a few young black militants turned into a riot. Several store windows were broken, there was some looting and one man was killed. That evening this riot was the top news story on Atlanta television and radio. Next morning, Friday, March 29, Ray drove the 160 miles from Atlanta to Birmingham. He didn't return to his "permanent address" at 2608 Highland Avenue. But he went within six blocks of it, to the Travelodge Motel, 821 South 20th Street, and there he registered as Eric S. Galt, 5533 Hollywood Boulevard, Los Angeles, California. In August 1967, he had come to Birmingham to buy a car and "get some capital and ID." Now, seven months later, because he "had ID in Alabama," he had come to Birmingham to buy "a large bore deer rifle fitted with scope."

The facts of Ray's purchase of this rifle leave no room for the slightest doubt or argument. The man who drove a white Mustang to the Aeromarine Supply Company, 5701 Birmingham Airport Highway, on Friday, March 29, 1968, and told the salesmen at Aeromarine that his name was Harvey Lowmyer was in fact James Earl Ray. He went there to look at rifles, to handle several rifles, to discuss rifles; and he bought a rifle, waited half an hour for a telescopic sight to be mounted on it, then left the store with his new rifle only to telephone later and ask to be permitted to exchange it next day for another rifle. Sixteen hours after the murder FBI agents appeared at the Aeromarine Supply Company, picked up the rifles which "Harvey Lowmyer" handled but did not purchase, and found fingerprints which proved to be Ray's.

Moreover, the father and son who operate Aeromarine Supply Company, Robert E. Wood and Donald F. Wood, are responsible, alert citizens who know their business. They observed Ray closely, stood near him, and Donald Wood dealt with Ray, explained rifles, scopes and ammunition to him, mounted scopes for him on two different rifles on successive days, packaged the rifle he finally bought in an unusual manner, and accepted $265.85 in cash from him. The day after the murder both Donald Wood and his father gave accurate descriptions of "Harvey Lowmyer" and his white Mustang to FBI agents.

In buying the rifle why did Ray use another alias? He told me and both his lawyers that he decided to buy the rifle in Birmingham rather than in Atlanta because he "had ID in Alabama." But his I.D. was for Eric S. Galt. He didn't have a scrap of I.D. for Harvey Lowmyer. If he was going to buy the rifle under a name for which he had no identification, why did he drive to Birmingham? Why didn't he buy the rifle in Atlanta? Ray never answered this question either for me or for his lawyers.

On December 21, 1968, I went to the Aeromarine Supply Company and talked with Donald Wood and his father. They prepared for me, and sold to me, exactly the same sort of rifle, with the same sort of scope mounted on it in the same way, and the same ammunition which they sold Ray. They gave me a bill of sale identical to the one they gave Ray, except that the sales records had to be different in one respect. When, on March 30, 1968, they sold the rifle to Ray, the law did not require them to require Ray to identify himself. The bill of sale they prepared for Ray shows only that they sold a rifle, scope and ammunition, with serial numbers noted, to Harvey Lowmyer. But as a result of Dr. King's murder, a federal gun law was enacted requiring sellers of rifles to require purchasers to identify themselves as to name, age, residence, place of birth and home telephone number. So despite the fact that I am widely known in Alabama and that I was accompanied by Mr. Hanes, a former mayor of Birmingham, I was required to produce my driver's license; and all the information on it, together with my home telephone number, had to be written into the bill of sale, copies of which had to be sent to law-enforcement agencies.

In short, had the law which was in force in December 1968 been in force in March 1968, Ray probably could have bought the same rifle from the Aeromarine Supply Company. But he could have bought it only as Eric S. Galt, the name on his driver's license. He would have known that the sales record would be delivered promptly to the local police and the FBI; and this, added to the question of his home telephone number, might have frightened him off or resulted in his exposure and capture.

When Ray came to buy the rifle, he told Donald Wood that he and his brother were going deer hunting. Mr. Wood soon concluded that Ray knew little about rifles and nothing about deer hunting. After examining several rifles, Ray decided on the Model 760 Remington Gamemaster, .243 caliber, slide or "pump" action, at a price of $139.95. He selected the Redfield variable scope, 2-power to 7-power, price $94.95. For ammunition, he chose a box of 20 Norma Hollow-point cartridges, with a bullet weight of 75 grains and a velocity at 100 yards of 3,070 feet per second. Ray waited about half an hour while Mr. Wood mounted the telescopic sight, set the variable sight at 7-power, and sighted it in at 100 yards.

This is an excellent big-game rifle, low-caliber, but with enough "knockdown power" to knock down the biggest buck on earth at 300 yards. But later that afternoon Ray telephoned Donald Wood and said he wanted to exchange the .243 caliber rifle for "a little heavier gun." Mr. Wood agreed, but asked him to come in the next morning when he (Mr. Wood) would have time to mount the scope on the heavier rifle. When Ray arrived on Saturday morning, March 30, he selected, in the same Model 760 Gamemaster, a Remington 30-06-caliber rifle, with slide action. In the Army Ray was trained to fire a 30-06 rifle, and Army ammunition can be used in the Remington 30-06. Of this rifle the manufacturers declare:

> The new restyled Gamemaster Model 760 is the fastest hand operated big game rifle made. It has many features similar to the automatic, such as: New vibra-honing process, inside and out, makes metal surfaces silky smooth; parts work friction-free. Pump it and your trigger finger never leaves the trigger. Aim it and your eye never leaves the sights. Accuracy is there: crisp trigger and precision rifling, helping you put that buck in the freezer. Because of its super strong artillery-type bolt, Model 760 is the only pump action big game rifle that's chambered for the popular and powerful 30-06 Springfield cartridge. Capacity: 4 cartridges in clip magazine plus one in chamber.

Again Ray waited while Mr. Wood mounted the Redfield scope on the 30-06. Then Ray chose a box of 20 Remington-Peters 30-06 Springfield High Velocity, 150 grain, Pointed Soft Point Core-Lokt cartridges. This bullet weighs twice as much as the bullet which Ray selected on Friday. The bullet mushrooms on impact, travels 2,670 feet per second at 100 yards, does not drop even .01 of an inch in its first 100 yards of flight, and has enough knockdown power (2,370 foot-pounds at 100 yards) to stop a charging rhinoceros.

The bullet, exactly like this, which hit Dr. King in the neck, traveled only 205 feet or about 68 yards. It would have killed him had it hit him almost anywhere in the head, neck, chest, stomach or abdomen. Had it hit him in the groin or thigh, he probably would have died from shock and rapid loss of blood.

When Mr. Wood was ready to deliver the Remington 30-06 to Ray, a problem developed as to what sort of box or case Ray would carry it in. The Remington 30-06, like every fine rifle, comes in its own heavy cardboard carton, with the rifle's serial number also on the carton. But after the Redfield scope is mounted on the Remington 30-06, it will not fit in that rifle's light-brown Remington carton. Most purchasers of fine rifles who have scopes mounted on them, solve this problem by spending $12 to $50 more for a fabric or leather gun case. Mr. Wood suggested a gun case to Ray, but Ray didn't want to spend the extra money. Mr. Wood then remembered that a Browning rifle carton is a little roomier than a Remington carton. The Remington rifle with scope will fit into a Browning carton, which is black. Mr. Wood found an empty Browning carton, put Ray's rifle in it, and Ray left the store with his new Remington rifle in a black Browning carton.

This unusual action resulted in confusion at the murder scene. After the murder, when Ray dropped the Remington rifle on the street, it was in the Browning carton. So initial reports were that a Browning rifle had killed Dr. King; and when later reports said that the rifle purchased in Birmingham by Lowmyer-Galt-Willard was a Remington, many persons concluded that the rifle which killed Dr. King could not have been the rifle Ray purchased in Birmingham.

Where did Ray get the $265.85 he paid for the rifle, scope and cartridges? He says his criminal contact, Raoul, gave him $750. And this $750, Ray says, was the last money given to him by Raoul or any other criminal contact. In his financial accounting to me, Ray says that between March 18 and April 5 he spent $550 for "travel and everything" and that, when he left Atlanta for Canada on April 5, the day after the murder, he had $1,100. There is no way to be certain that this is the truth, but, as I have reported, in Atlanta, then in Canada and later in England, Ray was handicapped by a shortage of money. The $750 he says he got from a criminal contact on March 29 is hardly the sort of money which one criminal gives to another if both have been hired to murder a famous figure. It is the sort of money one criminal might advance to another before the anticipated theft of a new-model automobile or the robbery of a food store.

The more difficult question for Ray, and one which he never answered satisfactorily for me or for either of his lawyers, was: Where did he go on Saturday, March 30, after he left the Aeromarine Supply Company with his new rifle? He didn't go back to the Travelodge Motel in Birmingham: he had checked out of there. So did he go to his room in Atlanta? If not, where?

In August 1968, Ray told Mr. Hanes and me that, after he bought the rifle, he did not go back to Atlanta but proceeded leisurely toward Memphis, stopping somewhere near Florence, Alabama, then somewhere near Corinth, Mississippi. He said that on a side road near Corinth he fired the rifle, using several of the cartridges he had bought in Birmingham and several Army 30-06 cartridges. He said that he spent the night of Tuesday, April 2, in an uncomfortable motel near Memphis but in Mississippi. He said that Raoul visited him after dark in that motel and instructed him to rent a room at 422½ South Main Street in Memphis at 3 P.M. on Thursday, April 4. He said that Raoul told him to register in the Main Street room as John Willard. He said that, when Raoul left the Mississippi motel on the night of April 2, Raoul took the rifle with him. Ray said that on the morning of Wednesday, April 3, seeking a more comfortable place to sleep, he checked out of the Mississippi motel, drove into Memphis and checked into the Rebel Motel as Eric S. Galt.

This Mississippi motel where Ray said Raoul visited him was obviously of enormous importance to Ray's defense as well as to the story. A witness might be found who could identify Raoul or who saw a man leaving Ray's room with a box large enough to hold a rifle. So Mr. Hanes and I, together with a Memphis private detective employed by Mr. Hanes, began searching for this motel. Repeatedly, Mr. Hanes, using lists and diagrams of motels, questioned Ray for more information about this motel. Ray was certain that the motel was no more than five miles south of the Tennessee-Mississippi line, but, for the first time, his remarkable memory seemed to fail him. He had drawn diagrams with which I could find motels in Canada, Mexico and Selma, but he couldn't give us any reliable recollection about his "Mississippi motel." We went to every motel in Mississippi within 20 miles of Memphis, and we could find no evidence that Ray under any of his aliases, or anyone driving a white Mustang with an Alabama license, had registered at any of them between March 30 and April 3.

Similarly, with the motels near Corinth and Florence. Ray could give us no help, and we found nothing. Meanwhile, we learned that in Atlanta, James Garner, the rooming-house manager, believed that Ray spent the nights of March 30 and 31, and April 1 and 2, in the Atlanta rooming house. Mr. Garner felt certain that Ray paid his second week's rent on Sunday, March 31, when it was due. Then I studied Dr. King's movements on the days and nights in question.

On Friday morning, March 29, the day after the riot in Memphis, Dr. King flew from Memphis to Atlanta. He was deeply depressed because, for the first time, a few marchers led by him had resorted to violence. Newspapers, radio and television publicized his pledge to return to Memphis to try to lead a peaceful march, but the news media did not say when he would return.

On Saturday, March 30, while Ray was in Birmingham buying the rifle, Dr. King held a staff meeting at the Ebenezer Baptist Church during which he considered *not* returning to Memphis and even calling off his proposed Poor People's March on Washington in the face of what he called "the rising tide of hate in America." On Sunday, March 31, Dr. King preached at the Washington Cathedral in Washington, D. C. On Monday, April 1, after an SCLC staff meeting in Atlanta, it was announced that Dr. King would return to Memphis on April 3. On Tuesday, April 2, Dr. King rested at his home; and on Wednesday, April 3, he flew to Memphis on a plane that was delayed while it was searched after a bomb threat. He went to the Lorraine Hotel and Motel, which is operated and chiefly patronized by Negroes, and was given room 306.

Dr. King had stayed at the Lorraine before, always in one of the new, more comfortable motel rooms fronting on Mulberry Street. These motel rooms along Mulberry Street have one characteristic that proved fatal to Dr. King. When you go in or out of any door, you are standing in full view of, and within 200-odd feet of, the rear, second-floor windows of two old, two-story, brick buildings which front on Main Street and whose second-floor rooms are bedrooms to be rented to any man or woman who can pay $8.50 a week and who can climb the stairs at 422½ South Main. Photographers took pictures of Dr. King, standing at the door to his room on Mulberry Street, and on television that evening the number 306 could be seen above his head.

Ray was in Memphis, at the Rebel Motel, the evening of April 3. He could have driven from Atlanta to Memphis in seven hours. Since Atlanta is in the eastern time zone and Memphis is in the central zone, he could have left Atlanta at 7 A.M., Atlanta time, and reached Memphis easily by 2 P.M., Memphis time. He could have stopped near Corinth and practice-fired his new rifle, and still reached Memphis by 3 P.M. He told me and his lawyers that in Memphis, on the afternoon of April 3, he got a haircut and purchased a shaving kit at a Rexall drugstore before registering as Eric S. Galt at the Rebel Motel, 3466 Lamar Avenue.

About October 25, 1968, after I had completed the two articles published in *Look* before Ray's trial was to have begun, I wrote this letter to him:

> Both the *Look* articles have now gone to press, and Mr. Hanes believes they will be helpful to you in the trial beginning November 12th. You and Jerry also believe they will be helpful to you. In these articles we have revealed much about your activities down to March 22nd that the FBI did not know, and I have presented you as a man who is willing, in time, to tell all the truth you know.
>
> I am now trying to recreate your days between March 23rd and June 8th; and, as you know, nothing that I write now will be published until after you have been tried and sentenced. And what bothers me now is your reluctance to tell the truth about where you were between 2 P.M. on March 30th and 2 P.M. on April 3rd. If the FBI knows where you were, the state will surely present such evidence at your trial. If the FBI doesn't know where you were, then after you have been sentenced, my publishing the truth with your assistance can win for you some further measure of respect.
>
> At your trial Garner will testify for the state that you were in Atlanta on March 31st. And I believe there is other evidence. You

picked up laundry in Atlanta on April 5th before you caught the bus for Toronto. I suspect that you deposited this laundry on Monday, April 1st, and that such evidence will be presented against you. Why then do you continue telling us lies about your leisurely procession from Birmingham to Memphis? And about your meeting Raoul at some non-existent "Mississippi motel" on the night of April 2nd? Such lies are likely to be more incriminating than any truth.

Remember this: when you were in Selma on March 22nd you were stalking Dr. King. That is truth already admitted by you and to be published by me. In Atlanta on March 24–28 you were stalking Dr. King. In Birmingham on March 29–30 you were buying a rifle with which to kill Dr. King. And you went to Memphis only after you learned that Dr. King was to be there on April 4th. That's the truth, so let's agree on it, and then learn just how you came to be stalking Dr. King, and who else may have been stalking him with you.

That letter was ineffective. To see just how ineffective it was, turn back to the opening of this chapter and read again the account Ray wrote for me and Mr. Foreman in February 1969. Also, on February 24, 1969, Ray wrote to me:

I will begin on March 30th and go on from there. When I left Birmingham on March 30th, if that was the date, I never returned to Atlanta. I was supposed to be in Memphis by the 3rd of April. I paid Garner rent twice. I think I paid him the second week's rent on a Friday, the 28th or 29th. I think the FBI knows all of the motels I stayed at between Birmingham and Memphis. But there would be no advantage for the state to bring this out as they, the state, would probably think it to their advantage not to show that I didn't arrive in Memphis until April 3rd. Also, Garner stayed drunk most of the time so I think it possible he might of been mistaken.

For purposes of clarity, I will delay telling the story of the day of the murder, April 4th, until after I have presented Ray's largely truthful story of his escape and capture. I will then tell the story of the murder as I reveal the efforts to prepare a defense for Ray. In closing this chapter, here is what Ray told me and Mr. Hanes about the murder:

Raoul had told me to rent the room at the rooming house [422½ South Main Street] at 3 P.M. I had a little trouble finding it so it was 3:15 when I got upstairs and rented a room [5B] from the woman [Bessie Brewer]. I signed my name as John Willard and paid her $8.50 for a week's rent. Then I went downstairs and found Raoul in the tavern [Jim's Grill]. He told me to get the binoculars, so I went up to the store [York Arms Company] and bought them, and when I got back Raoul was up in the room. That was about 4:15 P.M. I left Raoul in the room and went back downstairs and stayed in Jim's Grill quite a while, drinking a couple of beers. At about 6 [6:01 P.M.] I was sitting in the Mustang when I heard a shot. In a minute or so Raoul came running down the stairs carrying my zipper bag and the rifle which was in the box and wrapped up in a bedspread I had brought from California. Just before he got in the car Raoul turned around and threw the rifle and my zipper bag down on the sidewalk. Then he jumped in the back seat, and covered up with a sheet, and I took off. After I drove a few blocks I stopped at a stop light and Raoul jumped out. I then drove on south into Mississippi. I wasn't thinking about nothing but getting away. I knew that shot meant trouble. I kept driving south for a while, then I turned east and went through Birmingham and got to Atlanta about daybreak.

So from the beginning Ray admitted that he rented the room, that he bought the binoculars, that he parked the Mustang on South Main Street a few feet south of the upstairs entrance to the rooming house, and that he fled the scene in the Mustang. But he insisted that he didn't do any shooting, that the shot surprised him, and that he thought he and Raoul were waiting to show the rifle to some prospective Mexican gun buyers.

Eight

James Earl Ray drove away from the Memphis rooming house, 422½ South Main Street, about 6:04 P.M., April 4, 1968, three minutes after the shot which killed Dr. King was fired. Sixty-five days later, at 10:30 A.M., June 8, 1968, he was arrested at London's Heathrow Airport. Here I will tell the story of those 65 days as told by Ray and as reconstructed by me. Ray wrote:

> Leaving Memphis I had to drive slow and be careful so as not to attract attention and get arrested for speeding. I drove south into Mississippi for a while, then turned east across Mississippi and Alabama, through Birmingham to Atlanta. I had my radio on so I knew the police were looking for a white Mustang with an Alabama or an Arkansas license. But nobody stopped me. I got to my room in Atlanta about 6 A.M. on April 5th. I parked the Mustang and left it and sure hated that I didn't have time to sell it for at least $1,000. Upon leaving my room, on the table I left a letter from the John Birch Society in California telling me how to get information about the English-speaking countries of Africa. I wanted the FBI to investigate this letter while I got away. I also left a copy of the Los Angeles hippie paper, the *Free Press*, to steer the FBI toward California while I went to Canada.

Many people, including Judge Battle, have wondered how Ray got out of Memphis without being stopped. Three police cars were within two blocks of where the Mustang was parked; and three policemen on foot were within a hundred yards of Dr. King. Why didn't one of them either catch Ray or so spread the alarm that some other radio car could have caught him?

The answer is not that the police didn't want to catch the slayer of Dr. King. It is simply that Ray beat the police reaction time. No one anticipates a sniper murder. The first rush is toward the fallen victim, to assist him and obtain aid for him, and the natural assumption is that his assailant must have been within a few feet of him. Four minutes passed before there was a radio flash of Dr. King's having been shot; then there was another 15 minutes before police on the scene decided that the shot came from the rooming house and that the suspect had escaped in a white Mustang along South Main Street. By that time Ray was outside the downtown district, approaching the Mississippi line, which is about 12 miles from the murder scene. The Rebel Motel, where Ray had spent the night of April 3, is on one of the highway routes leading into Mississippi.

Adding to the confusion was the fact that 1968 license plates of both Alabama and Arkansas were red and white, so persons who saw the Mustang drive away were not sure which state's license it carried. And downtown Memphis is nearer to Arkansas than to Mississippi: only a dash across the Mississippi River bridge. So when a criminal must make a fast getaway from Memphis, police assume he will race for the bridge, and this gave Ray an extra minute or so to reach the Mississippi line.

Why wasn't Ray caught by the Mississippi or Alabama or Georgia highway patrols as he drove the white Mustang through the night? When the shot was fired, only 25 minutes of daylight remained. Except for these few minutes, Ray was protected by darkness; and the highways were not blockaded. A white Mustang was not particularly conspicuous. By 1969 white cars were no longer popular in the United States, but for the 1966-model Mustang, white was the most popular color. Ray took 11 hours to drive from Memphis to Atlanta: enough time to avoid main highways. And no one expected Dr. King's murderer to be traveling toward Atlanta, which was Dr. King's home.

About 8:30 A.M., April 5, Ray picked up his laundry in Atlanta, at Piedmont Cleaners. As I had suspected, the laundry record showed that he delivered the laundry to Piedmont Cleaners on Monday, April 1, a day on which Ray was to continue to insist he was traveling leisurely from Birmingham toward Memphis. FBI agents had that record by April 17. At the rooming house Ray wrote a note to James Garner and left it for him, telling him that he was leaving and giving up his room.

To abandon the Mustang, Ray parked and locked it in the parking lot of Capitol Homes, a housing project almost in the shadow of the golden-domed Georgia state capitol building. One woman, a resident of Capitol Homes, saw him park it, and other residents soon noticed it, but five days passed before one of them had heard enough broadcast descriptions of the car to notify the police. Four things about the car were noteworthy. On the windshield was a 1967 Mexican visa sticker, labeled "Turista." In the trunk was male clothing too small for Ray: it would fit a man weighing 125 pounds. The ashtrays were full of ashes, and Ray does not smoke. And the carpet was muddy, while Ray usually kept it clean.

Ray must have hated to walk away from the Mustang. It was by far the best car he had ever owned; it had given him status in Puerto Vallarta; and in seven months he had driven it 19,000 miles. Ray continues:

> I took a bus from Atlanta to Cincinnati. It was due to leave Atlanta about 11:30 A.M., but it left about 1 P.M. Nobody paid any attention to me on the bus or at the bus stops. I arrived in Cincinnati about 1:30 A.M. on the 6th of April. I had about an hour and a half layover, so I went to a tavern as I didn't want to stay in the bus station. I think the taverns close there at 2:30 A.M. I arrived in Detroit about 8 A.M., still the 6th of April. I then caught a cab to a train station where I was told I'd have to take a cab to Windsor, Canada. This train station was not in the main part of town, and from this station I walked across a little grassy park to a barber shop and got a shave. I remember I had trouble as the barber said he didn't shave customers any more.
>
> I took a cab to Windsor and got there about 10 or 11 A.M. The

train left for Toronto about 20 minutes after I got there. I arrived in Toronto about 5 P.M. on the 6th of April [Saturday], and I rented the room at 102 Ossington Avenue about 6 P.M. for $10. The people who ran the rooming house were immigrants [Polish]. The woman couldn't speak hardly any English and the man not much better. I never gave them a name as they never asked me for one.

At bus stations between Atlanta and Detroit Ray bought newspapers which carried front-page pictures of Dr. King and the murder scene, and headlines about rioting, burning and pillaging in 64 American cities. He drew me an accurate diagram of the railroad station in Detroit and the grassy park across which he walked to the barber shop. Two railroads provide passenger service between Windsor and Toronto. The distance is 225 miles; the running time is about four hours; the one-way fare is $8.20. Ray evidently rode the Canadian National Railways train which leaves Windsor at noon and reaches Toronto's Union Station at 4:05 P.M. He put his bag and raincoat in a locker and walked away from the station, looking for a place to hide.

Toronto, a city of two million, is called an "English city" to distinguish it from Montreal, which is a "French city," but actually Toronto is a city of diverse immigrants, many of them recent. Ray walked three miles from the railroad station, into "Little Italy," a seedy, rundown area of cheap bars, shabby rooming houses and small shops run by people with all the Central European accents. The weather on April 6 was dry and sunny; the high temperature was 55 degrees; sunset was at 6:52 P.M.

The FBI says that Ray reached Toronto on April 8. So when Ray told me he got there on April 6, I thought he might be lying and that he had used the two days in question to meet someone in Chicago or Detroit to get paid. But he didn't get paid; he reached Toronto with about $1,050. And further research and reflection convinced me that he got to Toronto on April 6. When he left Memphis, his aim was to cross the Canadian border as fast as prudently possible. While police looked for a white Mustang and checked airports, Ray craftily rode buses and a train from Atlanta to Toronto in 27 hours. He was in Toronto's "Little Italy" only 48 hours after the shot was fired.

The old, three-story house at 102 Ossington Avenue has a red-brick front and a new aluminum and glass door. It is across the street from Sully's Toronto Athletic Club, where Cassius Clay trained for his bout with George Chuvalo. The middle-aged Polish landlady is named Mrs. Adam Szpakowski. She is a short woman, with horn-rim glasses, and she wears her hair in a bun. Having survived the German and Russian invasions of Poland, she was, of course, frightened when police, reporters and cameramen began knocking at her door six weeks after Ray left her house. She retreated into the Polish language and tried to hide, but later she bravely told what she could remember.

"He was nicely dressed," she said. "He said he was a real-estate salesman for a Toronto firm, and I wondered why a man dressed like that would want a room in this district. He had no luggage with him, and I told him I would let him have the room if he brought luggage. He went away and came back in about an hour with a raincoat and a bag. For the first three or four days he ate in his room, and he ate apples, bananas and tarts that he bought at the nearby bakery. He'd go out and buy newspapers and tarts, then come back and I'd hear him turn on the television."

The room was exceptionally large, clean and light. It was on the second floor front, with three bay windows, red and white drapes and bedspread, a double bed, a dresser with mirror, tile floor, an embroidered "Home Sweet Home" on the wall, and the TV set. Ray rented this room because of the TV set. He wanted to watch the funeral of Dr. King; and he expected very soon to begin seeing his own pictures on the news programs, and on a Sunday thereafter he expected to appear on his favorite TV show, *The FBI,* when he was elevated to the Top Ten.

"He was good with the rent," said Mrs. Szpakowski. "He paid me twice, each time with a nice Canadian $10 bill. When he had been here about a week, I began to notice how sad and worried he looked. I thought maybe he was worried about his family. I thought once that he might be from the mental hospital down the street. He was very quiet, and he never had a visitor. His room was easy to clean because he didn't smoke. He'd go out in the mornings, come back at noon, then go out again in the afternoon and come home during the evening. Since he didn't give me any name, when two telephone calls came for Paul Bridgman, I said there was no such person at this address. Just before he left, a very official-looking letter came for Paul Bridgman. I gave it back to the postman, saying it was the wrong address. The day before he left, I saw a picture of Dr. King's assassin in the newspaper, and I told my husband it looked like our roomer. My husband said I was crazy. Then next day [April 19] the roomer left without notice. He just left his key on the hall table, and when I went to clean his room, there on the bed was a newspaper open at the same picture I had seen the previous day."

Ray continues:

On Monday [April 8] I went to the library and went through birth announcements for 1932. I was looking for two names to use in applying for a passport. I wrote down about ten names of men whose births were announced in the papers in 1932. Among these names were Paul Edward Bridgman and Ramon George Sneyd.

When Ray was in Canada in July and August 1967, he believed that the only way to obtain a Canadian passport was to have a Canadian guarantor. He failed to find such a guarantor. Now, in April 1968, he had no time to search further for a guarantor; he had to apply for the passport even at the risk of arrest; so he hoped either that, by fakery, he could serve as his own guarantor, or that he could find a way to obtain the passport without a guarantor.

He knew that in the United States to obtain a passport a birth certificate is an absolute requirement. He concluded that if in Canada he was to obtain a passport without a guarantor, certainly he would have to produce a birth certificate. He then concluded that the safest way to apply for a birth certificate in the Province of Ontario (Toronto) was not to apply under a fictitious name but under the real name of a man born in Toronto, a man about Ray's own age, a man whose birth had been announced and recorded; and under this man's name Ray would apply, not for an original birth certificate, but for a duplicate, claiming that he had lost the original. (Similarly, merely by writing for it, Ray had obtained a duplicate of Eric Starvo Galt's driver's license in Alabama.) Ray also reasoned that, since he would use the birth certificate in applying for the passport and would submit recent photos of himself with the birth certificate, he would need the birth certificate of a Canadian who had never been issued a passport and whose photo therefore was not on record in the passport division of the Canadian government in Ottawa.

Ray then began a fumbling, uncertain effort to obtain a passport, one way or another. He made stupid mistakes which could have resulted in his arrest. He almost lost his nerve, and this is why he looked so sad and worried to his landladies. Here is how he proceeded.

The Toronto Central Library maintains microfilms of all three of Toronto's daily newspapers. For any visitor a library assistant will put the microfilm roll of a newspaper of any requested month on a viewing machine, show the visitor how to operate the machine and leave him to copy whatever he pleases. It's a simple process which Ray learned in prison libraries. Ray asked for the papers of October-November 1932. He, of course, was born in 1928, but since he thought he looked younger than that and had already claimed 1931 as his birth year, he decided now to claim 1932. He wrote down the names of ten males born in 1932, along with their birth dates, the names of their parents, particularly the maiden names of their mothers. Then, checking the ten names against the Toronto telephone directory, he found that only Paul Edward Bridgman and Ramon George Sneyd were listed as being alive, in Toronto, with telephones, in 1968.

This is how Ray came to confer ironic notoriety on two totally surprised citizens of Toronto: Paul E. Bridgman, the $18,400-a-year director of the Toronto Board of Education's Language Study Center; and Ramon George Sneyd, a Toronto police officer. Among its births in 1932, *The Toronto Evening Telegram* listed:

> BRIDGMAN—On Thursday, November 10th, to Mr. and Mrs. Edward Bridgman (née Evelyn Godden), a son, Paul Edward.

The Daily Star listed:

> SNEYD—At the Women's Hospital on Saturday, October 8th, to Mr. and Mrs. George Sneyd (née Gladys Mae Kilner), a son, Ramon George.

To avoid the mistake of applying for a passport in the name of a Canadian to whom a passport had once been issued, Ray, posing as a passport official checking on some misunderstanding, planned to telephone both Mr. Bridgman and Mr. Sneyd and learn if either of them had ever been issued a passport. But he delayed making these telephone calls. He liked the name Bridgman better than Sneyd because he wasn't sure how to pronounce Sneyd (Snead). So he moved at once to try to obtain a birth certificate as Paul Bridgman. On April 9, to the Registrar of Births, Province of Ontario, Toronto, he wrote that he was Paul Edward Bridgman, son of Edward Bridgman and Evelyn Godden Bridgman, born on November 10, 1932, now living at 102 Ossington Avenue, Toronto, and that, having misplaced his birth certificate, he would appreciate a duplicate copy's being mailed to him. He also gave the telephone number at 102 Ossington Avenue.

Then on April 11 he walked into the Arcade Photo Studio, on Yonge Street (Toronto's principal downtown street), said he was Paul Bridgman, and asked the manager, Mrs. Mabel Agnew, for passport photos. He was wearing heavy, horn-rim glasses above his new, shortened nose, now minus the "prominent nasal tip." The shorter nose made his face look wider. And he had applied some makeup from a kit he had purchased at Brown's Theatrical Supplies on Yonge Street. Mrs. Agnew seated him on a revolving piano stool before the white backdrop demanded by all nations for passport photos, and snapped a full-face picture. Ray left and returned half an hour later and picked up three prints for $2. Mrs. Agnew offered him her special—three more prints for an extra 50 cents—but Ray didn't take it. He wanted only the three prints he would have to submit with his application.

Then, belatedly, Ray telephoned Mr. Bridgman, who remembers the call. "Yes," said Mr. Bridgman, "it was one night in the spring before there was any publicity about Ray. It was after supper and the guy said he was with the government. He had a European accent, a very convincing accent, and asked me if I had ever applied for a passport or whether I had lost my passport. Something like that. I asked him if he had the right person. He spelled my name, gave me my birth date, gave me my mother's maiden name, so I figured he must be on the level. I told him I had had a passport about ten years ago but not now. He thanked me and hung up. Afterwards I thought it strange that a government worker should phone on business in the evening, but I gave it no further thought. I'm just hoping like hell now I don't hear any more about this case."

Ray then telephoned Mr. Sneyd, who said he had never applied for or been issued a passport. So Ray learned on Friday, April 12, that he could not apply for a passport as Paul E. Bridgman, but he could safely apply as Ramon George Sneyd. This meant that Ray now must apply for a birth certificate as Sneyd, so Ray decided that, in order to receive mail as both Bridgman and Sneyd, he must maintain two residences, one as Bridgman, the other as Sneyd.

But from April 9 to April 18 Ray was imperiled by a misunderstanding of which he was not aware. He thought that on April 9, after he had applied for the Bridgman birth certificate, he had made clear to Mrs. Szpakowski that his name was Paul Bridgman. He told me that he wrote the name down for her. But Mrs. Szpakowski says she never did understand that her roomer's name was Bridgman. This is why she twice told a telephone caller that Mr. Bridgman did not live there. These calls were from the Registrar's office, checking on the birth-certificate application. When these calls did not confirm that Mr. Bridgman lived at 102 Ossington Avenue, the birth certificate, it appears, might not have been issued. But it was issued and promptly mailed to Paul Bridgman, 102 Ossington Avenue. But when Mrs. Szpakowski looked at the official-looking letter containing the Bridgman birth certificate, she returned it to the postman, saying Mr. Bridgman didn't live there. So Ray never did receive the Bridgman birth certificate, nor did he know why until I returned from Toronto and explained it to him.

On the morning of Tuesday, April 16, Ray walked seven blocks from 102 Ossington Avenue to 962 Dundas Street, West, and rented a $9-a-week back room from a Chinese landlady, Mrs. Sun Loo. He told her his name was Ramon George Sneyd. He wrote it down for her. Here's how Ray explained these maneuvers:

> Posing as a government employee, I telephoned Bridgman and Sneyd to see if they had ever had a passport. I couldn't use the

name of anyone who had ever had a passport as his picture would
be on file. Bridgman told me he had had a passport about eight
years ago, but Sneyd said he had never had a passport. I thought
this would work out okay for me because at that time I thought
that the man applying for a passport had to have another man
who'd swear that he had known him [the applicant] for two years.
I'd just let Sneyd apply for the passport and let Bridgman be his
witness [guarantor], and I'd be both Sneyd and Bridgman. I had
already written and applied for a birth certificate for Bridgman;
now I went and applied in person for a birth certificate for Sneyd.

I had told the Polish lady on Ossington Avenue that my name
was Paul Bridgman. I wrote it out for her on a piece of paper,
because I expected mail as I had applied for a birth certificate
under that name. Then I went to the Dundas Street address and
rented a room as Ramon George Sneyd. I told the Chinese lady
I worked nights. I was going to spend days at Dundas Street as
Sneyd, and nights at Ossington Avenue as Bridgman.

I then went to Brown's Theatrical Supplies on Yonge Street and
bought a makeup kit. This was so I could apply for the passport
as Sneyd, then I could change my appearance and go back to the
passport office as Bridgman and sign as a witness for Sneyd. In
this way I could be Bridgman vouching for Sneyd.

I then went to the travel agency and asked about going to London. It was there and then that I found out that I had gone to a
lot of extra trouble. If you don't have anyone to swear they have
known you for two years, you can still get a Canadian passport
simply by swearing that you are a Canadian citizen. I did this and
was told I'd get my passport in about two weeks.

Ray's visit to the travel agency was indeed a revelation to him.
He was nervous and anxious. He thought he knew something about
getting a passport, but he had never before tried to obtain one, so
he was uncertain, and aware that he was making a dangerous move.
The Kennedy Travel Bureau, which advertises that they have been
"travel counsellors since 1926," is one of Canada's most respected
agencies. The head of the agency, with an office at 296 Queen
Street, West, is forty-two-year-old Henry Moos. The manager of
the office at 424 Bloor Street, West, is Mrs. Lilliane Spencer.

As Ray approached Mrs. Spencer on Tuesday afternoon, April
16, one fact seems clear: he did not think that he was in a "passport office." He expected that Mrs. Spencer would tell him how

to apply for a passport, would direct him to the proper government office to file the application, and would arrange the air travel for him, but certainly Ray did not expect that Mrs. Spencer would be able to "get the passport" for him. Here is what Mrs. Spencer remembers:

> Well, this has been such a shocking experience for me, and I have been questioned so many times, that it's hard for me to be certain just what I do remember. Ray is not the sort of man one notices or remembers. A minute after he left the office his features had faded into the wallpaper for me. Had not all this happened, I would never have thought of him again. The one thing I am certain I remember is that, when he told me his name was Ramon George Sneyd, I thought it was an odd name because Ramon is Spanish and doesn't usually go with George. I would remember this because names are my business.
>
> When he told me that he wanted to fly to London and return, I asked him as I always ask if he had a Canadian passport. He said "No," so I said we'd get it for him. He said that he had been born in Toronto, but that he had moved away, had now been back for three weeks, and was living in a rooming house on Dundas Street. He said he did not have a birth certificate. Since he was such a recent returnee, he was not certain that he could find a guarantor who would vouch for having known him two years.
>
> I then explained to him, as is routine in such cases, that he could make a sworn statement that he was a native-born citizen of Canada, that his statement would be notarized by the notary in our firm [Mr. Moos], that we would mail the papers and photos [he had brought them with him] to Ottawa, that the passport would then be mailed to us in about two weeks, and that he could then pick up both his ticket and his passport at our office.
>
> He disappeared from my mind ten seconds after he left our office. Our business is giving service. So my concern was in satisfying a customer. I was able to get the booking that he wanted. He seemed happy and I was pleased to have been of service.

To see how easily Ray obtained his Canadian passport, see the information he supplied in the form and the Statutory Declaration in Lieu of Guarantor. Printing with a ballpoint pen, Ray wrote that his name was "RAMON GEORGE SNEYD." But his "D" in "Sneyd" is a triangle which can easily be—and was—mistaken for an "A," making it "SNEYA." Ray wrote that his passport was to be mailed to him in care of Kennedy Travel Bureau, 424 Bloor Street, West, Toronto; that his permanent address was 962 Dundas Street, West; that his home telephone number was 537-9825; that he was born on October 8, 1932, in Toronto; that he was five feet ten inches tall; that his hair was black, his eyes, blue, his weight, 168 pounds; and that he was a car salesman with a scar over his nose. To the question "Person to Notify in Canada in Case of Emergency," Ray wrote: "Mr. Paul Bridgman, 102 Ossington Avenue, Toronto, a Friend." He also said that he was single, that he had never before applied for a passport, that he was enclosing a postal money order for $5, and that he was making this application in Toronto on April 16, 1968. Over the area in the application form for Declaration of Guarantor is scribbled: "Stat Dec Attached."

The attached Statutory Declaration in Lieu of Guarantor reads:

I, Ramon George Sneyd, of 962 Dundas Street, West, Toronto, Ontario, do solemnly declare that:

1. The statements contained in the attached application for passport are true and correct;
2. There is no one in Canada, eligible under the Canadian passport regulations to vouch for passport applications, who knows me well enough to vouch for my application. The reason for this is that I HAVE BEEN IN TORONTO ONLY 3 WEEKS. And I make this solemn declaration conscientiously believing it to be true, and knowing that it is of the same force and effect as if made under oath, and by virtue of the Canada Evidence Act.

It is signed by Ramon George Sneyd and notarized by Mr. Moos "at Toronto in the Province of Ontario on this 16th day of April AD 1968."

Much has been written about how Ray "had to have help" in order to obtain a Canadian passport. But anyone can see that he didn't need any help. He found it easier to obtain a passport for Ramon George Sneyd in Toronto than it was for him to obtain a driver's license for Eric Starvo Galt in Birmingham. Any adult man or woman can obtain a birth certificate and a passport in Canada on his own statement. Canada has a land area larger than that of the United States and relatively few people, so Canada wants both immigrants and visitors and therefore makes it easy for them to enter and leave. Canadian citizens want a minimum of government interference with their lives, so they want government agencies to take a man at his word. To obtain a passport in the United States, you must present yourself to a government official, show him a birth certificate, which can be difficult to obtain, and fill out a comprehensive form as well as supply recent photos. But in Canada you need not face any government official: a travel agency will accept your application, notarize your declaration that you are a Canadian citizen, mail the forms and photos to the proper agency in Ottawa, and you can pick up your passport at the agency when you purchase your ticket.

As a result of the Ray publicity, some changes are being effected in Canada to make fraudulent passports more difficult to obtain. But understandably, many Canadians, appalled by the growing complexity of modern life, will accept these changes reluctantly.

When Ray left the travel agency, he was encouraged but still nervous and uncertain. He had been told that the agency would have the passport for him by May 1, but he didn't feel sure of it. He faced two weeks of anxious waiting. Next day he made the sort of blunder which has sent many a fugitive back to prison. A Toronto policeman stopped him, questioned him, gave him a ticket for jaywalking, on which he had to pay a fine of $3. Ray, surprised, handled himself stupidly and, had the policeman been more alert or had Ray not looked so trustworthy, this incident would have led to his arrest. Because, when the policeman stopped him, Ray was still carrying his Galt identification, including his driver's license; and by then, for several days, the name Eric S. Galt had been in the news as the suspected assassin of Dr. King. The FBI had not yet announced that Galt was Ray, but every police force in North America had been alerted to watch for Galt.

Having already applied for a passport as Sneyd, Ray came within a breath of telling the policeman his name was Ramon George Sneyd. Had Ray used the Sneyd name, the policeman to whom he was talking might have known the real Mr. Sneyd, who is himself a traffic officer (something Ray did not know); and this could have put Ray, then and there, in the hands of the Royal Canadian Mounted Police, the Canadian counterpart of the FBI.

Ray gave the policeman a name he had once used but not in 1967–1968. Then, trying to think fast, he told the policeman he lived in Toronto, and gave him the correct address of a woman who once wrote to Ray through a lonely-hearts column. He had kept this address in mind in case he needed it, and he needed it now. (Because to fabricate in such a situation is dangerous. You may pick a number which the traffic officer knows does not exist on the street you name, or which the officer knows is a public building or a vacant lot and not a residence. So Ray used an address which he knew was correct, and he knew was a residence.) Had the policeman been suspicious enough to detain Ray while he checked the name with the address, Ray would never have seen London and Lisbon. This jaywalking ticket is on record in Toronto, but it is unlikely to be exhumed because I won't reveal either the name Ray used or the address of the woman.

When I was in Toronto in April 1969 for a television appearance for the Canadian Broadcasting Corporation, I drove to the address of the lonely woman who had once written to Eric S. Galt in Hollywood. I found her, photographed her without her knowledge and watched her for a few minutes. I wanted to speak to her, to ask her if she remembered writing to Eric Galt, to ask her if she had ever realized that Galt was Ray, and to tell her how her address had been used. But, watching her, I decided that she could tell me nothing about Ray, that her life had touched his only in another rueful twist of fate and that, if I spoke to her, I would frighten her and might hurt her as I had hurt the woman Ray met at Gray Rocks. So I got back in the taxicab and left her alone.

After the jaywalking incident, Ray destroyed all the Galt identification which he had assembled so carefully in Birmingham. This left him without identification as anyone. He was nameless, waiting for a birth certificate and a passport to name him Ramon George Sneyd.

On Friday, April 19, 1968, 15 days after the murder, the FBI announced that Eric S. Galt, Harvey Lowmyer, and John Willard were, in truth, James Earl Ray, habitual criminal and an escapee from the Missouri State Penitentiary. By then the agents had had time to collect all the fingerprints left in the rooming house in Memphis, on the rifle and the binoculars, in the Mustang and on the map in the room in Atlanta; and the computers had had time to compare these prints with the millions on file in Washington. The agents had had time to trace the Los Angeles laundry marks on the underwear in the zipper bag left with the rifle; and they had had time to learn that the number on the transistor radio in the zipper bag was Ray's prison number at Jefferson City. He had bought the radio in the prison commissary the day before he escaped. So during that weekend, beginning April 19, the news media recounted the meager, melancholy, ridiculous criminal career of James Earl Ray.

Ray read the papers and watched some of this on television in his "Bridgman room" on Ossington Avenue. Then he gave up this room and stayed in his "Sneyd room" on Dundas Street. But on Sunday evening, April 21, he had to risk going out. He had had a television set at Mrs. Szpakowski's house, but he didn't have one at Mrs. Sun Loo's house. So he went looking for a tavern whose television set was tuned to the show *The FBI*. The first, second and third taverns he entered had their sets tuned to *The Ed Sullivan Show*. But the fourth one had its set tuned to *The FBI*. (Toronto sets receive the Buffalo, New York, stations as well as the Toronto stations.) And in that tavern James Earl Ray, the man no one ever notices, drank vodka and orange juice and watched himself elevated by the FBI to the Top Ten. He did even better than "make the Top Ten." A special international category was created for him. Actor Efrem Zimbalist, Jr., as an FBI agent, described Ray, showed photos of him, warned that he was probably armed and dangerous, emphasized that he might be anywhere in the United States, Canada or Mexico, and urged everyone to watch for him and report his whereabouts to the nearest law-enforcement office.

All this publicity left Ray elated, scared, uncertain and depressed. What added to his fear and uncertainty was the size of the reward: $100,000, posted by the City of Memphis and its newspapers (Scripps-Howard). Ray hadn't expected that the City of Memphis would be quite that anxious to apprehend the slayer of Dr. King, who had been leading a revolt against the City of

Memphis. What depressed him, he told he, was that the publicity "makes me look too much like Tobacco Road." He hated the emphasis on his childhood poverty, his lack of education and his ineptitude as a criminal. In his mind he could see thousands of other criminals, in hundreds of prisons across America, reading and watching his publicity, and he worried about his image among them. He worried about what Benny Edmondson thought of him in Jefferson City. He worried about what his two brothers, with their criminal records, thought of him.

Ray wrote:

> Since they were going to give me my passport on my own declaration that I was a Canadian citizen, I didn't need Bridgman any more. So I checked out of the Ossington Avenue room and kept the Dundas Street address where the passport people or the travel agency people could reach me or check on me as Sneyd, and where Sneyd's birth certificate could be mailed to me. Then I went to Montreal [on Monday, April 22] to check on some ships in case the passport deal fell through. In Montreal I got a room on Notre Dame West, all the way across town from Notre Dame East where I had lived in August, 1967. If I didn't get the passport, I was going to rent passage on a ship that sailed around the coast of South Africa and try to slip in at one of the stops. I found a Scandinavian line that had ships going to Mozambique. The price for a ticket was $600. But they wanted a passport number, so I gave up on that.

> During the nine days I was in Montreal the police must have had a tip that I might be there because several people were arrested. I remember reading in a paper where two males were arrested in a white car with a dog. For this reason I never left the room except to buy food and when I went to the shipping office. I returned to Toronto after being gone nine days, and next day I called the travel agency and was told that my passport had just arrived. When I picked up the passport I found the name was spelled wrong. It was SNEYA instead of SNEYD. There wasn't time to get it changed, so I had to leave Toronto with a faulty passport.

> When I got back to Toronto from Montreal I had about $800. I wanted to go to an English-speaking country in Africa so I could get employment, but the price of a round trip ticket was $820. You can't get into one of those countries without a round

trip ticket. So I bought a round trip ticket to London, but I didn't expect to stay in England because it has too close police and other ties with the U. S.

As will be obvious to everyone, what Ray needed before he left Canada was money. He was going to be given a birth certificate and a passport. With this passport and enough money, he could have reached any of several countries which do not have extradition treaties with the United States. A cardinal truth of Ray's story is that he could have escaped arrest. He could be free today if he had had enough money and had known how to use it. He got caught because of his poverty and his lack of knowledge or help, and because he lost his nerve. His mistake was that he didn't pull a holdup in either Toronto or Montreal.

He knew then that he should pull one or more holdups, to give himself at least the $3,000 he once had in Mexico. But, with all the publicity, he became afraid to stay out of a room long enough to "case" a store or a loan office. He had had nerve enough to kill Dr. King. Then he didn't have nerve enough to pull the holdups which could have assured his escape.

He knows this now. When I asked him why he didn't pull a holdup in Canada between April 22 and May 6, he replied bitterly: "That's where I made my mistake. I should have pulled a holdup. But I didn't. And I let myself get on that plane to London without enough money to get where I intended to go."

The birth certificate for Ramon George Sneyd was waiting for Ray at Mrs. Sun Loo's house when he returned from Montreal. The postman had brought it. And with the birth certificate Ray committed another nervous error which could have led to his arrest. He carried the birth certificate in his inside coat pocket in the official-looking envelope in which it had arrived. In the booth from which he telephoned the travel agency, he pulled out the envelope to note on it the departure time of his flight to London. Then he walked away from the booth leaving the envelope and birth certificate.

But again the fates intervened. The envelope was found by a good-hearted fellow who came to be known as the Fat Man. Noting that the envelope was addressed to a brother in the next block, the Fat Man walked to 962 Dundas Street, West, and asked Mrs. Sun

Loo if he could see Mr. Sneyd. Mrs. Sun Loo called Ray, whose heart skipped a beat, but who managed to confront the Fat Man, who said he had come to return the envelope. Ray thanked him, but forgot to offer him money, and the Fat Man went away. Because, to the knowledge of investigators, he was the only visitor Ray ever had outside of prison and because he delivered an envelope to Ray on the day that Ray paid the Kennedy Travel Bureau $345 for a 21-day round-trip ticket to London, the Fat Man is a towering figure in the Ray mythology. Decades from now, when the "real" story of the murder of Dr. King is again told, the Fat Man will be the agent of the FBI, the CIA, the Ku Klux Klan, Fidel Castro, or of rich Louisiana racists, delivering getaway money to their hired assassin. And some people will believe this despite the unlikelihood that such an emissary would have delivered such a payment in the full view and knowledge of Mrs. Sun Loo.

During the afternoon of May 6 Ray packed his bag, and with his raincoat over his arm, he told Mrs. Sun Loo that he was leaving because the noise of children playing in her neighborhood bothered him. Then he traveled by trolley and taxicab to Toronto Airport and boarded BOAC Flight 600 to London at 6 P.M. After a flight of seven hours and 40 minutes, he landed at London's Heathrow Airport at 6:40 A.M., Tuesday, May 7.

Ray wrote:

> Upon my arrival in England I called the Portuguese Embassy and asked how long it would take to get a visa. They told me one day. I then used my return ticket to Canada to go to Portugal that night. I didn't want to spend any more time in London than I had to. In Portugal I spent all my time [10 days] looking for a ship to go to Angola. On about my 8th day in Lisbon I finally found a ship going to Angola. The fare was 3,777 escudos one way, about $130. The ship was leaving in two days. I then went to get the visa and was told it would take seven days. This meant that by the time I got the permit to go to Angola, the ship would be gone. I was getting so short of money that I decided to go back to London. But before I left for London I went to the Canadian Embassy in Lisbon and complained about my name being misspelled [Sneya] in my passport. So they cancelled the old passport [Sneya] and issued me a new one with my name spelled right [Sneyd].
>
> In London I tried to find out all I could about getting in the

mercenaries. I was told to go to France, and I would have gone
from England to France, but they were having riots in France,
and planes were not landing there. I finally contacted a newspaper
reporter who told me the mercenaries had an office in Brussels.
He gave me the address of a man who might help me. I then
bought a ticket to Brussels, and I was going there on June 8th
when I was caught at the London airport. They shook me down
and found the .38. I also had a blueprint on how to make a si-
lencer for a pistol.

His last month of freedom—from May 7, when he reached London enroute to Lisbon, to June 8, when he was arrested in London
—was a miserably frustrating period for Ray. He lived on aspirin,
stayed in bed much of the time, and watched his money and his
hopes run out. He was a little man who had overreached himself,
without friends, without money and without much knowledge of
what he was trying to do. I think he wanted to be arrested and
returned to prison as a way out of his misery.

To many people in the United States, this was also a frustrating
month. After the FBI identified Ray on April 19 and described
him on television on April 21, many people expected an early arrest. When days, then weeks passed without an arrest, some people
accused the FBI either of aiding Ray's escape or of not really trying to catch the murderer of Dr. King, whom the FBI director,
J. Edgar Hoover, despised. A number of people who hated Dr.
King, including some of my friends and relatives in Alabama, said
they hoped Ray would never be caught. And other people, like the
author Truman Capote, predicted on television talk shows that
Ray would never be found because he had been killed by his fellow
conspirators.

Again the explanation for the delay was the need for time. The
"Sneya" passport was not issued in Ottawa until April 25. Searching for Ray, the Royal Canadian Mounted Police had to examine
the photographs on 50,000 passport applications; and this examination had to be done, not with computers but with human eyes
and magnifying glasses. It was May 20 before the Mounties and
the FBI knew that Ray had left Toronto for London on May 6
carrying passport No. DJ 905324 in the name of Ramon George
Sneya. It was May 23 when they learned from the Canadian Em-

bassy in Lisbon that on May 16 this passport had been canceled and another issued to Ramon George Sneyd. The new passport number was YT 602294. On May 23 the FBI also learned that Ray, with the new passport, had flown from Lisbon to London on May 17.

The information that Ray evidently was in London, having reached there on May 17, was flashed to Scotland Yard, and Detective Chief Inspector Kenneth Thompson of the Yard's Commonwealth Immigrants and Passport Offences Squad was assigned to see that Ray was arrested the next time he presented the Sneyd passport. The picture and description of "Sneyd" was published at once in the *Police Gazette,* which goes to every police and passport officer in Great Britain. Beneath "Sneyd's" picture were these words: "Wanted in connection with a serious immigration matter. Do not interrogate but detain for questioning by Detective Chief Inspector Kenneth Thompson of New Scotland Yard."

Scotland Yard agents then learned that, when Ray reached London at 6:40 A.M. on May 7, he did not leave the airport. He stayed there all day, obtaining his permit to fly to Lisbon, and he left London at 10:55 P.M. on BEA (British European Airways) Flight 074 and arrived in Lisbon at 1:20 A.M., Wednesday, May 8.

In Lisbon Ray spent ten nights at the Hotel Portugal, a cheap but clean hotel which travel guides assign to the "third category." If he had had more money, and if he had applied on May 8 for permission to go to Angola, by May 15 Ray could have had this permit, and he could have gone to Angola, the Portuguese colony in West Africa, by either ship or plane. Why didn't he do this? Since he was afraid of being arrested in London, why did he return there? Why didn't he remain in Lisbon and pull a holdup there to solve his money problem? There are two answers. Nowhere in Lisbon could Ray find anyone interested in hiring him as a white mercenary soldier to fight rebellious blacks in Angola. And Ray has a special fear of being arrested and imprisoned in a non-English-speaking country. So he preferred to risk a holdup in London rather than in Lisbon.

When he reached London on Friday, May 17, Ray rented a room in Heathfield House Hotel, Cromwell Road in Earls Court, a low-rent district heavily populated by Australians and therefore called "Kangaroo Valley." This hotel is near the Earls Court Stadium in West London, scene of Billy Graham's British crusades. The bus from the airport to central London travels along Cromwell Road. In addition to Australians and native Londoners, the population of Earls Court includes New Zealanders, Canadians, Indians, Pakistanis, and blacks from Africa and Jamaica. It is a shifting population of students and workers.

On Tuesday, May 28, Ray moved a short distance to the New Earls Court Hotel, 35-37 Penywern Road. Here he spent eight nights in room 54, a third-floor single, and he is remembered by the twenty-one-year-old receptionist, Jane Nassau. "He had no telephone calls, no mail, no visitors," she said. "He was very quiet, nervous, pathetically shy and unsure of himself."

By Tuesday, June 4, Ray was down to his last $20. So he held up a cashier of the Trustee Savings Bank, Fulham. He didn't speak, but with the muzzle of his pistol showing between his fingers, he nudged a note toward the cashier which read: "Hand over the cash." He snatched 100 pounds ($240) in five-pound notes and fled.

Detectives investigating the robbery found fingerprints on the note, and Scotland Yard's Criminal Records Office said the prints were Ray's. Then, certain that Ray was in London and that he had committed a felony inside Great Britain, Scotland Yard ordered detectives in their crack Flying Squad, led by Detective Chief Superintendent Thomas Butler, to join Inspector Thompson's squad in the search for Ray. Mr. Butler is the detective who arrested members of the Great Train Robbery gang.

On Wednesday, June 5, the day after he robbed the bank, Ray moved from the New Earls Court Hotel to an obscure, back-street hotel, the Pax Hotel in Pimlico. The Pax, a cream-colored, three-story building, seems lost in a block with other buildings exactly like it. There was no name on the door, only the word "hotel." The telephone number was unlisted, and the nearby newsdealer had never heard of the Pax. Anna Thomas, the Swedish-born, fifty-four-year-old wife of an Englishman, bought the place in early 1968, redecorated it, and opened it in April 1968. She has seven rooms to let. She is articulate and intelligent, and she remembers Ray distinctly. She said:

He arrived in the middle of a violent rainstorm on Wednesday evening [June 5]. He had only an airline bag as luggage, but I gave him No. 1 on the ground floor. We often get single gentlemen with only an airline bag, staying over between flights. He didn't have much to say. He said he was from Toronto, so I asked him about Toronto, and he said there was a lot of unemployment there. He hardly ever went out, and then only to buy food, lots of newspapers, and aspirins. He seemed ill and stayed in bed all day. He told me he had arrived on an early flight and was very tired. He seemed very, very nervous.

When I brought him breakfast on Thursday morning he refused to open the door and told me to leave the tray outside. I had given him the hotel register and asked him to sign it. He still had it with him inside the room, so I asked him to please hand it to me. He put it out with the breakfast tray, but he hadn't signed it.

I entered his room only once during the three days he was here. That was when he had run out for headache tablets. I found that he had made up his bed and tidied up. He had washed his own shirts. And he had been reading newspaper accounts of the murder of Senator Kennedy. He had no visitors, but there were two telephone calls from a girl at BEA about postponed flight bookings to Germany. He wouldn't come to the telephone, so I wrote down the messages and pushed them under his door. On Friday afternoon he said he would be leaving Saturday [June 8], and when he left Saturday morning I was glad to see him go. I felt sorry for him, but he was so obviously a troubled man that he gave me the creeps.

A reporter for *The London Daily Telegraph,* Ian Colvin, has reported extensively on armed conflict in Africa involving white mercenaries. Mr. Colvin said that between June 3 and June 7 he received several calls from a man who said he was Ramon George Sneyd and wanted information about joining mercenary forces in Africa. The caller claimed to have a brother missing in Portuguese Angola. Mr. Colvin said he gave the caller an address in Brussels at which he might find some assistance.

Heathrow Airport, of course, was the focal point of Scotland Yard's watch for "Sneyd." When, on Saturday, June 8, Ray left the Pax Hotel for the airport, with a ticket for BEA Flight 466 due to depart at 11:50 A.M. for Brussels, the police were waiting for him. At 11:15 A.M., when he produced his passport, Detective

Sergeant Philip Birch reached for it. "Please come with me, Mr. Sneyd," he said. He escorted Ray to the Scotland Yard office at the airport. Three other detectives joined Sergeant Birch. They searched Ray and found the .38-caliber Liberty Chief (Japanese) loaded with five rounds of ammunition. Ray said: "I'm going to Africa and I felt that I might need it. You know how things are out there." The detectives then fingerprinted him and rushed the prints to the Criminal Records Office.

At 1:05 P.M. Detective Chief Superintendent Butler and Detective Chief Inspector Thompson arrived. "I can't understand why I am here," Ray told them. They asked him where he was going, and he said to Brussels. They asked him if the pistol was his and if he had any sort of permit to carry it. He said it was his, that he had no permit, and added: "I'm thinking of going on to Rhodesia and things are not too good there just now." They told him he was under arrest for carrying the weapon and that he would be transported to a police station.

Each of these detectives is convinced that Ray, as of that moment, did not believe that they knew his real identity. They called him "Mr. Sneyd" and implied no doubt that that was his real name. They escorted him to the Cannon Row Police Station, which is within the courtyard of the former Scotland Yard headquarters on the embankment at Westminster, 300 yards from the Houses of Parliament. They placed him in a cell "in the company of a detective." They took his fingerprints again and checked them again with the Criminal Records Office.

At 4:45 P.M. Mr. Butler and Mr. Thompson visited him in his cell. Mr. Thompson reminded him of his rights, that he did not have to make any statement, after which Mr. Butler said that they had reason to believe that he was James Earl Ray, wanted for murder in the United States. Ray's shoulders sagged.

"Are you Ray?" Mr. Butler asked.

Ray sighed audibly. "Oh, well, yes, I am," he replied. He shook his head and added: "Oh, God." He seemed about to collapse as he said: "I feel so trapped." Then he said: "I guess I shouldn't say anything more now. I can't think right."

Later, during the six weeks he was in prison in London, and even later in the United States, Ray came to feel ashamed of his behavior in London. His crippling anxiety before his arrest, his meek surrender at the airport, his allowing himself to be fingerprinted, his admitting that he was Ray, his sighing that he felt so trapped—was that the proud, insolent behavior expected of a member of the Top Ten? A smart criminal who makes it to the Top Ten, if he chooses not to shoot it out with the detectives, at least spits in their eyes and admits nothing! And he damn sure never whimpers that he feels so trapped!

Because he felt ashamed of his behavior, Ray hated all published accounts of it. To his lawyers, to me, to his brothers, to his jailers in Memphis, he insisted that he never said, "I feel so trapped," that he never admitted he was Ray, that Mr. Butler lied about him and tried to make deals with him. He demanded that his lawyers "get something" to discredit Mr. Butler, and he urged me to print the truth about how defiantly he really acted. In January 1969, he wrote this to me:

> Upon arrest at London Heathrow Airport I was taken to a detention cell and told that a Scotland Yard officer would be there shortly to talk to me. About a half hour passed, then I was searched and a pistol was found on me. About one hour later several officers from Scotland Yard arrived, one whom I learned later was Supt. Thomas Butler. They proceeded to ask me questions about where I was going and why I had the pistol. I told them the reason I had the pistol was that I was going to Africa. I was then asked if I would give my permission to be fingerprinted. I said no. Whereupon five or six took a hold of me and said I was going to be printed one way or the other (Butler said this). I was then fingerprinted. An officer left with the prints and returned. Upon returning he nodded to Supt. Butler who then asked me to sign the print card. I refused. He then asked me to sign my personal property receipt. I refused to sign that paper. Whereupon Supt. Butler signed both of them. (I found out later that under English law if a suspect does not want his prints taken the arresting officer must get a court order.) I was then taken to a lockup in London which is about 15 miles from the airport. I was again printed after being forced. I again refused to sign the printcard. (I did this to show I opposed having my prints taken.) I was then placed in a cell with an officer.
>
> About an hour later (this would be about three hours after my

arrest) Mr. Butler came to the cell with another officer who told me I didn't have to make any statements. Mr. Butler then said he had reason to believe I was wanted in the U. S. for murder and my name was James Ray. I then asked him for permission to consult with my attorney. He said I couldn't have or see an attorney, but if I would help him he would help me. I then turned and walked away from him and sat on a bench.

At a later courtroom appearance on my extradition hearing Butler said I made a statement (oral). I denied this in open court as I hadn't made any statement. When Mr. Butler returned me to the prison after the hearing, I wrote a letter (reg.) to the following official: Mr. James Callagan, Home Secretary, House of Commons, London, England. I asked Mr. Callagan to bar Mr. Butler from having any further contact with me as it was my belief he was lying about me in court in regards to a statement at the behest of the U. S. Attorney General's office. (I never did receive an answer. Would it be possible to get a duplicate of this letter from Mr. Callagan's office?)

Sometime later Mr. Butler came to the prison and requested to see me. I refused as under British law you don't have to see anyone while you're in prison. Also I didn't want him to make up another statement. He told the guard that came to tell me that Butler wanted to see me, that he was going to Canada and could go on to Washington. The next day I read in the paper where Mr. Butler did go to Canada. (What did he want to see me about? So he could give out a statement when he got to the U. S.?)

Supt. Butler also threatened once to put my picture in every paper in London if I didn't answer his questions.

Under English law I'm not sure if you are entitled to an attorney at the time of your arrest as you are in the U. S. even if you request it.

Would it be adviseable to get the print cards and personal property cards from London to show that I didn't co-operate and help discredit the statement?

In his fantasies Ray sees himself as a great "jailhouse lawyer." At both Leavenworth and the Missouri State Prison he read law books in the prison libraries, and he bought law books regularly by mail. He wrote to me: "In prison you have to do most of your own law work." He instructed both Arthur Hanes and Percy Foreman in how to conduct his defense. His account of his behavior in London shows the jailhouse lawyer at work.

I gave Ray's account of his arrest to a capable crime reporter in London. He showed it to all parties involved, and reported this to me:

> The police stand by the court report that Sneyd made an oral statement and that he said exactly what they reported he said. They deny that Sneyd asked to see a lawyer and had his request refused. They add that an international investigation of this nature is so sensitive that no detective would be foolish enough to do anything that was "outside the book." All detectives in the London Airport operation strongly deny that Sneyd refused to have his fingerprints taken. They say that he readily agreed.
>
> I have talked to Michael Eugene of Dresden & Company, solicitors who represented Sneyd, and Mr. Eugene cannot recall Sneyd writing a letter of complaint to the Home Secretary. There is a strict routine at the Home Office whereby any such complaint is automatically acknowledged and a copy of the complainant's letter is passed to the Commissioner of Police.
>
> Despite exhaustive enquiries, I have been unable to find any person with any knowledge of such a letter being received at the Home Office or the Yard. Regarding Sneyd's comment about Butler signing the personal property receipt and the fingerprint card, under the law these documents must be signed by the officer in charge of such a case. So Butler was proceeding strictly by the book.
>
> It is not possible to obtain photocopies of any official documents as suggested by Ray. All such documents are governed by the Official Secrets Act.

What's important about Ray's account of his arrest is not that there is any truth in it. It's a lie: imagine Mr. Butler threatening to put Ray's picture in every newspaper when it was already in every newspaper. What's important about the account is that it again reveals why Ray murdered Dr. King. His motivation was his yearning to wear boots too big for him. Cursed with that little learning said to be such a dangerous thing, he was a dull criminal, ashamed of himself, striving to prove that he belonged in the Top Ten and deserved to be found interesting by criminals as well as by noncriminals who enjoy crime by watching it and reading about it.

In the "Property Found in Possession of Ramon George Sneyd" at the London airport, in addition to the pistol, the two passports, and the birth certificate, there was the Polaroid 220 camera with which Ray photographed himself, a radio, a bottle of Sloan's Liniment, aspirin, and a quantity of deodorants, skin creams, shampoos and hair dressing. There were eight books: the 1967 *Almanac;* a book on Rhodesia; a spy story, *The Ninth Directive;* three books on self-hypnotism; *How to Cash in on Your Hidden Memory Power;* and *Psychocybernetics,* the book about how to find your goal in life.

As for money, in pounds, shillings and pence, Ray had $123.54.

Nine

From the moment the shot was fired on April 4, 1968, Dr. King's murder was widely assumed to have been the result of a conspiracy. Then, after Ray was arrested in London on June 8, 1968, this assumption gained support from much of what appeared in the press. On Monday, June 10, *The Toronto Star,* combining reports from London, Ottawa and Washington with its local story, ran seven columns of type under the head: "POLICE SUSPECT INTER-NATIONAL KING CONSPIRACY." Here are excerpts from the coverage:

> Canadian and Washington investigators are urgently checking the possibility that James Earl Ray may have been part of an intercontinental murder conspiracy. In the month he spent in Toronto after the murder of King, Ray used sophisticated techniques far beyond his own powers in hoodwinking the Canadian government into issuing him two passports under phony names.
>
> Ray was arraigned in London's Bow Street Magistrates Court this morning on charges of illegal possession of a firearm and of possessing a falsified passport. He was ordered to be held until June 18th for another court appearance.

Ray, a grin on his face, was half dragged into court for an 82-second appearance. He wore the checked gray-green sports jacket, blue cotton sports shirt and dark slacks he wore into captivity when caught in the airport. His hands were jammed into his trouser pockets. He was ushered to the front of the bench, and after one brief look at the magistrate he stood there, head hanging. He asked the court to appoint a lawyer for him, an indication that he will fight extradition. American legal experts, however, say they hope to have Ray back in the U. S. very soon.

Royal Canadian Mounted Police sources revealed the conspiracy fears last night. Their belief that Ray was not alone in murdering Dr. King, or in making his getaway, is based on four points:

1. He showed expert knowledge of the loopholes in the Canadian system of obtaining birth certificates and passports. These loopholes have been used before by extensive Soviet espionage apparatuses to get secret agents into North America and by heavily-financed narcotics smuggling organizations.
2. He appeared to have had plenty of money.
3. There is some evidence that he had contacts in Canada who knew in advance what his assumed names would be.
4. His obtaining a second Canadian passport in Lisbon might mean he planned to establish residences in several places, an expensive business for a man on the run.

   The Mounties are convinced that accomplices aided Ray while he was hiding in Toronto. "He didn't come cold into this city and make all his own arrangements for the birth certificate and passport," a Mountie spokesman said. "There was help of some kind."

   The hunt for persons who may have aided Ray has spread to Brussels and Lisbon where, according to police, Ray may have been picking up funds channeled through a Swiss bank.

In addition to being regarded as the result of a "giant conspiracy," the murder also came to be regarded as a "political crime." Ray, opposing extradition, was represented in London by both a solicitor, Mr. Eugene, and a barrister, Roger Frisby. Britain has long been a haven for persons charged with "political crimes" in other countries because its extradition treaties with other countries provide that "a fugitive criminal shall not be surrendered if the

crime or the offense in respect of which his surrender is demanded
is one of a political character." This provision is in the 1931 extradition treaty between Britain and the United States, and extradition can take place only under the strict terms of this treaty. So
Ray's attorneys contended that he should not be surrendered to
the United States because the crime with which he was charged
in the United States was "of a political character." At a hearing in
London before Magistrate Frank Milton on July 2, 1968, Mr.
Frisby, in Ray's behalf, declared:

> Dr. King was the leader of a political movement. He was en-
> gaged in trying to compel the United States government to change
> political policy. He was opposed by millions of citizens. It is there-
> fore abundantly clear that whoever did the killing did it not on
> personal grounds but on grounds which arose out of disapproval
> of the type of political activity Dr. King was conducting. Whoever
> did this killing was acting consciously or otherwise as representa-
> tive of a large body of persons who disagreed with the objectives
> and aims of Dr. King's movement.

Mr. Frisby was answered by British barrister David Calcutt, ap-
pearing for the United States. Mr. Calcutt declared:

> There is not a shred of evidence to show that Dr. King was
> murdered to further the ends of his political opposition. There is
> nothing to show that this shooting was done to oppose the cause
> of coloured people. There was no conspiracy, and no group or
> other man was involved. There is no evidence of this man having
> worked with any other man. There is no evidence of this man be-
> ing associated with any organization. There have been undertones
> that this must be so, but the evidence before this court points to
> a lone assassination for private purposes.
>
> Dr. King and his Southern Christian Leadership Conference
> were not plotting or promoting insurrection. And the murderer of
> Dr. King was acting, not for some organization which opposed
> Dr. King, but for himself alone and for his own purposes. So the
> murder of Dr. King cannot be called a political crime under our
> traditional interpretation of political offence.

Magistrate Milton granted extradition. But several aspects of
that hearing should be remembered. The U. S. Department of Justice had taken the "one man alone" position since Sunday, April 7,
when Attorney General Ramsey Clark appeared on the television

program *Meet the Press*. Maybe Mr. Clark and the FBI, less than three days after the murder, already had concluded that it was the work of one man alone. But this must be remembered. When Mr. Clark made his statement, a hundred American cities were enduring race riots set off by the murder. To see the smoke of these riots, Mr. Clark had only to look out his window in Washington, D. C. The attorney general would have aggravated this racial conflict had he said anything else but that the murder was done by a lone criminal who would be speedily apprehended and punished. Moreover, only by taking the one-man-alone position could the Justice Department have extradited Ray from Great Britain. Either before or after Ray's arrest in London, any concession by the Justice Department that Ray might have been assisted, or that he had acted for some organization opposed to Dr. King, would have given Ray the protection of the provision in the British treaty against extraditing persons charged with crimes "of a political character." In short, in order to try to dampen the flames in our cities and in order to bring Ray to trial, conspiracy was something the Justice Department had to deny from the moment the shot was fired.

An early maneuver by the FBI jeopardized this one-man-alone position. Learning on the first day after the murder that Eric S. Galt, as Harvey Lowmyer, had declared at the Aeromarine Supply Company that he was buying the rifle because he and his brother were going deer hunting, FBI agents, in order to put out an immediate arrest order, had a warrant issued charging "Galt and his brother with conspiracy in connection with the murder of Dr. King." A day later, after the dangers of that word "conspiracy" were realized, this arrest order was rescinded.

The extradition treaty of 1931 between the United States and Great Britain also provides that a fugitive criminal, once he has been extradited, can be tried for no other crime than the one for which he was extradited. This means that Ray, extradited as the one-man-alone murderer of Dr. King, could not and cannot be tried for any crime other than the *murder* of Dr. King. He could not and cannot be tried for conspiring to murder, or for aiding and abetting the murder, or for conspiring to deprive Dr. King of his civil rights: only for the one-man-alone murder itself.

For those who like to ponder how the best-laid provisions of extradition treaties can go awry, here is an ironic fact. Had the Ku Klux Klan gone promptly to Ray's assistance and taken the position that Ray was a Klansman who, without the knowledge of other Klansmen, had nevertheless acted for the Klan in murdering Dr. King, Ray could not have been extradited and might never have been brought to trial for murder.

Had Magistrate Milton ruled against extraditing Ray to the United States, then Great Britain would have had to try Ray for armed robbery committed in Great Britain, and would have had to imprison him. I'm not suggesting that this influenced the magistrate's decision, but from the moment Ray was arrested, neither he nor anyone else in London doubted that he would be extradited. So in his first conference with his court-appointed solicitor, Michael Eugene, Ray asked for assistance in obtaining a lawyer to represent him in the United States.

What sort of defendant who is penniless expects a famous lawyer to take his case and spend thousands of dollars and hundreds of hours defending him? This happens in the United States only in highly publicized cases when the famous lawyer can appear to be serving a popular cause, like crusading against capital punishment (as in the Sirhan case). In other cases, well-known lawyers come in when a sizable defense fund from public subscription can be anticipated (as in the Scottsboro case) or (as in the Dr. Sam Sheppard case) when the lawyer expects to sell the defendant's story for $100,000 or more. (The lawyers for Sirhan also sold his story to a writer who was permitted to interview Sirhan repeatedly before the trial.)

Ray figured that, since he had become a famous member of the Top Ten, a famous lawyer, on his invitation, would gladly rush to London to begin preparing to defend him at a famous trial. So he asked Mr. Eugene to telephone his invitation to F. Lee Bailey, the Boston lawyer who defended Dr. Sheppard. When Mr. Eugene told Mr. Bailey that Ray wanted him to defend him, Mr. Bailey summarily declined. This jolted Ray, who decided he had better try for a less famous lawyer.

Ray told Mr. Eugene that he had heard of a lawyer in Birmingham, Alabama, a man named Hanes who had defended the three Klansmen who murdered Mrs. Viola Liuzzo, of Detroit, after she had participated as a civil-rights advocate in the Selma-to-Mont-gomery March led by Dr. King. Ray didn't know the full name or the unusual spelling, so Mr. Eugene learned through the U. S. Em-bassy that the man Ray wanted was Arthur J. Hanes, of the law firm of Hanes and Hanes, Birmingham. (The other Hanes in the firm is Arthur J. Hanes, Jr.) Ray wrote to Mr. Hanes through the Birmingham Bar Association, after which Mr. Eugene telephoned Mr. Hanes, who agreed to consider representing Ray and to come to London to confer with him. *The Birmingham News* reported that Mr. Hanes, a former mayor of Birmingham, had been asked by Ray to represent him.

My home is 70 miles north of Birmingham. As a writer who has written about several race-conflict cases, including the Liuzzo case, I knew Mr. Hanes. In 1968 he was fifty-two, a black-haired, dark-visaged, energetic, affable man whose elder son, Arthur, Jr., then twenty-seven, is a graduate of Princeton and the University of Alabama Law School. The Hanes family is far from wealthy. The law firm is a father-and-son firm with one secretary, who also an-swers the telephone, and they make a comfortable living represent-ing poor and middle-income clients in both civil and criminal mat-ters. Until 1966 Mrs. Haines, Sr., was the secretary who answered the telephone.

Mr. Hanes's politics is not mine. As a former FBI agent and another angry man—angry at the United States for trying to im-pose racial change on Alabama—he was elected one of Birming-ham's three city commissioners. One of these commissioners wore the honorary title of mayor, so Mr. Hanes was "mayor" while Bull Connor was the police commissioner who used the dogs and fire-hoses against Dr. King's marchers. The mayor differed from Bull not in attitudes but in being more literate and not saying "nigger" in public. Both the mayor and Bull were then deposed by Birming-ham voters in an effort to improve the city's image. Mr. Hanes is, or was, a supporter of George Wallace; and while he isn't a Ku Klux Klansman, he allowed himself to be retained to defend Klans-men, and he received Klan votes.

None of which kept Mr. Hanes from being friendly to me. We were not close associates, but we called each other by first names and we generally believed what we said to one another in private.

In the specialized trade of defending a white man before a Southern jury against the charge of slaying a white or Negro civil-rights advocate, Art Hanes is an effective lawyer. He knows how to recognize and select white jurors who want to vote not guilty, then he makes them feel respectable. He doesn't embarrass them with raw racism. He is courteous, seldom yells, and strives only to provide his white jurors some excuse to vote that the state has not proved beyond a reasonable doubt that the defendant did what he obviously did. When I read that Ray was trying to get Mr. Hanes for his lawyer, I thought that Ray, from somebody in Alabama, had received sound instruction or advice.

I also knew what Mr. Hanes knew: that he was neither able nor inclined to represent Ray for publicity only, he had to be paid; that the Ku Klux Klan has no money; that neither Wallace nor any other racist politician in the South would raise a penny to defend Ray, therefore no substantial money would be raised; so Mr. Hanes could defend Ray only if he could obtain and sell Ray's story.

I telephoned the Hanes office and talked with Art, Jr. "Dad's out," he said. "He's rushing around trying to get ready to go to London. We're both going. And we have to get passports and vaccinations. Shall I have him call you?"

"No, just give him a message," I said. "Tell him I'm interested."

I had just come back from London. My novel *The Klansman* had been published there on May 13, and I had spoken at Oxford and made several radio and television appearances. I was in London while Ray was at large in Lisbon and London. A day or so after I talked with Art, Jr., his father called me from Washington.

"I'm picking up our passports here," he said, "then we're going on to London tonight. Did you mean what you told Artie?"

"Yes," I said. "I'm interested."

"How interested? You know I can't afford to chase around the world and defend that boy unless I can get some money somewhere. Nobody that I'll associate with is gonna raise any money; and contributions would add up to nothing. So I can't go into this unless Ray's willing for me to sell his story to be published after he has been sentenced. If he's willing, how much can we get?"

"Well, neither of us knows what the story is," I said. "Or what he will tell. But after you talk with him, if you think the prospects are good, I'll gamble with you. Up to $40,000."

"And you'll start putting up part of it at once?"

"Yes."

"That's all I want to hear," he said. "I'll see you when I get back."

"Do you need any help in London?" I asked. "Do you have a place to stay?"

"We haven't made any arrangements," he said. "There hasn't been time. And we've never been to London. We're just getting on the plane and hoping we can find a place to stay when we get there."

"Then you need help," I said. "This is Ascot week in London, and without help, you can't find a barn to sleep in. I'll call my agent, and you'll be met at the airport."

"That's great, buddy!" he said. "See you when we get back."

The Haneses spent four exciting days in London, but were not allowed to see Ray. The magistrate had not yet made the decision on extradition, so Mr. Hanes was adjudged to "have no standing in British courts." But Mr. Hanes conferred with Mr. Eugene, who told Ray that Mr. Hanes was there and had tentatively agreed to represent him "if and when he was extradited." The Haneses then flew back to Birmingham.

A day later Mr. Hanes was told by Mr. Eugene that the extradition decision would be made on July 2; that the decision would be appealed; and that Mr. Hanes would be allowed to confer with Ray on July 5. So Mr. Hanes, without his son, flew back to London and conferred with Ray for half an hour on June 5 and again for half an hour on June 6.

Meanwhile, on June 27, one organization had offered to raise money for Ray. Here is the report of the announcement:

> SAVANNAH, Ga., June 27. (UPI)—The "Patriotic Legal Aid Fund" of Savannah offered today to defend James Earl Ray, the escaped convict accused of assassinating Dr. Martin Luther King Jr.
>
> "We have offered to defend Ray free of charge, pay all legal costs, attorney fees, court costs and cost of appeals, if there are any, and bond," said Dr. Edward R. Fields.

Fields is secretary of the Legal Aid Fund and president of the Savannah-based National States Rights Party. This Party has been identified by FBI Director J. Edgar Hoover in testimony before a House subcommittee as an anti-Negro "hate-type" organization.

Fields said former Birmingham, Ala., mayor Arthur Hanes, who has tentatively agreed to defend Ray if he is extradited and tried in Memphis, is "a personal friend of mine and would be a good attorney."

The lawyer for the National States' Rights party and long-time associate of Fields in the Ku Klux Klan is a man with a limp and a speech impediment named J. C. Stoner, also of Savannah. Fields and Stoner are "raw racists." They say "nigger" even when talking with reporters, and they add such statements as: "We didn't shed no tears when Saint Martin Lucifer Coon was shot." They had telephoned Mr. Hanes and offered to associate with him and use their defense of Ray to "launch a nation-wide fund-raising drive." Mr. Hanes had turned them down both because he didn't want to associate with them and because he knew they couldn't raise much money.

When Mr. Hanes saw Ray in London on July 5, both of them knew of the offer from Savannah. Mr. Hanes told Ray that he (Hanes) would never associate with Fields and Stoner; that he would have no part in the defense if Ray insisted on bringing Stoner in; that he would agree to defend Ray only if he and his son were the only defense lawyers in the case, and only if Ray agreed to tell and agreed to the publication of his complete story after the trial. Ray agreed to all these conditions, and in Wandsworth Prison on July 5, with Mr. Eugene as a witness, Ray signed for Mr. Hanes a power of attorney and this agreement:

KNOW ALL MEN BY THESE PRESENTS: That the undersigned, R. G. Sneyd, or whatever other name he be known by, and Arthur J. Hanes, in consideration of the mutual covenants of the parties, do hereby agree and covenant as follows:

1. The said R. G. Sneyd does hereby assign, transfer and set over unto the said Arthur J. Hanes, his heirs and assigns, an undivided 40% interest in all his right, title and interest in and to money, rights and benefits which may accrue to him under and by virtue of an agreement to be entered into between the said

R. G. Sneyd, William Bradford Huie and Arthur J. Hanes. This shall be in addition to any money, rights or benefits which may accure to the said Arthur J. Hanes independently under said agreement.

2. The said Arthur J. Hanes does hereby agree to act as exclusive agent and attorney for the said R. G. Sneyd in the handling of his affairs, contracts, negotiations, and sale of any and all rights to information or privacy which he may have in and to his life or particular events therein to persons, groups or corporations for the purpose of writing, publishing, filming or telecasting in any form whatever.

IN WITNESS WHEREOF, we have hereunto set our hands and seals this 5th day of July, 1968.

> [Signed]
> JAMES EARL RAY, alias
> R. G. SNEYD
> ARTHUR J. HANES

After Mr. Hanes saw Ray on July 5, reporters were waiting for him outside the prison. Here is a resulting news story:

LONDON, July 5 (UPI)—The Alabama lawyer for James Earl Ray met with his client for the first time today and announced that if Ray is extradited he will plead innocent to the charge of murdering Dr. Martin Luther King Jr.

Arthur Hanes, former mayor of Birmingham, said he felt more confident of a successful defense after talking half an hour with Ray at Wandsworth Prison in West London. "For me a successful defense means a verdict of not guilty," the attorney told newsmen. Asked how Ray would plead, Hanes replied, "Not guilty, not guilty to anything."

A London court Tuesday ordered Ray extradited, but Ray appealed. Hanes, who beamed with optimism, qualified all discussion of appeals by saying "only if he is extradited. I am not certain he will be." Asked if Ray was optimistic about the outcome of the appeal against the extradition order, Hanes kept repeating: "He feels good, he looks good, he is in good health, he is getting plenty of sleep."

Hanes said he and Ray talked about the defense and payment of the lawyer's fees. The lawyer engaged in a heated argument with reporters after he insisted "no organization, no one, only Sneyd himself" had contacted him about paying his fee. The reporters questioned how Ray would be able to take care of the expenses of Hanes' two trans-Atlantic flights plus trial costs. "He assured me he can take care of my fee," Hanes said. "He has indicated he may be able to raise money from his family. He ain't going to pay me with love, I can tell you that."

His face reddening, the attorney almost shouted at the British reporters, "I'm not on trial! Bear that in mind. The source of any money is not relevant to the case." Then Hanes said: "This is a challenge and a big case. The man needs help and I intend to give it. It's a big ball game. I would do the same for anyone, black or white. I am made that way."

Those London reporters who questioned Mr. Hanes could never, I suppose, have been made to believe the truth: that Mr. Hanes was no more than one individual, spending his own money, and supported by nothing more organized or powerful than a verbal agreement with one, lone Alabama writer. For hadn't Ray been a member or a tool of a "giant conspiracy" from which Ray drew "plenty of money," some of which he obtained in contacts with "Swiss banks"? So hadn't this organized force twice sent Mr. Hanes to London either to assist or to shut up their man Ray? Evidently no one wants to believe in simplicity any more, only in complexity and organization.

Mr. Hanes reached Birmingham on Sunday, July 7. On Monday we met in his office, and he showed me the documents Ray had signed. Then he gave me his first impressions of Ray. "He's neat, takes care of himself, and he can talk. He knows what's going on: he reads the papers every day. He gives some sign of enjoying his prominence. He's burned up at some of his publicity and wants me to sue some magazines for libel. He's a great one to write letters, and that worries me. I can't tell what he might decide to write without my knowledge. He's cagey, like an old con. He doesn't look you straight in the eye, sort of hangs his head and grins out of the side of his mouth. He's incapable of trusting any man on earth. He's definitely not like any Negro-killer I've ever known. I don't think he hates Negroes. I don't think he has strong feelings about anything. If he didn't kill King for money, I can't see that he had any motive. So it had to be money. Of course, I only talked to him about an hour in all, and most of that time somebody else was in earshot. We couldn't get down to the case itself. I told him we had to have the truth, and had to sell it. He said he understood and said he'd cooperate. I think he wants to tell his story."

"He knows that he can fire you any day he wants to, doesn't he?"

"Sure he does. He's a jailhouse lawyer."

"Well, Art," I said, "neither of us knows when I'll be allowed to talk with Ray. I have to gamble on you as well as Ray. So I put it to you: now that you have met Ray, do you believe you can get the truth out of him?"

"I believe I can," Mr. Hanes answered. "It may take a while. But before that trial is over, I believe we'll know the truth."

My own lawyer had not seen the agreement signed in London by Mr. Hanes and Ray. That was prepared by Mr. Hanes. But on July 8 Mr. Hanes and I signed a three-way agreement between him, Ray and me. Ray signed this agreement in Memphis on August 1. This agreement was prepared by my lawyer. Here are some of the provisions:

AGREEMENT entered into this 8th day of July, 1968, by and between William Bradford Huie (herein "Author"), James Earl Ray (herein "Ray") and Arthur J. Hanes (herein "Hanes").

—Author proposes to write literary material dealing with the assassination of Martin Luther King Jr., and the alleged participation of Ray therein, for the purpose of establishing the truth with respect thereto.

—Ray and Hanes are desirous of assisting Author in such writing by furnishing him such material relative to the subject matter of such writing which Author might not otherwise be able to obtain.

—Ray and Hanes and each of them agree that they will use their best efforts to arrange as many personal interviews between Author and Ray and on the earliest occasions which may be permitted by the authority having jurisdiction over the institution in which Ray is then confined; and that they and each of them on such occasions and otherwise, through Hanes or other persons, will impart to Author such information (herein the "Private Material") with respect to the assassination of Martin Luther King Jr., the alleged participation of Ray therein, and the life and activities of Ray, as they or either of them may have or reasonably may be able to obtain; and that Author shall have the right to use the Private Material or any part thereof in his writing of said literary material.

—In full consideration for all rights, titles and interests given or agreed to be given by Ray and Hanes to author hereunder and for all agreements and acts of Ray and Hanes hereunder or pursuant hereto, Author agrees to pay Ray and Hanes each, thirty per cent of the gross receipts from said work.

In short, both Ray and Mr. Hanes agreed to impart to me all the information with respect to the murder of Dr. King which "they or either of them may have or reasonably may be able to obtain," for which I had agreed to give each of them 30 percent, a total of 60 percent, of the gross receipts from whatever I, in my "sole discretion," decided to write.

Since Mr. Hanes, under his prior agreement with Ray, had obtained 40 percent of Ray's 30 percent, Mr. Hanes would receive 42 percent of the whole, and Ray an unencumbered 18 percent. This meant that, if I realized $100,000 from the story, Mr. Hanes would receive $42,000, I would receive $40,000, and Ray an unencumbered $18,000.

However, Ray understood this: that as a criminal who, if he escaped a death sentence, would spend many if not all of his remaining years in prison, he could never keep any significant amount of money in his own name, or hope to collect any amount owed to him. Why? Because in a civil action Mrs. King and her children could easily seize it. In whatever remains of his life James Earl Ray has no legal or moral right to property. Therefore, for Ray ever to have any money for himself, he must owe it to some lawyer so the lawyer can protect it from Mrs. King and her children under a lawyer's lien. This meant, and means, that any money ever owed to Ray must be paid to some lawyer who may or may not give Ray any of it.

The agreement I signed with Ray and Mr. Hanes anticipated income which might be received months and years in the future. But Mr. Hanes was already spending money and had to spend much more within a few weeks. So, in the form of a letter from me to Mr. Hanes, I made this supplementary agreement with him on July 8, 1968:

Dear Art:

This letter is meant to be part of our Agreement, signed on this date, and is an extension and clarification of Article 5 of said Agreement.

It is known and understood by you, Ray, and me that all advances made by publishers to an Author on a book contract are merely loans, returnable in full if, for any reason whatever, the book is not completed and accepted; and these advances or loans become income to the Author only after completion of the book and after its acceptance by the publisher.

Therefore, any monies paid by me to you and Ray while I am researching and writing this book are, in effect, loans from me to the two of you. However, under the circumstances, I am willing to consider these monies or advances made by me to the two of you *non-returnable* if you and Ray will agree that these payments or advances shall not exceed the following schedule of payments:

1. On the signing of this Agreement I will pay you $10,000.
2. On the first day after Ray has been lodged in a jail in the United States, I will pay $5,000.
3. One month after Ray has been lodged in the United States I will pay $5,000.
4. Similarly, a month later, another $5,000; a month later, another $5,000; a month later, another $5,000; and a month later, another $5,000.

In short, on signing, on Ray's return, and during the first five months after his return, I am obligating myself to pay you and Ray, under terms of our Agreement, a total of $40,000.

Five months after Ray's return, assuming that I receive all the cooperation from you and Ray guaranteed by the Agreement, I expect to have completed the book. Normally a publisher has 30 days in which to accept or reject a book. Once the book has been accepted, the entire publishing advance will be paid; and thereafter, all payments made to me, from any and all sources, will be income, not loans; and this income will be divided and paid promptly as provided under the Agreement.

Your signature, along with that of Ray, will attest Agreement.

(Signed)
WILLIAM BRADFORD HUIE
ARTHUR J. HANES
JAMES EARL RAY

This contract was a poor one for me. I signed it and fulfilled it against the advice of my agent and my lawyer. Under it I assumed all the risks, all the costs of my travel, research, lawyers and agents, and agreed to do the work, and still give Ray and Mr. Hanes more than half of possible gross receipts. My agent pointed out that I could work for five months, pay Ray and Mr. Hanes $40,000, spend another $25,000 on travel and various forms of assistance, and not get my money back. But I didn't make this contract to make money; I made it to spend money for what I hoped would be convincing truth. I would have given Ray 100 percent if I could have known that I would get the truth.

On Friday, July 12, I met Mr. Hanes again in Birmingham, and he outlined his plan for Ray's defense. "When he is arraigned in Memphis," he said, "I'll ask the court for the earliest possible trial. Maybe the third or fourth week in September. I want to put Ray in the position of seeking the speedy trial which is the Constitutional right of every defendant, and place the blame for any delay on the state. They may want to postpone the trial until after the election. I'll oppose that, and say that my client is suffering cruel and inhuman treatment. I'm going to declare that Ray is innocent, that he is the victim of a Communist conspiracy, that he has nothing to hide. I won't make any motion for a change of venue: I want him tried in Memphis while tensions over what King was doing there are still high. I think we can get a hung jury. Even if the jury reaches a verdict, I think the jurors who hated King will hold out for a compromise sentence of 25 or 30 years. Since I'm claiming he's innocent, his fighting extradition any longer is wrong. Only a guilty man fights extradition, and my client is not guilty. And while he fights extradition, the press is beating him to death. Ramsey Clark [the Attorney General] says that Ray is the sole killer, so there is no presumption of innocence until proved guilty. Much of the press describes Ray as *the* killer, not the *alleged* killer. So I'm going back to London tomorrow and advise Ray to waive extradition. Then I'm going to insist that I be allowed to ride back to Memphis on the plane with him. I don't want him to be alone with those FBI boys all those hours in the air. I know what they can do."

Mr. Hanes then made his third trip to London. He was denied

permission to ride back on the airplane with Ray, who was flown from London to Memphis on an Air Force jet on Friday, July 19. That weekend, July 20 and 21, Mr. Hanes and his son talked for five hours with Ray and heard his first version of his experience from April 23, 1967, when he escaped from the Missouri State Prison, to June 8, 1968, when he was arrested. Outside the Memphis jail Mr. Hanes met reporters. Here is a resulting story:

James Earl Ray was pictured yesterday by his attorney as the victim of an international Communist plot. Arthur J. Hanes, pulling angrily on a filter cigaret and gesturing to make his point, said at a press conference here: "In my judgment Ramsey Clark is 100 per cent wrong. This is a giant conspiracy and my client is being used."

Mr. Hanes refused to divulge the source of his information. He would say only: "I hope Ramsey Clark will not sit back on his laurels and allow this conspiracy to cause us further harm and confuse the American people. Ramsey Clark is not going to use my client as a patsy."

Mr. Hanes, while not actually saying so, indicated that telephoned threats being made against his life and the lives of his family were coming from the "conspiracy." He said: "Gentlemen, I've got my neck way out on this one. My son and I are the only two people who have talked to Ray. It doesn't take a Phi Beta Kappa to realize that the conspirators may fear me and my son for what we know." Mr. Hanes did not deny that he was armed.

Mr. Hanes blasted his client's treatment in the Shelby County Jail and charged that Ray's rights were being violated and that his health would be weakened by the elaborate security precautions—particularly by two television cameras that monitor his every movement and the light that burns constantly in his cell. Mr. Hanes said: "Ray does not like, nor do I like, having the light burning and two cameras focused on him 24 hours a day. It's like prisoners are treated in Russia. Ray has to hide his head under a pillow to sleep. He even has an electronic eye on him when he uses the toilet."

On Monday afternoon, July 22, after their long talks with Ray, and after the press conference, Mr. Hanes and his son, driving from Memphis to Birmingham, stopped at my home and spent three hours telling me what Ray had said.

"He says," said Mr. Hanes, "that from August 1967, when he met Raoul in Montreal, down to King's death, he moved at Raoul's direction. He went to Birmingham, Mexico, and California because Raoul said so. He made a round trip from California to New Orleans to see Raoul. He left California for New Orleans and Atlanta because Raoul said so. Raoul went with him to Birmingham and told him which rifle to buy. Ray went to Memphis and rented the room at Bessie Brewer's rooming house at 3:15 P.M. following Raoul's instructions. He delivered the rifle to Raoul, bought binoculars for Raoul, then from about 4:30 to nearly 6 he sat downstairs in Jim's Grill drinking beer, waiting for Raoul. He says it was Raoul who fired the shot, and ran down the stairs, and threw down the rifle and zipper bag, and jumped in the Mustang where Ray was waiting, and the two drove off together."

"Do you believe any of that?" I asked.

"I believe some of it." Mr. Hanes answered. "Unless Ray is a complete damn fool, I don't see how he could have made the decision to kill King. Before King was killed, Ray was doing all right. He was free, and able to support himself with smuggling and stealing. He was driving a good car all over Canada, the United States and Mexico. He was comfortable, eating well, finding girls, and nobody was looking for him. Why then would he jeopardize his freedom by killing a famous man and setting all the police in the world after him? If Ray made the decision to kill King, he has to be crazy. Since he evidently is not crazy, I have to believe either that he didn't do the killing, or if he did, he did it because he was caught in a conspiracy and couldn't get out."

"If he's telling the truth," I said, "we ought to be able to find at least a little supporting evidence. If he associated with Raoul for seven months, surely he can give us one of Raoul's addresses or telephone numbers. If he was in Jim's Grill drinking beer at 5 P.M., and if he was sitting in the Mustang at 6:01 when the shot was fired, surely we can find one witness who saw him."

"We're going to try," Mr. Hanes said. "I'm hiring a good private detective in Memphis to find and keep track of all those winos and other derelicts who were in Bessie Brewer's rooming house. But don't forget that nobody in Memphis wants to risk talking to anybody."

"Maybe we can persuade one or two to talk," I said.

"Meanwhile," said Mr. Hanes, "Ray likes the idea of you and him writing his story. The more he thinks about it, the better he likes it. He's going right to work. But while you're writing the book, he wants you to start immediately in the newspapers and magazines trying to improve his image. He's mad about all the lies that have been printed about him. One magaine says his father died as an alcoholic. Ray says the old man is not only alive but he's too stingy to buy whiskey. Another magazine talks about Ray always wearing $150 alligator shoes. He says he bought those fake-alligator shoes on Hollywood Boulevard for $11, wore them a few times, then threw them away. He says all the stories about him chasing whores and wasting money in nightclubs are lies. He says: 'Every newspaper and magazine is trying to make it look like nobody in the world likes me.' So he says: 'Tell Mr. Huie that I'll give him the names and he can go find people who like me.' So he wants you to find people who like him and present him as a man who is liked."

"Tell him I'll find the folks who like him," I said. "Tell him that before the trial I'll publish the truth about his father, his shoes, his whores, his drinking, and about the people who like him. Tell him that you and he can tell lies at the trial—he has a right to do that—but he has waived his right to tell lies to me."

On Thursday, August 8, 1968, I went to Memphis for my first examination of the murder scene. Memphis began as a trading post on the east bank of the Mississippi River, sitting on a bluff which once belonged to the Chickasaw Indians. So today its streets parallel the river: they run north and south. Its avenues run east and west. Front Street is the first street on the bluff, nearest the river. It was once lined solidly with cotton brokers. Near the intersection of Front Street and Adams Avenue is the modern center of Memphis, a new city hall. Within a few steps of this city hall, at 87 Adams Avenue, in 1860 a slave dealer named Nathan Bedford Forrest had his place of business. Forrest, to me, was the ablest general of the Civil War, and the most truthful. He said: "If I ain't fightin' this war to keep my niggers, then what the hell am I fighting fer?" After the war, he became the first Imperial Wizard of the

Knights of the Ku Klux Klan. I would have liked Forrest. I wouldn't have admired him, but I would have liked him for his candor. So when I go to Memphis looking for truth, I like to start at the spot where N. B. Forrest once dealt in what he advertised as "No. 1 niggers."

The first street east of Front is Main Street, and to give myself time to reflect, I walked the two miles down Main Street to the rooming house at 422½ South Main.

Forty percent of the residents of Memphis are Negroes. Since slave days they have been a pool of relatively cheap labor—the lowest stratum of a white-supremacist society. Into Memphis in the 1880s came members of a Jewish family named Loeb. Over the decades they made a fortune using Negro labor in the laundry business. By 1968 Henry Loeb III was mayor of Memphis, a proud, stubborn man, an Episcopalian married to a gentile, leader of an Establishment devoted to keeping the city orderly. Then agitators brought disorder. They persuaded 1,200 garbage collectors, all but a few of them Negroes, to strike for higher pay, union recognition and a union dues checkoff. Mayor Loeb said no, and a battle was joined in which many persons, including merchants, suffered.

The mayor was winning this battle and the cheap laborers were losing when Dr. King came to help them. He preached defiant sermons, but by then he was a descending star. Times had changed for him since Birmingham and Selma and the 1963 March on Washington. Even with Dr. King's help, the cheap laborers continued to lose. Mayor Loeb was never going to recognize a union of municipal employes and put Memphis's city government in the difficult position of New York City's government.

The murder of Dr. King reversed the tide of this battle. Mayor Loeb had defeated Dr. King only to be overwhelmed by an international wave of sympathy which demanded success for Dr. King's last effort. The shot fired by James Earl Ray compelled Mayor Loeb to give the garbage workers their union. This concession caused the mayor to expect more protest and disorder. Because when he recognized a union of garbage workers and raised their wages, firemen wanted more so that their salaries would exceed those of garbage workers. Then policemen wanted much more so that their salaries would exceed those of firemen. And teachers wanted much, much more so that their salaries would exceed those of policemen.

Had Ray killed Dr. King at another time and in another place, Mayor Loeb and the Memphis Establishment might not have been too concerned with the severity of Ray's punishment. But since Ray had multiplied Memphis's troubles, Mr. Hanes had to anticipate that, when Ray confronted a jury, 40 percent of the 12 jurors would be Negroes.

In his special cell, playing gin rummy with one of his guards, Ray didn't know all this. But walking down Main Street in hot sun, I knew it. Other ironies occurred to me. Mayor Loeb and Dr. King would have agreed on many issues. For Dr. King was not the "liberal" so many "liberals" believed he was. He was a Christian theologian who blamed liberals for what he called their "superficial optimism concerning human nature." And himself being human, he had his weaknesses.

Six blocks north of the murder scene I paused in the shade of a movie theater marquee. The theater boasted that it showed "All Adult Movies" and in the ticket window a sign said: "Proof of Age Required." I could have proved my age, escaped the heat, and enjoyed the two films: *The Taste of Flesh* and *Naughty Pagans of the Suburbs*. Or I could have walked a few steps farther and enjoyed Lee Van Cleef in *The Big Gundown*.

The old Gayoso Hotel, once the pride of Main Street, the pleasure dome of cotton kings and "the finest hotel between New Orleans and Chicago," is gone now, replaced by a department store. The intersection of Beale Street and Main Street is five blocks from the murder scene. Beale Street is really Beale Avenue because it runs east and west, but for the sake of legend and tourism the signs say "Beale Street." Negro vendors still sell love potions and evil eyes along Beale, but the urban renewalists are tearing at it so Beale will soon be something W. C. Handy would never recognize.

The Chisca Hotel, still standing, with a modern motel addition, is four blocks from the murder scene. And after you pass the Chisca, Main Street deteriorates rapidly into ramshackle stores offering credit clothes and credit furniture, then used clothes and used furniture, then there are wholesale houses and warehouses.

I stood on the west side of Main Street and looked across at the two old, two-story brick buildings which have become part of America's assassination history. They are 418 and 422 South Main. Their second floors were long ago joined together into one "rooming house" by cutting a passageway through their walls on the second floor. The marked entrance to the "rooming house"—the entrance with the sign "Rooms" on it—is the front stairway of the 422 building, making the address of the "rooming house" 422½ South Main. The old front stairs of the 418 building are still there, but the door to them is usually closed and there is no number on it. There are rotting rear stairs in both buildings, so there are no fewer than four old stairways leading up to the "rooming house."

On the ground floor of the 418 building is Jim's Grill, a bar and restaurant serving people who try to pay $8.50 a week for a room. It features corn bread, soup, stew, vegetable plates for 60 cents, along with beer, coffee and Wink. Jim's Grill is important because Ray claimed that he spent nearly an hour in there while the "other man" was upstairs watching and waiting for Dr. King.

But Ray was never in Jim's Grill. I didn't know this on August 8, but I knew it by November 1. With his remarkable memory for detail, Ray accurately described the interiors of taverns in Montreal, Chicago, Puerto Vallarta and Los Angeles. So we asked him to describe the interior of Jim's Grill. He described it—and missed it a mile. Then Mr. Hanes drilled him in the correct description of Jim Grill.

After Ray had discharged Mr. Hanes as his lawyer and obtained Percy Foreman, he told Mr. Foreman that he was in Jim's Grill between 5 and 6 P.M. instead of being upstairs watching for Dr. King. He attempted to convince Mr. Foreman of this by giving him an accurate description of the interior of Jim's Grill. Word for word, his description was what Mr. Hanes had given Ray, not the inaccurate description Ray originally gave Mr. Hanes.

On the ground floor of the 422 building is Canipe's Amusement Company. Guy Warren Canipe is a jukebox operator. At his place of business, he polishes, tunes, and repairs jukeboxes before trucking them out to restaurants and taverns. He also keeps shelves of worn phonograph records which he has taken from his jukeboxes and which he sells for a few cents each to young Negroes who come in and often spend long periods selecting the used records. The display window at Canipe's is set back on an angle from the sidewalk, and it was in this off-the-sidewalk area that, after the shot was heard, "the man" dropped the rifle and the blue zipper bag before he leaped into the Mustang and drove away. Mr. Canipe says he clearly saw the man, and saw him drop the rifle and the bag, and that the man was James Earl Ray.

Two young Negroes had been in Canipe's selecting records, and they walked out onto Main Street about 5:55 P.M. I found them. They were afraid of being identified. But they told me that they saw the white Mustang parked at the curb, and they saw no one sitting in it.

I climbed the 25 steps that Ray climbed at 3:15 P.M. on April 4. At the top of the stairs, the woman manager opened a screen door for me. The manager lives in the room nearest this entrance, the room on the southwest corner of the 422 building. When a prospective renter arrives, the manager comes out of her room, shows him her vacant rooms, and if he takes one, he signs her book and pays her for a day, a week or a month. Ray, as John Willard, handed her a $20 bill, from which she took $8.50 for a week's rent.

Ray was first shown a room on the west side of the 418 building, a "front" room with a window looking down on Main Street. He rejected this room, asking for something in the "back." All the rooms farther back in both buildings, the rooms with windows looking down on Mulberry Street and the Lorraine Motel, were occupied. The vacant room which was farthest back was room 5 in the 418 building. This room adjoins room 6, which is on the southeast corner of the 418 building and has a window looking down on the Lorraine Motel. Room 6 on April 4 was occupied by forty-six-year-old Charles Q. Stephens and a woman named Grace Hays Walden. Room 6 adjoins a common bathroom which is at the east end of the hall of the 418 building and which has a window looking down on the Lorraine Motel. Ray took room 5, the door of which is ten feet from the bathroom door, and the window of which opens to the south. By leaning out this window a few inches, you can look east and down to the Lorraine Motel.

These windows in the back of both buildings in the "rooming

house" look "down" on the Lorraine Motel because of the terrain. The land on which the buildings of the rooming house stand is 12 feet higher than the land on which the Lorraine Motel stands. The Lorraine Hotel and Motel—two two-story buildings, one old, one new—is on the east side of Mulberry Street and runs the length of the 400 block. There are no buildings between the rear of the rooming house and the motel, only a vacant lot then covered with high bushes and trees. And the distance between the rear of the rooming house and the doors entering the motel rooms is only about 200 feet because at that point Main and Mulberry Streets are not parallel but are converging toward an intersection.

Dr. King, when hit, was standing on the second-floor balcony of the motel. The shot was fired from a second-floor window of the 418 building of the rooming house. So the rifle was about 12 feet higher than Dr. King and to his right. This is why the bullet, after breaking his right jaw, ranged down and to his left in his throat. The bullet found in his cervical vertebrae was three inches below and two inches to his left of the entrance wound.

Part of the time between 4:30 and 6:01 P.M. Ray watched for Dr. King by leaning out of the window of room 5. Evidence of this comes from finger prints and from the fact that, after the murder, a chair and a table in room 5 were found to have been moved to the window. I sat in this window: the fatal shot could have been fired from it. But according to other residents, Ray went into the bathroom twice, and the bathroom was locked for a total of perhaps 25 minutes. Ray told me that he went into this bathroom, and a print of the heel of his palm was found on the bathroom wall.

The only evidence that I or anyone else found that a man other than Ray was in either room 5 or the bathroom was supplied by Grace Walden. Her statement contradicted that of her common-law husband, Charles Stephens. From the fourth day after the murder, Stephens was called the FBI's "star witness." The doors of most of the rooms in the rooming house are often kept open because of the heat and the poor ventilation. Stephens was paid at different times by several reporters, one of them from London, for saying that his door (room 6) was open when the shot was fired and that he saw a man resembling Ray run out of the bathroom.

Two Memphis lawyers then became Stephens's lawyers, and he became their candidate for the $100,000 reward. Memphis police became baby-sitters for Stephens, and for a while they held him in jail under protective custody.

But Stephens's value as a witness declined sharply when a taxi driver named James M. McCraw made this signed statement:

> I have been employed by the Veterans Cab Company of Memphis for most of the past seventeen years. I have also driven for Yellow Cab. On April 4, 1968, I was driving for Yellow Cab when I received a call from the despatcher to go to 422½ South Main and pick up a fare. I later learned the fare was Charles Stephens. When I arrived I went upstairs and saw Stephens who seemed to want a cab. He was too drunk for me to haul. He was laying on the bed and too drunk to get up. I have known Stephens for seven or eight years and have drunk a lot of whiskey and beer with him. I refused this fare, and the despatcher gave me another order to go to Frankie & Johnny's Boat Store. When I had hauled this fare just a few blocks the news of the shooting came over the radio.

Then Grace Walden gave Mr. Hanes a signed statement on November 5, 1968. By then she was in a state mental hospital. She said that she was ill and in bed in room 6 when the shot was fired. She said that she saw the man run out of the bathroom, that Stephens from where he was sitting could not have seen the man, and that the man who ran out was older than Ray, but not so tall or so heavy as Ray, and that he wore "a plaid sport shirt and an army-colored hunting jacket."

Since the hall outside the bathroom was poorly lighted at 6:01 P.M. on April 4 (only 33 minutes of daylight remained), and since the door to room 6 is only three feet wide, just how plainly either Charles Stephens or Grace Walden could have seen a man darting past their door seems questionable. In 1969 Grace Walden was still confined in a Tennessee mental hospital, but her statement will live in the mythology of this case.

Statements useful to the defense but contradictory to that of Grace Walden were made by two other residents of the rooming house and by a Negro man named Solomon Jones, who was standing near Dr. King when he fell. Seventy-four-year-old Bertie Reeves, who had lived at the rooming house for eight years, said that he was in his room in the 422 building when he heard the shot. "The best I can tell," he said, "that shot didn't sound like it came from the bathroom on the other side. It could have come from the parking lot." Eighty-three-year-old "Cornbread" Carter said that he was on the ground in the bushes at the rear of the rooming house. "Suddenly," he said, "I saw a man there in the bushes close to me. He whirled around, fired a shot, and took off so fast that he kicked gravel on me." And Mr. Jones told reporters that immediately after the shot he saw "a man with a sheet around him run out of the bushes."

These statements about the shot coming from the "bushes" at the rear of the rooming house supported the "bush-man theory" which was talked for a while in Memphis. You could hear statements like: "That killing was a well-organized, professional job. They had marksmen at both levels: up there in the bathroom and down on the ground in the bushes. If one man didn't get a shot at King, another one would. One thing is certain: they came here determined to get King and they got him."

When I stood in that rooming-house bathtub, in Ray's footprints, and looked down at where Dr. King had stood, I said: "My god, how easy it was!" It's so easy to kill a man: why do so many people imagine that it's difficult? President Kennedy understood how easy it is, even to kill a President. All it takes is one man who wants to kill and who positions himself for it. A motel is an easy place to kill a man. Through an exposed door he must walk several times a day, and almost certainly he will walk through the door sometime between 5 and 7 P.M. Dr. King had accommodated his killer. He had walked out the door, then stood still, leaning on the balcony rail, talking to people on the ground below.

Ray was an expert on motels and rooming houses. In the zipper bag which he dropped with the rifle was a copy of *The Memphis Commercial-Appeal* of the morning of April 4, reporting again that Dr. King was at the Lorraine Motel. One drive past the motel and Ray would have spotted the rooming-house window. The shot from the window was easy. Ray fired at a stationary target, from a rest position, resting the rifle on the windowsill. I hadn't fired a rifle in 23 years. But with a rifle and scope exactly like Ray's, and duplicating the distance and angle of the shot, I put ten straight shots in a circle the size of a silver dollar. Any twelve-year-old boy, reasonably familiar with a .22 rifle, could have killed Dr. King from that bathroom window with the rifle that Ray used.

Ten

After we had worked a month on the case, both Mr. Hanes and I concluded that Ray would never *directly* tell us the truth about the murder. But while he wouldn't tell us *directly,* he seemed willing for us to have the truth if we could worm it out of him in a protracted contest of wits between him and us. Or if we could guess the truth despite his best efforts to hide it. What he wanted was the contest: it made him feel like he belonged in the Top Ten. Evidently he felt that, if he ever told anyone the whole truth, the contest would be over, and he wants the contest to continue so he can continue to receive attention. He killed Dr. King to get attention, and he's afraid of losing it.

Both Mr. Hanes and I came to feel that we were being exploited by Ray for his own gratification. He lived comfortably in an air-conditioned cell at public expense, reading and watching and listening to his press notices, with television to watch and guards to talk with and play gin rummy with, while we chased about the earth gathering information for him. He looked forward to visits by Mr. Hanes and his son, and to the communications from me which they delivered to him, so he could play another inning of catch-me-if-you-can with us.

Because I couldn't question Ray face to face, both Mr. Hanes and Arthur, Jr., tried to describe for me how Ray played the game. Art, Jr., wrote:

> Ray always greets us with a silly, sheepish grin which is higher on the left side of his face than on the right. He seems to be enjoying a joke which only he knows. When I walk into his cell I always feel that he has just pulled a fast one on me and I arrived a minute too late to catch him at it.
>
> When Ray is talking, if he is lying his eyes blink and keep shifting downward. If his lie is challenged, he will shake his head briefly, then drop his head and admit his lie. When we seem to be having a productive conversation, containing questions and relatively truthful answers, he opens his eyes wide, holds his head erect, believes that he is making a good impression, and is therefore pleased with himself. But these good conversations in which Ray seems pleased with himself come only when we talk of relatively unimportant activities, such as all the places Ray has been, or when he is pointing out errors he claims he has detected in what has been written or said about him.
>
> When you ask Ray a hard question, like for a better description of Raoul, or when did he decide to kill Dr. King, or when did he first learn that somebody else wanted him to kill Dr. King, he hangs his head, runs his fingers through his hair, and says nothing. After a moment he may lean back until his chair is sitting on only two legs and rub his paunch. Then he changes the subject.

In 1954 Ray burglarized a dry-cleaning firm in East Alton, Illinois. He was arrested and questioned by Police Chief Harold Riggins. In 1968 Mr. Riggins said:

> There's one thing I remember clearly about Ray. When I'd ask him a question he'd just duck his head down and grin. Whatever I asked him, that was his only response. He'd just duck his head and grin.

In 1959, after he held up a food store in St. Louis, Ray was questioned by Detective Harry Conners. After reviewing the evidence with Ray, the detective told Ray that he could hardly deny that he committed the crime. In 1968 Mr. Conners said:

> I'll never forget his reaction. He sat there with a silly grin on his face and said: "I can't deny it but I'll never admit it."

Mr. Hanes and his son, separately and together, talked with Ray for more than 100 hours. In retrospect Mr. Hanes wrote for me:

> Those hundred hours were a baffling experience because Ray never gave us his confidence on critical issues. Preparing his defense was like preparing for moot court in law school. We worked, but we had no defendant to work with us.
>
> At all times Ray was courteous and respectful. Probing for motivations I often attempted to discuss race or politics with him. He is well informed, but his views are neither extreme nor bitterly held. I never heard him express or saw him display resentment, hatred or malice toward anyone.
>
> At each conference with Ray we had to consider first a written list of topics he had prepared, some relevant to the case, some not. His questions were serious to him, and he seemed interested in my responses. He showed most interest in such personal matters as my bringing him new shirts and ties for his courtroom appearances. On a human-to-human basis we seemed to be close. But when I began asking the questions he changed in attitude and demeanor. He insisted that his accomplice, Raoul, actually fired the fatal shot, but when I questioned him about Raoul he became tense and devious. Each time I saw him I felt I had to make a new start at trying to gain his confidence. I never met a man quite so alone.

After I knew that Ray would never tell me directly the truth about the murder, why did I continue working on the story? The answer to that question is in the story as I have told it here. I continued because I believed that, if I kept him communicating with me, I would get the truth indirectly. I believe I got most of it. I believe that indirectly, over a period of eight months, Ray told me why he murdered Dr. King more clearly than he is capable of telling me directly. For another instance, while he was insisting to Mr. Hanes that he had an accomplice in killing Dr. King, he wrote this to me:

> I have had accomplices twice on convictions. The first time I got three years and nine months, and the other party got three years. This was a federal crime. The other time I got twenty years and the other party got seven years. So I'm a little gunshy on committing crimes with other people.

Moreover, as I have reported, Ray backed down when I refused to accept his statement that he stopped in Selma on March 22 because he "got lost." He backed down and acknowledged that he spent a night in Selma because he was stalking Dr. King. Once Ray had been sentenced and I could face him, I'd have the advantage in the contest. He'd know then that, if he gave me silly grins instead of some sort of answers, I could cut off the contest, the attention and the money.

Another of Mr. Hanes's difficulties was that Ray was more interested in discussing libel suits to be filed against magazines than in preparing his own defense. All such discussion, of course, was silly. Mr. Hanes would listen to Ray no more than a moment before he cut him off; and when Ray wrote to me about libel suits, I ignored him. This irritated him, so he liked to receive visits from J. C. Stoner, the old Ku Klux Klan lawyer and counsel for the National States Rights party. Despite Mr. Hanes's refusal to associate with Stoner, Stoner could talk with Ray in the Memphis jail whenever he chose. And Stoner pleased Ray by telling him that he (Stoner) would file all the libel suits for Ray; that "hundreds of thousands of dollars" could be raised by the National States Rights party for Ray's defense; that "millions of red-blooded Americans" were proud of Ray and pulling for him; and that Ray deserved and should have "not just one lawyer but a whole battery of fine lawyers." As an old adversary of mine, Stoner told Ray that "Huie and Hanes are just using you to make money."

Ray loved to listen to Stoner—and ultimately succumbed to him —but at first Ray was afraid of him. Ray wrote to me:

> I guess Mr. Hanes is right in not wanting Stoner associated with the defense. I agree that we should leave politics out of it at this time. But Stoner wants to file the libel suits right now, while Mr. Hanes wants to put the libel suits off till after the trial. I want the libel suits filed now. In fact I want the libel suits filed at the same time that you publish how much people who have known me like me. So while I'm not going to push Stoner in on Mr. Hanes in the main case, I'm going to retain Stoner to file the libel suits. Also Stoner says he can raise hundreds of thousands of dollars for me if I need it. But Mr. Hanes is right about keeping Stoner and poli-

tics out of the main case. I don't want to use politics in my defense unless I have to.

Ray loved to hear Stoner tell him that he deserved "a battery of fine lawyers." Because Ray kept informed about his competition: he read and watched the publicity in the Sirhan case. He had noted that Sirhan had a "battery" of no fewer than three famous lawyers. So Ray thought he deserved three lawyers, at least one of whom should be famous.

What Stoner said about raising money interested Ray's two brothers. In August and September 1968, John Ray's tavern in St. Louis was an unofficial Wallace-for-President headquarters. So John and Jerry Ray decided that, if their fellow Wallaceite, Stoner, could raise "hundreds of thousands" for the slayer of Dr. King, then they ought to be able to raise "thousands." They came to Memphis, where a lawyer drew up a "legal plan" whereby they could appeal for contributions to be deposited in a bank as a "nation-wide defense fund." They held a press conference, called for contributions and waited. After a week of waiting, with no contributions to deposit, they went back to St. Louis.

This publicized failure of his brothers to raise money was a bitter dose for James Ray. But he rationalized that what had defeated his brothers was the publicity about how I was paying $30,000 to him and Mr. Hanes.

Noting how Ray's brothers had come to Memphis expecting a "golden rain" to fall on them and remembering that Ray had kept in contact with his brothers before the murder, Mr. Hanes suggested to me that the expectation of this "golden rain" could have been the motive for the murder. We had learned early in the investigation that Ray had not been paid after the murder; later we learned that he had not expected to be paid. Not in the usual manner of a hired assassin. So couldn't he have murdered Dr. King in the expectation that, after he was caught, he and his brothers would be the beneficiaries of a "golden rain"? We weighed the "golden rain" theory for a while, then discarded it.

Ray had to swallow his bitterest dose about October 1. His trial, put off until after the election, was set to begin November 12, 1968. Early in September Mr. Hanes filed his "discovery motions." In all states of the United States the defense has a right to a pretrial examination of the "physical evidence" the state expects to use against the defendant. In addition, the state must furnish the defense a list of all witnesses it expects to call. Tennessee may have the most liberal "discovery statute" in the union. Under it there is very little the state can hide from defense counsel. Late in September Mr. Hanes was permitted to examine all the physical evidence against Ray—the Mustang, the rifle, the fingerprints, the fatal bullet and the items found in Ray's zipper bag which was dropped with the rifle. This examination was a sobering experience for Mr. Hanes. When he saw what the state had and compared it to the little he had, he shuddered.

Normally, when a white man in the South has murdered a white or Negro civil-rights advocate, the defendant never speaks at the trial. He is more of a spectator than a participant. While the state presents its witnesses, the defense lawyers, by cross-examination and innuendo, try to show the sympathetic jurors that "reasonable doubt" remains as to the identity of the killer. When their turn comes, the defense lawyers present a parade of alibi witnesses: men and women who perjure themselves by swearing that they saw the defendant somewhere else while the killing was being done. Then comes a parade of character witnesses: preachers, public officials and ordinary folks testifying to the spotless character and nonviolent nature of the defendant. And that's the trial, except for the summation, the final attack on the victim and all such "Communists and atheists" who are trying to change "the Southern way of life."

That's the sort of trial Arthur Hanes understands. But, in trying to defend Ray, he would have no alibi or character witnesses. He could discredit only one state witness, Charles Stephens. He could argue with the ballistics and fingerprint experts. Then he could present Solomon Jones and Cornbread Carter to say they thought the shot came from the "bushes."

Would he present Ray as a witness? In the United States the state cannot call a defendant to the witness stand: the defendant testifies only if he is called by the defense or if he insists on testifying against the advice of his counsel. Well, what could Ray say in his own defense? He suggested to Mr. Hanes that he might take the stand and say that he thought he and Raoul were at the rooming house to show the Remington rifle to some prospective Mexican or Cuban purchasers; and that at 6:01 P.M. he was sitting in the Mustang when he was surprised to hear a shot, after which Raoul came running down the stairs, threw down the rifle, and he and Ray drove off.

No defense lawyer in his right mind would willingly put Ray on the stand to tell that story. Every juror would know that the Remington rifle can be purchased anywhere in the United States, so why would Mexicans or Cubans be looking at a Remington rifle in a Memphis rooming house? And in Tennessee the penalty for aiding and abetting a felony is the same as for committing the felony. So how could Ray help himself by saying that he was trying to sell a Remington rifle and that he didn't fire the shot but he aided the man who did?

"You have the right to testify," Mr. Hanes told Ray. "But you can't testify with me as your lawyer. If you insist on testifying, you can discharge me now and get another lawyer. If, during the trial, you insist on testifying, I'll inform the court that you wish to proceed against my advice, and I'll ask to be discharged as your counsel. As long as I'm your lawyer, my duty is to defend you to the best of my ability. I can't perform that duty if I allow you to testify. Any defense lawyer who allowed you to testify would be further jeopardizing you, not trying to help you."

After Mr. Hanes had examined the physical evidence and weighed it against the defense possibilities, he went to Ray's cell and said:

> Old Buddy, it's my duty now to lay it on the line with you. I've spent ten weeks trying to build a defense for you. You haven't helped me much. Now here's the situation. Capital punishment is still legal in Tennessee. They haven't used their electric chair since 1960. But that doesn't mean that they won't use it. I believe I can keep them from using it on you. But I can't be sure. With all the evidence that exists against you, there is no way you can go to trial on a not guilty plea without risking a death sentence. The people of Tennessee are talking a lot about law and order now. They are tired of so much crime. So this could be the time that they decide to use the chair again.

Now what do you want to do? You say there was a conspiracy, but you have given me no evidence of it. You say you had an accomplice, but I've seen no sign of him trying to help you. How about telling me the truth about the conspiracy and the accomplice and let me make a deal for you? Or do you want to change your plea to guilty or to not guilty by reason of insanity?

What I'm telling you is this: I'll go to trial with you on a not guilty plea. I think I can save your life. I see some chance of a compromise sentence like thirty years. I see some chance of a mistrial. I see no chance whatever of an acquittal. But what you must understand is that unless you give me more information, or unless we change your plea, we must risk you going to the electric chair!

Now you think about it. Tell your brothers if you want to. They won't even come to see me, much less cooperate with me. And tell me what you want to do.

Subsequently Ray informed Mr. Hanes that he would tell him nothing more, that he'd risk the death penalty. But from that point on, Mr. Hanes suspected that Ray and his brothers were planning to discharge him as a means of delaying the trial until the spring of 1969.

W. Preston Battle, the judge assigned to the Ray case, was a scholarly man, a reformed alcoholic who at sixty neither drank nor smoked. He despised Arthur Hanes, who is a courteous and decent man, and he hated me. He went out of his way to slander me from the bench. I didn't hate him. I treated him respectfully, spoke to him candidly and thought that his assignment to the Ray case was a mistake. He was unsure of himself. He was overly concerned with the "image of Tennessee." He told me three times that he had been ashamed of Tennessee's image since the Scopes "monkey" trial in 1928 and that it was his destiny to improve the state's image by his correct handling of the Ray case. I told him that my folks had lived near the Alabama-Tennessee border for eight generations, that we didn't think Tennessee's image was all that bad, and that perhaps he shouldn't overexert himself to correct it. I had two extended conversations with him and, had he not died suddenly in March 1969, I would report these conversations in full. But since he is no longer alive to continue the conflict, I will report little more than what I said to him. I showed him the contract between me and Ray. Then I said:

> I don't want any secrecy about this contract, Judge. I'm show-
> ing it to you, and I'll show it to any reporter who wants to see it.
> This contract is an effort to do what your court can't do: to find
> the truth about why Dr. King was murdered. When you try Ray
> your trial will be necessary but disappointing because you can
> establish only what is already known: that Ray came to Memphis
> and killed Dr. King. At great financial cost you will spend weeks
> hearing witnesses from five countries give testimony which already
> has been published. And after your trial every thoughtful Ameri-
> can, white and Negro, will feel cheated because you will not have
> answered the question that matters most: why?

The judge broke in to agree with me: the only time he ever agreed with me. "I agree with you," he said. "I agree with you that such a trial doesn't produce truth. All we can get are a few facts and perhaps a conviction. But we can't get much truth." Then I said:

> You know that, Judge, and I know it because we are involved.
> But most everybody else, not being involved, believes that "every-
> thing comes out at the trial." Everything doesn't come out because
> our trial system is wrong. It produces only disappointment and
> fills our prisons with hopelessness. As the judge in this trial you
> should be able to call Ray to the witness stand. You should be
> able to explain to him that your court's judgment of him, the
> conditions under which he will be incarcerated, the nature of the
> effort to rehabilitate him, will all depend on how effectively he
> cooperates in helping your court to understand the crime and the
> reasons for and the extent of his participation.
> But you can't do that. Before you Ray will be no more than an
> occasionally interested spectator. He won't even be in jeopardy
> because how can he fear a sentence of extra years in prison?
> Whether you give him ten years or a hundred years is meaning-
> less. He can't live to serve the years already against him. He
> doesn't fear execution; he knows you aren't going to execute him
> even if you pass such a sentence on him. So your trial can result
> only in disappointment and exacerbation of the racial conflict.
> Since you have these limitations, sir, I'm trying to complement
> you. I'm trying to do what you can't do. And I don't see why my

effort should conflict with yours. I think my effort should have your cooperation.

By then Judge Battle had decided that I was a threat to his plan to improve Tennessee's image. He felt sure I was leading up to "one more journalist's request to interview Ray." His answer was no. Then I continued:

> But, Judge, I'm not requesting that I be allowed to interview Ray. I concede that I have no such right. But the State of Tennessee clearly recognizes Ray's right to confer with me. The law says that any prisoner has the right to confer with his business partner or with anyone with whom he has contractual obligations. Ray had a valid and proper contract with me under which he gets the money to pay for the defense of his life.
>
> I'm not asking you for anything. I'm telling you that Ray's lawyer will formally request that you comply with the law and recognize Ray's right to confer with me. If you deny Ray's right to talk with me now, at what stage in the proceedings will you recognize his right? After the trial begins? After the jury has been sequestered? After he has been sentenced?

The judge took the matter under advisement. Later I brought to his attention the fact that Sirhan, prior to his trial, was being allowed to confer frequently with a writer who had a contract similar to mine with Ray. I said: "Judge, it's difficult for me to understand why Ray should be denied a right which is freely granted to Sirhan. Is Ray a more dangerous criminal than Sirhan?"

Judge Battle gave me an answer which will always puzzle me. He said: "I guess the court can be lenient in handling Sirhan because there are not many Arabs in Los Angeles." He must have been contrasting the small number of Arabs in Los Angeles with the large number of Negroes in Memphis. But how that related to Ray's right to talk with me—I can't figure it out. I said:

> Well, Judge, I wish I had time, in Ray's behalf, to take this issue to the Supreme Court of Tennessee and, if necessary, to the Supreme Court of the United States. If you continue denying rights to Ray, and continue trying to jail reporters [he had held two Memphis newspapermen in contempt], you are going to damage Tennessee's image more than the Scopes trial ever did.

In February 1969, Mr. Foreman filed a motion asking Judge Battle for permission for his client to talk with me in his presence for one period of four hours. This motion was argued in open court. Mr. Foreman said:

> Now, Your Honor, my client's right to hold such a conversation with a man with whom he is in business, a man to whom he is trying to tell his story, seems to be clearly supported by the statute. As for Mr. Huie, I know him well. He is a competent, hard-working, respected journalist. I can testify that he knows more about my client than anyone I know of. And he is a mild, soft-spoken, inoffensive, peaceful little man. He comes only up to my shoulder [Mr. Foreman is six feet four inches and weighs 240; I'm five feet eight inches and weigh 156] and he couldn't whip anybody. I fail to see how a conference between my client and Mr. Huie in my presence inside the Shelby County Jail could threaten the peace and tranquility of Memphis or the orderly disposition of this case.

Judge Battle then made a speech in which he said he didn't trust me, that I wrote novels in six weeks on which I made two or three hundred thousand dollars, and that when Ray's trial was over, he was going to try me for contempt. Then he denied the motion. He didn't live long enough to try me for contempt, but he served me with a "show cause" order, which was dismissed after his death. As far as I know, he died determined that I should never exchange an oral word with James Earl Ray, though he never tried to prevent Ray's writing to me and sending me his copy by either Mr. Hanes or Mr. Foreman.

On October 16, 1968, Ray wrote to me:

> My position on this book and articles you are writing is that while it was Mr. Hanes's idea (he had me sign two contracts in London for that purpose I guess) I naturally approve of it. But I don't want to get too tied up with multiple contracts which I will now attempt to explain.
>
> I have now signed four contracts including a power of attorney which gives you and Mr. Hanes the nearest thing possible to unlimited rights to say or make deals of any kind in my name. I have no objection to this up to a certain point, as I know there is

going to be all kinds of books wrote relating to me and Tobacco Road type movies, and under the libel laws in the U. S. which make it difficult for a convicted felon to get any relief in the courts, I can't do much about it.

It seems to me that for the last 12 or 15 months I've been told that if I would do this or that everything would be all right. Therefore before going to trial I want to get out from under some of these contracts. One is the power of attorney. It seems to me that the contract you, Mr. Haynes and I have signed would be enough. I certainly don't want any more deals as I think the one contract should cover everything. And I want my brother to have a power of attorney which I will explain later.

Therefore this is what I want to do before November 1st. I want your attorney or agent to start in November to putting ½ of my 30 per cent in a bank designated by my brother. This would be about $3,000. The other half would go to Mr. Hanes until I get him paid off. I don't think this would be a hardship on Mr. Hanes as he has already received about $20,000, his 30 per cent and mine. Now I will attempt to explain my reason for making this request and which I have attempted to explain to Mr. Hanes without success.

One. If I am convicted of a crime I am going to hire a Tennessee lawyer to help with my appeal. This is usually done as local lawyers sometimes know their way around a little better than out of state lawyers. Also, if I go to some prison and I am confined under the same conditions as I am here, I will need someone on the state level to try to get it changed. In other words, a state lawyer with a little political influence.

Two. I am going to try to have the Ethics Committee to investigate my adverse publicity. I will probably need a lawyer for this. This will take a little money and you can't show lawyers just contracts.

Three. I want to hire a private detective to investigate my case. And this is going to take money.

On the negative side I guess you have read where you have gave me thousands of dollars for publishing rights. Therefore if the unforeseen should happen it would be difficult for me or an attorney to make a public appeal. Also as you probably know some States Rights Party has offered to finance my defense. However Mr. Hanes is probably right in that I shouldn't get involved with politics unless I have to.

Let me know if what I have wrote sounds reasonable and logical. Whatever you and Mr. Hanes decide won't have any effect on books or interviews or anything in the contract. However if it is decided by someone to keep me from rocking the boat and that I'm too dumb to handle my financial and legal affairs, I am going to have to make some other long term arrangements, rather than go on like I have been. So I would like to know your views on this before November. This is the last time I want to comment on this subject as I want to concentrate on the trial.

On a related subject my relatives are still being pestered by writers. My brother tells me he heard one writer had claimed he had interviewed some relative of mine which he hadn't. Could your attorneys do something about this?

That letter again reveals Ray the jailhouse lawyer at work. It also reveals his turmoil over money. Until he "hired" Mr. Hanes, Ray had never paid a lawyer more than $100, and in his previous trials he was represented by public defenders as he was in London. Now he was a famous prisoner who thought and was told by Stoner that he should be rich, but he still had nothing. He read in magazines that I had paid *him* $30,000, a fortune to him and his brothers, but neither James Ray nor his brothers had seen "a penny of it." It's hell to be penniless. It's a worse hell to be famous and penniless. And it's a far worse hell to be famous and in jail and penniless.

Ray was penniless on October 16 because, without my knowledge, he had amended an agreement. Under our three-way agreement I paid to Mr. Hanes 30 percent of the total receipts for Mr. Hanes and an additional 30 percent for Ray. This meant that half of whatever I paid to Mr. Hanes belonged to Mr. Hanes, the other half belonged to Ray. Then, under the two-party contract signed in London between Mr. Hanes and Ray, Mr. Hanes was entitled to keep for himself an additional 40 percent of Ray's 30 percent; and Mr. Hanes was to keep the remaining 60 percent of Ray's 30 percent for Ray, and spend this money at Ray's direction. This meant that, after I had paid Mr. Hanes $30,000, a total of $9,000 would be Ray's, and he could give it to his brothers or spend it on other lawyers.

But about September 1 Ray decided that his 30 percent of the total might some day be worth $200,000. So he and Mr. Hanes, without my knowledge, amended the agreement between the two of them so that, from Ray's 30 percent, Mr. Hanes would deduct, not a permanent 40 percent, but *only* "a fee of $20,000 plus case expenses." After Mr. Hanes had collected this fee plus expenses, the entire 30 percent would be Ray's. In short, Ray had assigned all his immediate money to Mr. Hanes in return for a chance to collect more in the future. This gave to Mr. Hanes the right to keep for himself every dollar I paid to him and to Ray up to perhaps $75,000. So Ray had nothing on October 16, and he wanted me to persuade Mr. Hanes to allow me to begin paying money to his brothers.

Had I been consulted, I would not have agreed to any change in the original two-party agreement between Mr. Hanes and Ray. Because I wanted Ray and his brothers to get money at once and to develop an appetite for more, so that I would be in a stronger position to compel Ray to tell me the truth. But I couldn't prevent lawyers from reaching new agreements with Ray. They could see him; I couldn't. When Mr. Hanes realized that he might be discharged, he had made sure he wouldn't owe Ray anything from what I had paid him.

From all this conflict came the events of November 10–12, 1968, when Ray "fired" Mr. Hanes and "hired" Mr. Foreman. Here, in excerpts from *The Memphis Commercial Appeal,* is how these events were reported:

> Famed Texas criminal lawyer Percy Foreman was named by James Earl Ray yesterday to replace former Birmingham mayor Arthur Hanes as his chief counsel in his defense against charges of killing Dr. Martin Luther King Jr.
>
> Mr. Foreman met with Ray and two of his brothers about six hours before the change of attorneys was announced at a 10 P.M. news conference. He said he would seek a delay of the trial before Criminal Court Judge W. Preston Battle at 9:30 A.M. tomorrow. It was indicated that Judge Battle might grant the delay request.
>
> The change followed indications that Ray might be unhappy with Mr. Hanes's handling of the case and with his contract with Alabama author William Bradford Huie. Part of the conflict appeared as early as September when Ray talked with J. C. Stoner,

an Augusta, Georgia, lawyer, at the instigation of the two Ray brothers. Mr. Stoner is known as an organizer for the National States Rights Party and the Georgia Ku Klux Klan.

Mr. Foreman would not answer calls from newsmen at a downtown hotel where he and John and Jerry Ray were staying. It was John Ray, a St. Louis tavern operator, who first suggested retaining Mr. Foreman in a letter he wrote to his brother in London. James Ray had already retained Mr. Hanes as his counsel. In a letter replying to his brother, James Ray said: "You mention Percy Foreman. He is a good attorney but I will wait until I get back as I want a battery of attorneys who can work together, so I will let Hanes decide on the ones he thinks will be best."

There was no immediate indication what financial arrangements had been agreed on for Mr. Foreman's participation. Mr. Foreman, whose large frame contradicts a puckish grin, has often voiced "what the traffic will bear" theory of fee assessment. From the Candace Mossler case he may collect the largest criminal case fee of all time, perhaps as much as five million dollars. Often fees come in the form of a barter system. "I prefer cash," he says cheerily, "but if a client hasn't got any, I'll take anything of value that he does have." The result is that the attorney has amassed a fortune in what were once the jewels of families whose members have run into difficulties, hundreds of home appliances, some choice pieces of real estate, and thirty automobiles which, he says, his law practice doesn't allow him time to drive.

The Foreman record and the Foreman workload are famous among his fellow attorneys. He handles about 40 cases a week. In 1958 a friend counted 778 accused murderers among his clients. Of these, one was executed and 52 were sentenced to prison. The other 705 were acquitted. Since then the Houston lawyer estimates he has defended "250 to 300 accused murderers. One was convicted: he got life."

Mr. Foreman, who is 67, lives in a $500,000 home in Houston with his attractive second wife, Marguerita, and their ten-year-old daughter, Marguerita Jr.

CHANGE OF LAWYERS IS BASED ON MONEY

Money and disgruntled brothers emerged yesterday as the reason behind the change in attorneys hours before James Earl Ray was scheduled to stand trial in the April 4th slaying of Dr. Martin Luther King Jr.

Jerry Ray and John Ray, brothers of accused James Earl Ray,

have told several newsmen here they feel attorney Arthur Hanes
and writer William Bradford Huie are using their brother to make
money and get publicity. Jerry Ray, it was learned, became curi-
ous enough about the flow of cash from Huie to Hanes that he
flew to Huntsville, Alabama, to inquire about it of Mr. Huie 11
days ago. Mr. Huie has said he has paid $30,000 to Hanes as part
payment to Ray for the exclusive rights to his story.

Jerry Ray told newsmen at the Claridge Hotel yesterday he was
concerned that Hanes "seems to be in the case just for publicity."
He said that he admired Foreman because "he doesn't talk to reporters. He works to win."

James Earl Ray and Hanes have been at odds over financial arrangements over Mr. Huie's exclusive rights to Ray's story of the
mystery-shrouded slaying. Jerry Ray said his brother has been un-
happy because he hasn't seen a penny of the $30,000 Mr. Huie
has already paid to Mr. Hanes.

Mr. Foreman, wearing his Texas-size hat and with his feet
propped on the bed in his Claridge room, wasn't reluctant to talk
about the money he has made. "I've given away at least $300,000
this year," he said. Referring to his tax bracket, he said: "I've
made so much money this year that it costs me only $17 on the
thousand to spend deductible money." But the question of who is
paying him for his work in the Ray case remains unanswered.

Jerry Ray came to see me on Friday, November 1. I had his
plane ticket delivered to him at the St. Louis airport, I met his plane
and I put him up at the hotel at the Huntsville airport, which is 20
miles from my home. I paid all his expenses, gave him a bottle of
whiskey, and during Friday afternoon and early evening we talked
for several hours. He is six years younger than James Earl and
three years younger than John, and he is handicapped by a slight
speech impediment and a criminal record which began when he
was a juvenile and includes armed robbery. He has spent about
seven years in prison, and his being James Ray's brother is now an
additional handicap. He was friendly and kept assuring me that he
and John and "Jimmy" regarded me as "the best friend we've got."
He wanted only what Jimmy had listed in his letter of October 16:
that I help Jimmy get his power of attorney back from Mr. Hanes
so Jerry could have the power of attorney, and so I could pay
"Jimmy's money to me instead of to Mr. Hanes."

There is an old saying in Alabama politics: "I'm opposed to all forms of graft I'm not in on." John and Jerry Ray didn't like the contract between Mr. Hanes, James Ray and me because they were not "in on it." I very much wanted them to be "in on it," so I told Jerry I'd insist that Mr. Hanes go back to the original two-party agreement with James Earl so that Mr. Hanes could begin paying Jerry at once.

Jerry told me that he, John and Jimmy were "for Wallace and we believe he'll be elected President next week [November 5]." He said he felt that "politics" would help Jimmy "get out in a year or two." Jerry thought the trial would start on November 12, and he said he was worried because "they have assigned most of the seats in the courtroom to reporters, and there are not enough conservative reporters, and the few who have been given seats don't have good seats." He named three "conservative" reporters he assumed would be "friendly to Jimmy," and he wanted me to use my influence to get these conservatives the best seats. I told him I'd try. Then he said that the announced assignment of seats had omitted my name, and he assumed this was a mistake. "Of course, you have a good seat?" he asked.

"No, Jerry," I said. "I won't be there at all. It would be a waste of time. I already know what the state will present, and the defense has nothing to present. I'll go back to Tennessee only when the judge decides to allow James Earl to talk with me."

Between October 28, 1968, and April 1, 1969, Jerry Ray telephoned me collect 17 times. The record of each call, with what was said, is preserved.

Before conclusion, one other news story needs to be understood. It, too, is from *The Commercial Appeal:*

HANES ISN'T FIRST ATTORNEY
TO BE DISMISSED BY RAY

One of the major questions for Percy Foreman, as he ponders his defense strategy for James Earl Ray, has to be how to control his client. Two other attorneys have failed—and found themselves fired in the middle of the case. When the man accused in the slaying of Dr. King fired Arthur Hanes Sunday night, it wasn't the first time.

In 1959 Ray waited until a five-day trial was almost over to tell the judge in a St. Louis courtroom he felt he had not been represented properly, and asked that his court-appointed attorney be dismissed from the case. The judge overruled his request, but the attorney was relieved after Ray's conviction, and Ray himself argued his appeal before the Missouri Supreme Court. He lost.

Ray tried to fire Richard D. Schrieber nine years ago, just before the closing arguments to the jury in his armed robbery trial. Mr. Schrieber remembers Ray as "a jailhouse lawyer . . . he pretty well ran his own trial. He knew what he wanted to do, and I pretty well had to go along with it." Mr. Schrieber said Ray took the witness stand in his own defense although he (Mr. Schrieber) advised against it "in the most vigorous language possible."

"When Ray took the stand," recalls Mr. Schrieber, "of course the prosecution was then entitled to bring out his past criminal record before the jury. This utterly stupid action by Ray resulted in his getting the maximum sentence of 20 years, while his accomplice was sentenced to only seven years." Ray was convicted in December, 1959, of the armed robbery of a St. Louis Kroger store. It was this 20-year prison term he was serving when he escaped from the Missouri State Penitentiary on April 23, 1967.

Ray's dissatisfaction with Mr. Hanes's strategy in the present case was first revealed several weeks ago when Mr. Hanes told Criminal Court Judge W. Preston Battle that "serious differences have arisen between my client and myself, and it may be necessary for me to withdraw as defense counsel." At that time it was understood that Ray and Mr. Hanes had argued over bringing in another attorney, and over whether Ray should take the stand in his upcoming trial. Ray said yes, Mr. Hanes advised no.

That story shows that Ray in 1959 was willing to hurt himself to get attention. He was being tried for the crime which, as I have reported, he said he couldn't deny but would never admit. To get off with no more than a seven-year sentence, he had only to say nothing during the trial. As long as he said nothing, the prosecution was handicapped by not being able to present his criminal record to the jury. But at the price of having to fire his lawyer, he took the stand. The prosecution then had him describe to the jurors all his previous crimes, and his years at Leavenworth, and the prosecution read to the jurors the psychiatric judgments that "this prisoner seems unlikely ever to be able to adjust successfully to life outside an institution." Then the jurors gave him 20 years. A criminal who wanted attention that much in 1959 might want it enough in 1968 to murder Dr. King. And when he went to trial for Dr. King's murder, certainly he would insist that he must take the stand.

All three of the Ray brothers believed they had won a great victory in getting rid of Mr. Hanes and persuading Mr. Foreman to take his place. They thought this famous and rich Texan would inject new drama into the case, get Jimmy acquitted, make the Rays rich, famous and free, and do it all at his own expense. How could they have known that they were about to be hit by a Texas twister: that four months later James Earl Ray would be in the Tennessee State Prison for life, robbed of his chance to take the stand before the world, shorn of his last hope of wealth, and John and Jerry would be back in St. Louis, dejected, wondering "how in the hell we could have been so mistaken about Foreman?"

Somehow the Rays had assumed that I was a casualty of the change in lawyers, that my contract depended on Mr. Hanes's remaining in the case, and that now they could make a new contract with someone else and keep all the money. How could the Rays have known that in my first telephone conversation with Mr. Foreman he would say: "Now, you know, of course, that I'm depending on you for my fee. So tote that bale, boy! Get to work!"

Early on Wednesday morning, November 27, 1968, I met Mr. Foreman at the statue of the Texas Ranger at the Dallas airport. We drove to Fort Worth, where he made a brief courtroom appearance. Then we had lunch, and all together, we talked for several hours. I said:

> Percy, I have made a serious mistake. In September and early October I believed that the decision to kill Dr. King was made in New Orleans by someone other than Ray. I believed that on March 21st, when Ray spent the entire day in New Orleans, he was directed to do the killing. On March 22nd he began stalking Dr. King and spent the night in Selma. I studied some of Ray's movements in New Orleans on March 21st. I believed the FBI would make an arrest in New Orleans. In addition, when Art Hanes showed Ray the witness list Ray was interested only in certain witnesses from Louisiana. None of the other witnesses interested him, but he looked carefully at every name from Louisana. Then

the psychiatrists in Missouri who had examined Ray told me: "From what we know of him it's hard for us to believe he was capable of the initiative required to commit such a crime. We have to believe that he was directed."

So in what I wrote in September I supported conspiracy. My articles were useful in that I presented Ray as a human being, and I revealed places he had been and things he had done which the FBI didn't know about. The FBI didn't even know that he had plastic surgery until I told them. But all that doesn't justify my mistake of plugging conspiracy. Sure there may have been conspiracy in the strictly legal sense that one or two other men may have had prior knowledge. But not in the sense that so many people want to believe, or that I implied.

Now I wish that I had never gone into this case at all. A lot of nonsense is being talked about the value of my rights to "the story." The story is of relatively little value because it's only the story of another Oswald, another Sirhan, another twisted nut who kills a famous man to get on television. That's all there is to it. I'm going to complete a book for what it's worth, and try to present a true picture of a twisted nut and all the damage he can do. But far from making any money, I don't expect to get back what I will have spent.

And speaking of mistakes, I believe you've made one. This is not your sort of case. You let them get you to Memphis where the old fire horse couldn't resist another race to the fire. But a week after you begin trying to work with Ray you'll know that there is no defense, and you'll be as sick of the case as Hanes was. You did Art a favor by replacing him; you just haven't realized it yet.

Mr. Foreman liked my three-way contract with Ray. All he wanted was for Mr. Hanes to get out so he could have what Mr. Hanes had had. "I like the idea of owning 60 percent of one of your books," he said, "while you own only 40 percent. So you get Hanes out and let me in, then, goddam it, get to work and write us a good book and make us a good movie and make us some money."

"I don't mind you having the money," I said. "But your client hasn't met his obligations. I want to know how, why and when he decided to kill Dr. King."

"He may be incapable of telling anybody that," Mr. Foreman

said. "You know why he did it. I've seen him only briefly, and I already know why he did it."

"But I want the particulars," I said. "And I expect you to get them for me. If you want me to work for my 40 percent, goddam it, I expect you to work for your 60 percent."

In December Mr. Foreman had pneumonia and lost a month's work. But on Friday, January 24, 1969, he flew into Huntsville airport, where I met him and we talked for another four hours between planes. The result was that on January 29, 1969, we signed a four-way amendatory agreement under which Mr. Hanes "got out" by transferring all his rights to Ray, and Ray reaffirmed all his grants to me, with all actions being approved by Mr. Foreman. Then on February 3, 1969, Mr. Foreman plucked Ray clean by having him sign a notarized two-way agreement which reads in part:

> KNOW ALL MEN BY THESE PRESENTS: That I, James Earl Ray, presently in Memphis, Shelby County, Tennessee, for and in consideration of his agreement to represent me at the trial or trials of any cases presently pending against me in Shelby County, Tennessee, have signed over, given, conveyed and transferred, and do by this instrument here now give, assign, set over and transfer to Percy Foreman, of Houston, Harris County, Texas, all of my aforesaid right, title and interest in and to the proceeds that would otherwise have accrued to me pursuant to said Basic Agreement and to said Amendatory Agreement, and to all of my rights thereunder as well as to any other right or rights that might be or have been mine because of the writing and subsequent publication of such writing by said Author William Bradford Huie, whether included in said assignment by the said Hanes to me under the Amendatory Agreement of January 29, 1969, or otherwise, said assignment and transfer herein to the said Percy Foreman being absolute and irrevocable, and I here now authorize and direct any person, firm or corporation having funds due and owing me by virtue of said Basic Agreement, or otherwise owing to me because of the writings of said Author, to pay the same to the said Percy Foreman, at his office in Houston, Harris County, Texas, in his own name and as his own property.

I read that agreement with dismay because with it went my last hope of ever being able to exert financial leverage on Ray. It's hard to pay a prisoner through his lawyer. Every effort I made to pay Ray was defeated. I wrote two more checks of $5,000 each to James Earl Ray, making a total of $40,000 I had advanced on the contract to obtain the truth. Mr. Foreman had Ray endorse these checks to him.

During February I was in Memphis three times with Mr. Foreman. Ray was still writing for me and sending me oral messages, and I was wrangling with Judge Battle. Mr. Foreman and I had some good evenings together. He is an enormously vital man, loves action, is blunt, vain, cantankerous and petulant, and has a fund of yarns, caustic comment and obscene account which he has told in a thousand judges' chambers to judges, state attorneys, sheriffs and bailiffs who slapped their thighs and cackled while wretches waited in docks for justice to be done. We dined always at Justine's, a restaurant which is a reason for visiting Memphis, and we dined with gracious company, including Memphis's singing citizen, Miss Marguerite DiPiazza.

Mr. Foreman said he spent some of each day in Memphis "sitting with my client, listening to him, waiting for him to decide that I may know as much about the law as he does." Then Mr. Foreman explained: "When a client hasn't paid a lawyer anything, the lawyer doesn't really have a client, he only has an associate whom he must consult before he knows what the hell is going on. That's why I always at the start require a prospective client to pay me a substantial portion of his estate. Then he has to listen to me, and I know what's going on."

Ray pointed out to Mr. Foreman that he didn't have to fear a death sentence because "no white man has ever been executed in Tennessee for killing a nigger." Ray also pointed out that Wallace had carried Shelby County for President, so he'd have plenty of friends among the prospective jurors.

After listening to Ray for about 30 hours, Mr. Foreman said to him: "I assume you know that I can't get you out of this?"

"Yeah, I know you can't," said Ray.

"Then why go to trial? A defendant in your position should never risk the death penalty unless he has some chance for acquittal. You have absolutely no chance for acquittal. You get either death or a long prison sentence, probably 99 years. In this state a defendant can be convicted of murder and get a sentence of no more than 20 years plus one day. That's the minimum. But 20 years plus what's waiting for you in Missouri is more than life for you. So why should you risk a death sentence? And why should you jeopardize my record for not letting men go to the electric chair?"

Ray reflected a moment, then asked: "If we go to trial, will you put me on the stand?"

Mr. Foreman surprised him by answering: "You're goddam right I will."

"You mean . . . you mean you think I can do some good?"

"Hell, no, you can't do any good. But after your trial I'm not going to have you telling me that you could have won if I'd only listened to you and let you testify. So I'll put you on. You can't do any good, but you also can't do any harm. Every juror will know your record anyway, so having to listen to you recite it for a week won't do any harm. You can't do any harm because the situation for you can't get any worse. The only question is whether you get death or a life sentence, so what you say can't make any difference. So you're damn right, you can get on the stand."

The most distinguished lawyer in Tennessee is John J. Hooker, Sr. His son, John J. Hooker, Jr., was a candidate for the Democratic nomination for governor in 1966. He was defeated by the present governor, Buford Ellington. Mr. Hooker, Sr., is a friend of Mr. Foreman, and Mr. Foreman considered trying to persuade him to associate with him in Ray's defense. But despite Ray's always wanting a battery of lawyers, he angrily refused. "I won't have him," Ray said. "His son got every nigger vote in Tennessee when he ran for governor. I want you to get some Wallace lawyers for me."

That Judge Battle and the Memphis Establishment wanted to avoid a trial was never denied. A trial would last for weeks, be expensive and could only worsen race relations in Memphis. Whereas Judge Battle had been hostile to Mr. Hanes, he was friendly with Mr. Foreman. So the question openly asked in Memphis was: "Can Percy deliver the guilty plea, or will Ray fire Percy and go to trial represented either by the public defender or by Stoner and the Ku Klux Klan and the Wallaceites?"

It was a near thing. Ray signed the letter authorizing Mr. Foreman to approach the state with a guilty plea. Then he signed, and initialed every page of the expensive document prepared by the state in which he admitted the truth of 56 statements, including these:

> That at approximately 6:01 P.M., April 4, 1968, defendant fired a shot from the second floor bathroom of the rooming house and fatally wounded Dr. Martin Luther King who was standing on the balcony of the Lorraine Motel.
>
> That defendant ran from the second floor and dropped the rifle, box, 9 rounds of ammunition, a green and brown bedspread, and a blue zipper bag containing various items including: tack hammer and pliers, April 4th issue of *The Commercial Appeal*, Bushnell binoculars, shaving kit from Rexall Drugs, Channel Master pocket size transistor radio, two unopened cans of Schlitz beer, hair brush and miscellaneous toiletry items, and a pair of men's shorts and undershirt.

On Friday, March 7, 1969, Judge Battle alerted the reporters to be present in his courtroom at 9 A.M. on Monday, March 10, to hear "a development in the Ray case." Every reporter immediately speculated on radio, on television and in the papers that Ray would plead guilty and receive a sentence of 99 years. When this broadcast was heard in the jail, somebody told Ray that he had been a sucker, that he should have gone to trial where he would have got "no more than 20 or 30 years." Mr. Foreman was in Houston, but reports came out of Memphis that Ray was apoplectic, that he had "fired Foreman" and that he "wasn't going through with it."

I talked with Mr. Foreman by telephone on Saturday, March 8, and he said: "The Lord only knows what will happen. I am going to Memphis tomorrow to ascertain if I still have a client, and if so, he will no doubt tell me what to do."

When Mr. Foreman saw Ray on Sunday afternoon, March 9, Ray was quiet. He denied that he had "fired Foreman" and said he was ready to enter his plea on Monday morning. Mr. Foreman sat with him for an hour, listening to him. Finally Mr. Foreman said: "Now that it's about to be all over, and not that it makes any difference, I'd like for you to answer one question for me. Why did you leave your fingerprints in those upstairs rooms, and on the rifle, and on the binoculars, and why when you ran down those stairs did you drop the rifle and that bag which contained a transistor radio with your Missouri prison number on it? Why didn't you carry the rifle and the bag another four or five steps and throw them in the Mustang?"

Ray hesitated a moment, then said: "I don't suppose I could ever persuade you that I didn't do it?"

"You sure couldn't," Mr. Foreman answered. "Not in a thousand years."

After more reflection, Ray said: "I thought I was going to get away. I thought I could get to Africa and serve two or three years in one of them mercenary armies, and those folks over there wouldn't send me back."

After that conversation Mr. Foreman delivered to Ray these two letters, dated March 9:

Dear James Earl:

You have heretofore assigned to me all of your royalties from magazine articles, book, motion picture, or other revenue to be derived from the writings of William Bradford Huie. These are my own property unconditionally.

However, you have heretofore authorized and requested me to negotiate a plea of guilty if the State of Tennessee through its District Attorney General and with the approval of the trial judge would waive the death penalty. You agreed to accept a sentence of 99 years.

It is contemplated that your case will be disposed of tomorrow, March 10, by the above plea and sentence. This will shorten the trial considerably. In consideration of the time it will save me, I am willing to make the following adjustment of my fee arrangement with you:

If the plea is entered and the sentence accepted and no embarrassing circumstances take place in the courtroom, I am willing to assign to any bank, trust company or individual selected by you all my receipts under the above assignment in excess of $165,000. These funds over and above the first $165,000 will be held by such bank, trust company or individual subject to your order.

I have either spent or obligated myself to spend in excess of $14,000, and I think these expenses should be paid in addition to a $150,000 fee. I am sure the expenses will exceed the $15,000, but I am willing to rest of that figure.

Yours truly,
PERCY FOREMAN

Dear James Earl:

You have asked that I advance to Jerry Ray $500 of the "$5,000", referring to the first $5,000 paid by William Bradford Huie. At that time I had spent in excess of $9,500 on your case. Since then I have spent in excess of $4,000 additional.

But I am willing to advance Jerry $500 and add it to the $165,000 mentioned in my other letter to you today. In other words, I would receive the first $165,500. But I would not make any other advances—just this one $500. And this advance also is contingent upon the plea of guilty and sentence going through on March 10, 1969, without any unseemly conduct on your part in court.

P. S. The rifle and the white Mustang are tied up in the suit filed by Renfro Hayes [the private detective who worked for Mr. Hanes]. Court costs and attorneys fees will be necessary, perhaps, to get them released. I will credit the $165,500 with whatever they bring over the cost of obtaining them, if any.

Both those letters are signed by Mr. Foreman and acknowledged with the signature of James Earl Ray.

On Monday morning, March 10, Ray stood up before Judge Battle and answered a long list of questions, including these:

JUDGE: Has anything besides this sentence of ninety-nine years in the penitentiary been promised to you to get you to plead guilty? Has anything else been promised you by anyone?

DEFENDANT: No.

JUDGE: Has any pressure of any kind, by anyone in any way been used on you to get you to plead guilty?

DEFENDANT: No.

JUDGE: Are you pleading guilty to murder in the first degree in this case because you killed Dr. Martin Luther King under such circumstances that would make you legally guilty of murder in the first degree under the law as explained to you by your lawyers?

DEFENDANT: Yes.

JUDGE: Do you understand that you are waiving, which means giving up, a formal trial by your plea of guilty? Do you understand that by your plea of guilty you are also waiving your rights to 1) motion for a new trial, 2) successive appeals to the Tennessee Court of Criminal Appeals and the Supreme Court of Tennessee, and 3) petition for review by the Supreme Court of the United States? Do you understand that by your plea of guilty you are also abandoning and waiving your objections and exceptions to all the motions and petitions in which the Court has heretofore ruled against you, among them being: 1) motion to withdraw plea and quash indictment, 2) motion to remove lights and cameras from jail, 3) motion to permit conference with Huie, and 4) motion to permit photographs? Do you clearly understand that by your plea of guilty you are waiving all these rights, objections and exceptions?

DEFENDANT: Yes.

Only once did Ray depart from the script. He said that, while he was pleading guilty to the murder, he was not saying that there had been no conspiracy, because there had been.

On Tuesday, March 11, Mr. Foreman left Memphis and Ray was transported to the state prison in Nashville. He was quoted in news stories as having told his guards during the trip that he wished he had not pleaded guilty because "with what they had on me I think I could have got off with a lighter sentence." On Thursday, March 13, Ray wrote this letter to Judge Battle:

> I wish to inform the Honorable Court that that famous Houston attorney Percy Fourflusher is no longer representing me in any capacity. My reason for writing this letter is that I intend to file for a post conviction hearing in the very near future and I don't want him [Mr. Foreman] making any legal moves unless they are in Mr. Canale's behalf.

The attorney general (district attorney) in Memphis is Phil M. Canale. Ray had decided to maintain that Mr. Foreman, in advising him to plead guilty, had acted in the state's interest and not in his client's interest. So Ray intended to charge that Mr. Foreman had "pressured" him into pleading guilty, and Ray, acting as his own attorney, intended to ask for a trial despite his having admitted the state's entire case against him and despite his having waived both his right to a trial and his right to move for a new trial.

Two weeks after Ray was lodged in the Tennessee State Prison, Jerry Ray telephoned me collect and said: "I have just talked with Jimmy. He has fired Mr. Foreman, but he wants to see you. He regards you as the only real friend he has. He has put you on his visitors' list. He's ready to tell you a lot now that he couldn't tell you before."

"All right, Jerry," I said. "My lawyer in Nashville, Mr. Hooker, will call Harry Avery, head of the Tennessee prison system, and as soon as Mr. Avery says Jimmy can talk with me, I'll be there."

Mr. Avery stalled when Mr. Hooker telephoned him, for Mr. Avery intended to write Ray's "story." Governor Ellington had ordered that no prison official should talk with Ray "except as is necessary in handling him as a prisoner." In defiance of this order Mr. Avery held several three-hour-long conversations with Ray. He announced that he was writing a book. Governor Ellington fired Mr. Avery.

On March 26 Ray wrote this letter to Judge Battle:

> I would respectfully request this court to treat this letter as a legal notice of an intent to ask for a reversal of the 99-year sentence petitioner received in this aforementioned court. I understand on one avenue of appeal I have only 30 days in which to file a review notice to have previous sentence set aside. That is the appeal route to which I now address the court.
>
> I also would like to bring to the attention of the honorable court that Mr. Percy Foreman, the attorney who was supposed to be representing me on this charge, stated in open court: 1) That since he was receiving no funds to help prepare the case for trial, and he did not think he should be required to use his own funds, he requested the court to appoint counsel to help defray costs. The court appointed the public defender to investigate the case and assist Mr. Foreman. And 2) Mr. Foreman said in open court that he did not want, or expect to receive, a cent for his efforts.
>
> I think Mr. Foreman's statement to the press that he had a contract from me and Mr. William B. Huie "upon entering" the case for $400,000, and that he was now to receive $150,000 should lay to rest the above two lies Mr. Foreman told the court. And

3) I, James E. Ray, in turn, have not personally received a cent from Mr. William B. Huie.

My only reason for bringing the aforementioned facts to the attention of the court is that I would respectfully move that the court appoint an attorney, or the public defender, to assist me in the proceedings. I have no stocks or bonds, nor have I received any funds from any source to engage counsel.

Petitioner uses the word "assist" as I hereby request the court that I be personally present at the hearing to assist court-appointed counsel so that there be no repetition of Mr. Percy Foreman's actions.

On the evening of March 31 Judge Battle was found dead of natural causes in his office.

A few days later the veteran Ku Klux mouthpiece, J. C. Stoner, of Savannah, Georgia, got what he had been seeking since the day of Ray's arrest: he became an attorney of record for Ray, and the publications of the National States Rights Party began soliciting contributions for Ray's "defense." As long as Stoner is Ray's attorney, Ray can't talk with me. Then Stoner, along with two other lawyers, initiated an action to get Ray a trial, charging that Mr. Foreman "pressured" Ray into pleading guilty. (As this is written, this action, having been denied in two courts, is before the Tennessee Supreme Court. It may go to the Supreme Court of the United States.) Stoner also filed a petition in federal court in Memphis charging Mr. Hanes, Mr. Foreman and me with "violating Ray's civil rights" and asking for an injunction against publication of this book. The petition further asked that the contracts between Ray and me be voided.

On October 11, 1969, Jerry Ray called me collect and said: "I been talking with Jimmy. He wants you to know that he's not responsible for any of the charges made against you personally. He thinks you're the best friend he's got, and he's anxious to talk to you."

"All right, Jerry," I said. "I'm glad to hear from both of you. Stay out of jail and keep in touch."

When Stoner filed the petition against Mr. Hanes, Mr. Foreman and me in Memphis, we could have delayed a trial for years. Instead, we replied to the charges and asked U.S. District Judge

Robert M. McRae, Jr., for an early trial on the merits. Judge McRae issued an order setting ground rules and dates for the taking of depositions, and setting the trial date as December 1, 1969. The judge ruled that Ray would not be transported to Memphis for the trial, but that his deposition would be taken by his lawyers in the presence of all defendants and our lawyers in the maximum security area of Tennessee State Prison in Nashville.

On November 11, 1969, at 9:30 A.M., we met at the prison. There were seven of us: two of Ray's lawyers including Stoner, Court Reporter Barbara Thomas, myself, Arthur Hanes, Jr., representing his father, and Mr. Hooker, representing Mr. Foreman and me. After being searched we were led through a guarded labyrinth to the maximum security area, to a room where Ray was seated at a table. When young Hanes introduced me to him, Ray smiled and we shook hands for the first time. I was shocked at his appearance. He had lost at least twenty pounds; his coarse, faded blue prison clothes hung loose; his nose was long, thin, and sharp; and his face looked pale, bleached, chalky.

Throughout the two-hour session Ray was cordial to me. Stoner questioned him about his relations with Mr. Hanes, Mr. Foreman and me, but Ray didn't try to make a case against any of us. He refused to say anything "bad" about anybody. He said he signed the contracts with me and Mr. Hanes "to get money for my defense," and he declined to say that he had ever been misled, cheated or coerced. And since he made no charges against any of us, he was not cross-examined either by young Hanes or by Mr. Hooker. When I shook hands with Ray and told him goodbye, his pale, chalky face lit up with a melancholy smile, and I felt sorry for him.

That afternoon, in Mr. Hooker's library, Stoner questioned me, under oath and for the record, for almost two hours. I answered many questions about the writing business, about my three articles in *Look,* about my research, and about publication plans for this book. I furnished copies of all contracts between me and Ray and between me and various publishers. I reported correctly all that I had spent, all that I had been paid. I put in the record my statement that all the information I had given to Stoner I had previously given to Judge Battle and to any reporter who had visited my home and asked for it. And for me, Mr. Hooker offered, as an exhibit to be read by Judge McRae, about 20,000 words which Ray had written for me, addressed to me, and delivered to me through Mr. Hanes and Mr. Foreman.

The most interesting of Stoner's questions were those dealing with my "alleged connections and relations with agencies of the federal government, particularly the Justice Department and the FBI." I replied that, except for being in the Navy during World War II, I had never had any "connection or relation" with any agency of the federal government. I conceded that I had talked with FBI agents during my investigation of the Ray case, as I had while investigating previous cases involving the murder of civil rights advocates. "I have given information to FBI agents," I said, "but they have never given me any."

Stoner then questioned Mr. Foreman, who had arrived in Nashville too late to be at the prison when Ray's deposition was taken. Stoner seemed satisfied to place in the record Mr. Foreman's "admission" that he had been a "life-long friend" of former U.S. Supreme Court Justice Tom C. Clark. Stoner asked: "And you are also a close friend of Justice Clark's son, Ramsey, who was Attorney General when King was killed and when Mr. Ray was arrested in London?" Mr. Foreman replied: "Yes, I have known Ramsey all his life."

When Stoner took Mr. Hanes's deposition he "established" that Mr. Hanes was once an agent for the FBI. And with that Stoner completed constructing the myth that will be believed and propagated from now on by Ku Klux Klansmen, other members of the National States Rights Party, and other Wallaceites: that the murder of Dr. King was planned by the FBI, that Ray was used, and that Mr. Hanes, Mr. Foreman and I were then used to "force" Ray to plead guilty and thereby "cover up" all evidence that others had planned the murder.

Realizing that he had failed to make any case against Mr. Hanes, Mr. Foreman or me, Stoner asked Judge McRae for permission to take a "supplemental deposition" from Ray. The judge agreed. So on Saturday, November 22, 1969, we all had to assemble once more with Ray in the prison. And this time we were there for seven hours! Before we began taking the supplemental deposition

Ray's three lawyers spent two hours alone with him, preparing him to testify. Then he testified before all of us for five hours. He said that he discharged Mr. Hanes and engaged Mr. Foreman in November, 1968, because he had grown to fear that "Mr. Hanes was influenced too much by Mr. Huie." He said that he wanted to testify at his trial, that Mr. Hanes did not want him to testify, and that he figured Mr. Hanes did not want him to testify because Mr. Huie didn't want him to testify because if he testified he would give away the story which Mr. Huie hoped to sell. He said that he blamed Mr. Foreman for not going to trial with him. "When Mr. Foreman became my lawyer," Ray said, "he promised to go to trial with me. Then in a little while he began insisting that I must plead guilty. I think he should have stuck with me through a trial and not sold me out." The case against me which Ray seemed to be trying to make was that I should never have been brought into the case by Mr. Hanes because I was really "for" Dr. King and not "for" Ray.

Through all these hours of testimony Ray appeared to enjoy himself and to grow stronger as the rest of us grew weary. Not many prisoners in maximum security ever get that much attention for so long. "He's more articulate than I have ever seen him," young Hanes told me. "He's enjoying himself because he's getting attention and he has nothing to lose."

The trial, on December 1, 1969, in Memphis's magnificent new federal building, lasted only three hours. Stoner argued before Judge McRae that Mr. Hanes should never have allowed his client, Mr. Ray, to "make such a contract with Mr. Huie whose sympathies were known to be with Dr. King and not with Mr. Ray." Stoner contended that my third article in *Look,* published soon after Ray had pleaded guilty, "showed an obvious bias against Mr. Ray." He said that publication of *He Slew the Dreamer* "will make it impossible for Mr. Ray ever to receive a fair trial, and for the real truth about this case to ever come out." He asked that the contracts be voided and that a permanent injunction be issued against publication of *He Slew the Dreamer.*

Mr. Hooker and young Hanes made motions on behalf of their clients that the petition be "dismissed with prejudice." Judge McRae granted these motions.

Is this the end of the story? Perhaps it is. Beyond reasonable doubt Ray will spend the rest of his life in the maximum security area of the Tennessee State Prison. The conditions under which he lives, and must live, would cause many men to go mad. He lives alone in a cell. He does no work. He can talk with two or three other prisoners who are in nearby cells, but he is not allowed to mingle with any other prisoner in any common area. He is not allowed such "freedom" because another prisoner, white or black, would surely kill him for the same reason that Ray killed Dr. King: to get attention and relieve the monotony of his existence. When Ray is allowed to walk briefly in the sun, in a small encolsure, he walks only with a guard, never with a fellow prisoner.

Once Ray's present attorneys find that they can raise no more money by "representing" him, or are discharged by him, he may ask to see me. I have sent him an advance copy of this book, and he can see me any time he desires. If we ever meet under relaxed conditions, he may be able to talk truthfully about his actions, his thoughts, his motives, and what he calls his "politics." But with the passage of time truth becomes more and more difficult to re-call and to enunciate. Many men outside prison prefer fantasies to truth. So James Earl Ray may prefer to live out his years cling-ing to the fantasy that President George Wallace will soon release him with the thanks of "millions of Americans." Or that he will find money to bribe a guard and thereby escape to visit again beautiful Gray Rocks Inn in the Laurentians or the Tropicana Hotel on the beach at Puerto Vallarta.

Appendix

Letters to James Earl Ray

[Hundreds of letters and telegrams from all over the United States, and a few from other countres, were delivered to James Earl Ray during the eight months he was confined in the Shelby County Jail, Memphis, Tennessee. Here are excerpts from a representative few. The addresses and initials of the writers are correct.]

Dear James Earl Ray:

God answered my prayers when Communist Rev. Martin King (nigger) was shot. He had it coming. Governer Rockefeller donated to King's Communist organization and bragged about it in the papers. So I intend to donate regularly to the James Ray Defense Fund. Set up a good propaganda committee.

D. W.
Rensselaer, N. Y.

You might be alone but you will never be without friends.

J. S.
Florence, S. C.

Congratulations from one ex-con to another. And here's a $5 money order for smokes and candy. Whoever killed King Coon deserves the admiration of the free American people plus a bonus of 10 million dollars. Good luck!

J. H.
Pontiac, Ill.

I'm praying for you, for you are not guilty of murder. You killed a Communist.

E. L.
Philadelphia, Pa.

I object to our government spending a million dollars to track you down so they can charge you with murdering a nigger Communist. I was a witness to some of King's Selma March in which the widespread immorality was sickening. And I object to this country lowering the flags to half-mast during the mourning period they proclaimed for King. I can't understand how any white man can vote for anybody but George Wallace. Just rest assured that you have millions of friends across this nation who will be wishing you the best of luck, just as I do.

A. F.
San Antonio, Texas

We the people of Central Mississippi wish to thank you. We think you should have a medal and a reward. The million dollars spent in getting you back to Memphis should have been spent on needy children. We don't have money to contribute to your defense, but if you are still in jail in a year we will help.

J. A. and H. W.
New Albany, Miss.

King stirred up violence and caused many to lose their lives. The FBI classed him as a trouble-maker. If you killed King, you did a good job, for he had it coming to him. My prayers will be with you.

N. G.
Loma Linda, Calif.

The case against you is ridiculous. When the jury is shown what kind of man King was, the jurors will vote to give you a medal of honor.

A. G.
Hollywood, Fla.

You did the right thing. Don't forget that there are a lot of people behind you, and you are still in the South. Let me know if you need anything.

L. S.
Clements, Calif.

They should not blame you when no one saw you, just because you have a record. You should be protected and assisted by all real Americans.

H. T.
Brooklyn, N. Y.

Millions of Americans heard a television reporter say that the gun that killed King "seemed to explode in his face." A rifle fired from 200 feet away doesn't explode in the victim's face. So King was killed by a Negro, and you are innocent.

L. F.
Huron, S. D.

Every day the leaders of our country proudly announce that good American soldiers have killed hundreds of Communists in Vietnam. And we honor those Americans who kill Communists. But when you killed a Communist, the United States spent a million dollars to track you down. You should be freed, honored, and rewarded.

J. T.
Selma, Ala.

Martin Lucifer Coon was an arrogant, greedy nuisance who needed to be disposed of. You did your duty as a good American. I'm proud of you.

L. S.
Gary, Ind.

You should be given the Congressional Medal of Honor, and I believe you will get it in another year or two.

T. D.
Portland, Oregon

No African could by nature inherit an English or Scot-Irish name. So the African you killed was not really named Martin Luther King. He was just a nigger Communist imposter. God bless you.

T. P.
Malvern, Ala.

I have been a government informer on Commies since 1942. At your trial I will tell the truth about King, after which no jury could convict you.

J. S.
Washington, D. C.

I'm a very poor man, but as long as I live I'm going to give a dollar every month to you and George Wallace. When Wallace becomes President you'll get your freedom, a medal and a million dollars.

H. P.
Anderson, S. C.

You deserve anything they decide to give you. You're a bad man.

M. T.
Simi, Calif.

Many people out here are in your corner rooting for you. We will send you money for cigarettes, candy and magazines. We're sure you will be acquitted.

L. S.
Coleta, Calif.

There are at least 100 million suspects in the killing of King Coon. So how can one man be called the guilty one. Spend this $5 on something you like to eat or drink.

E. G.
Ocala, Fla.

Just paste this Wallace for President sticker on the wall of your cell and look at it every night before you go to sleep. Then you won't be afraid because before long we'll get you out.

J. B.
Pine Bluff, Ark.

[*Ray received 182 letters containing Wallace for President stickers.*]

Hope this $10 will make things a little easier for you. Will try to send more.

E. S.
Trenton, N. J.

Here is a money order for $20. Wish I could send more. Good luck.

G. F.
Atlantic City, N. J.

Your friends in this area have collected $300 for you. Here it is. You are a fine, red-blooded American.

C. R.
Newport News, Va.

Here is $2. Wish we could send more.

D. B.
Wetumpka, Ala.

Here is $10 with my best wishes to a man who has served his country.

R. H.
Columbus, Ohio

[*Ray received a total of about $800 in small gifts. There were three larger gifts: one for $300, and two for $200 each. All gifts totaled about $1,500.*]

You are another victim of a Red conspiracy. So good men everywhere must come to your assistance.

I. H.
Wellington, N. Z.

[This is one of about 20 encouraging letters Ray received from overseas.]

I am sending you $5. You are a patriot and should not be kept in jail.

> J. M.
> Marysville, Calif.

Silver and gold have I none, but such as I have I give thee. Acts 3:6. All to the glory of God and the USA. Please read this Bible every day of your life.

> E. P.
> Cleveland, Ohio

[Ray received a total of 52 Bibles.]

My only complaint against you is that you didn't kill Abernathy, too. Count on me for help.

> L. D.
> Oshkosh, Wis.

Be of good cheer. You have millions of friends and we won't let you suffer long. We're going to elect a President who'll free patriots like you and put the traitors in jail.

> E. L.
> Shreveport, La.

I hope you will read the enclosed material and find the Peace That Passeth Understanding. I feel so much better from having written you. You are in my prayers.

> C. C.
> Tacoma, Wash.

[About half the mail delivered to Ray contained no letters at all, only religious pamphlets. He read none of them.]

THIS BOOK WAS SET IN

ULTRA BODONI CONDENSED AND TIMES ROMAN TYPES,

PRINTED AND BOUND BY

AMERICAN BOOK—STRATFORD PRESS.

IT WAS DESIGNED BY BARBARA KOHN ISAAC